# THE VIRTUAL LIFE OF FILM

# THE VIRTUAL LIFE OF FILM

D. N. Rodowick

HARVARD UNIVERSITY PRESS
Cambridge, Massachusetts
London, England
2007

Printed in the United States of America

Library of Congress Cataloging-in-Publication Data

Rodowick, David Norman
The Virtual Life of Film / D. N. Rodowick.
p. cm.
Includes index.
ISBN-13: 978-0-674-02668-1 (hardcover : alk. paper)
ISBN-10: 0-674-02668-3 (hardcover : alk. paper)
ISBN-13: 978-0-674-02698-8 (pbk. : alk. paper)
ISBN-10: 0-674-02698-5 (pbk. : alk. paper)
1. Photography—Digital techniques. 2. Digital cinematography. I. Title
TR267.R64 2007
778.5′3—dc22 2007015230

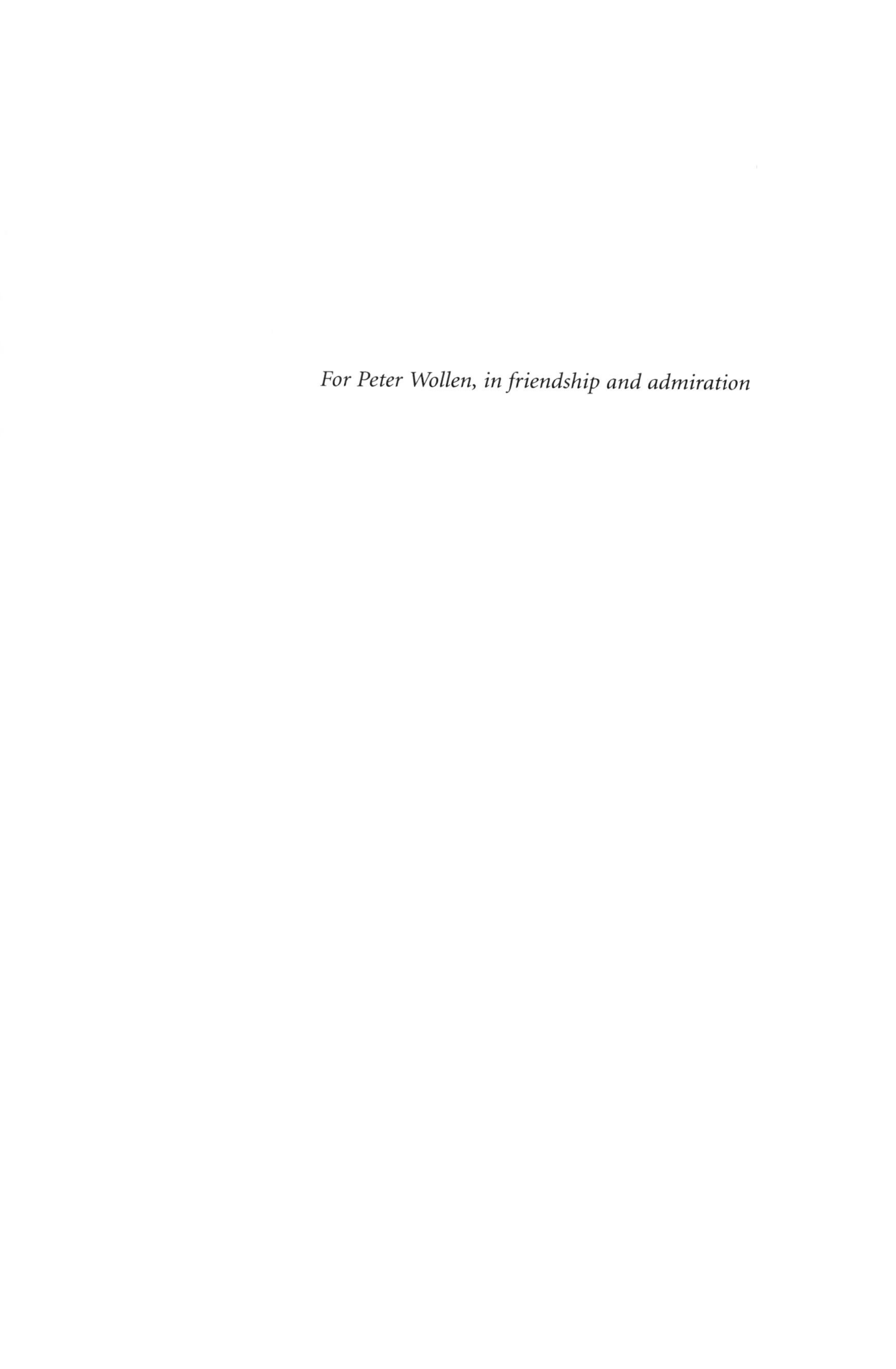

*For Peter Wollen, in friendship and admiration*

# PREFACE

*The Virtual Life of Film* is the first of two books in which I discuss the fate of cinema studies in the twenty-first century as a field of humanistic inquiry. In the pages that follow, I explore the philosophical consequences of the disappearance of a photographic ontology for the art of film and the future of cinema studies. In the current climate of rapid technological change, "film" as a photographic medium is disappearing as every element of cinema production is replaced by digital technologies. Consequently, the young field of cinema studies is undergoing a period of self-examination concerning the persistence of its object, its relation to other time-based spatial media, and its relation to the study of contemporary visual culture. The film industry also roils with debate concerning the aesthetic and economic impact of digital technologies, and what the disappearance of film will mean for the art of movies in the twenty-first century.

The *Virtual Life of Film* is organized into three parts, each of which proposes and examines different though related critical responses to the disappearance of film as a photographic and analogical medium for recording moving images.

Part I argues that time-based spatial media, including photography and film, occupy a special place in the genealogy of the arts of the virtual. In this respect, there is no inherent discontinuity cleaving the digital from the analogical arts, at least from the standpoint of contemporary film practice. While film disappears, cinema persists—at least in the narrative forms imagined by Hollywood since 1915.

Part II makes the case for a photographic ontology of film. Here I argue that the disappearance of film does matter and has had profound aesthetic and historical consequences. We feel these consequences now because cinema has been in the process of disappearing for quite some time, and, in fact, has largely already been displaced by video. But in order to understand how this is so, we must have a deeper and more flexible notion of what a medium is and how filmic and digital media inform our past and current ontologies.

Part III observes that most so-called new media have been imagined from a cinematic metaphor. An idea of cinema persists or subsists within the new media, rather than the latter supplanting the former as is typically the case in a phase of technological transition. But this circumstance also means we cannot envision what new media will become once they have unleashed themselves from the cinematic metaphor and begin to explore their autonomous creative powers.

The second book, *An Elegy for Theory,* will survey critically the place and function of the idea of "theory" in cinema studies since the 1970s. Why has theory become a contested concept, in competition with history on the one hand and philosophy on the other? The book takes the fate of theory in cinema studies as exemplary of the more general contestation of theory in the humanities.

Taken together, the two books examine a series of questions that have defined the professional context of my career as a writer and teacher: What defines the coherence of film studies as a discipline? How does it inform and enrich the broader study of contemporary visual culture? Is the philosophical coherence of film theory and visual studies challenged by the increasing cultural presence of digital and electronic media? In both books, I address the difficulties of grounding a discipline whose object is so variable and indeed in many respects ungraspable. *The Virtual Life of Film* concludes by reaffirming the importance of theory, in that every discipline sustains itself "in theory"—a discipline's coherence derives not from the objects it examines, but rather from the concepts and methods it mobilizes to generate critical thought. *An Elegy for Theory* continues this argument through a critical and historical examination of what "theory" means for the visual arts, and why and how it has become a contested concept over the past twenty years. The idea of theory must be reevaluated, for the retreat from theory, in either cinema studies or the humanities in general, may signify a relinquishing of our epistemological and ethical commitments.

# CONTENTS

# ILLUSTRATIONS

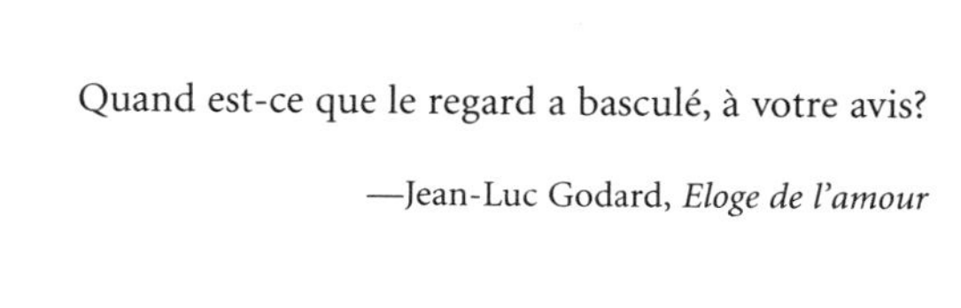

Quand est-ce que le regard a basculé, à votre avis?

—Jean-Luc Godard, *Eloge de l'amour*

# I

# THE VIRTUAL LIFE OF FILM

But even if Aldous Huxley's nightmare should come true and the experiences of taste, smell and touch should be added to those of sight and hearing, even then we may say with the Apostle, as we have said when first confronted with the sound track and the technicolor film, "We are troubled on every side, yet not distressed; we are perplexed, but not in despair."

—Erwin Panofsky, "Style and Medium in the Motion Pictures"

## 1. Futureworld

Films entertain and move us, but they also move us to thought. Imagine you are a young sociologist working around 1907. In the course of a year or two, on your daily ride to the university you witness an explosion of "nickelodeons" along the trolley route. They seem to operate continuously, day and night, and it is rare not to see a queue outside their doors. Because your children spend an extravagant amount of time and money unsupervised within their walls, and exhibit an extraordinary and sometimes incomprehensible fascination with the characters presented there and the people who play them, perhaps you yourself have gone inside to see a "photoplay" or two? How would it be possible to comprehend, despite the breadth and depth of your knowledge, that an entirely new medium and an important industry were being created which, in many respects, would define the visual culture of the twentieth century?[1]

This is how I respond when friends and colleagues ask why my critical attention has turned to "new media" and digital culture in recent years. My hypothetical social theorist may have been fortunate enough to participate in early studies of cinema and radio as mass cultural phenomena. In retirement, this imaginary scholar's interest may again have been piqued by the emergence of television. But the question remains: how would it be possible to imagine in 1907 what cinema would become in the course of the fifty years that followed? Or to imagine in 1947 what television would become in just ten or fifteen years? As the twentieth century unfolded, technological, economic, and cultural changes took place on the scale of a lifetime. This was already incomprehensibly fast from the perspective of the eighteenth or nineteenth centuries. Now, at the edge of the twenty-first century, these same changes are taking place in less than a generation.

The rapid emergence of new media as an industry and perhaps an art raises a more perilous question for cinema studies. The twentieth century was unquestionably the century of cinema, but is cinema's time now over? And if so, what is to become of its barely matured field, cinema studies?

Despite my interest in new technologies and the new media, I have never

1. This is not unlike the case of Hugo Münsterberg, the preeminent American psychologist at the turn of the twentieth century, whose final book, *The Photoplay: A Psychological Study*, is perhaps the first work of English-language film theory. Münsterberg was no longer young, however, and rumor has it that his fascination was sparked by the image of a young actress, Annette Kellerman, in the 1915 film *Neptune's Daughter*.

given up, and indeed still insist on my identity as a "film theorist," much to the confusion of my family and the amusement of taxi drivers the world over. If feeling more self-important, I'll say that my principal interests are philosophy and contemporary visual culture, with cinema as the decisively central element of study. Now, even in cinema studies itself this could be considered a marginal position. Film theory has fallen on hard times, even within the field of cinema studies itself. In the 1970s and early 1980s, many identified the field entirely with film theory, especially its Franco-British incarnation represented by the journal *Screen* and its importation from France of the work of Christian Metz, Roland Barthes, and others. More currently, research in film history has for many, and with brilliant results, dominated the field. In addition, many of the questions film theory raised in the heady days of political modernism concerning representation, ideology, subjectivity, and so on have evolved in the direction of cultural studies and media theory with their more sociological orientation. Thus, through the 1980s and 1990s one of the recurrent debates in the Society for Cinema Studies was how to represent the growing interest in television and electronic media. Was cinema studies disappearing, and was film becoming less central? This was a hard pill to swallow for the prevideo cinephile generation of which I am a card-carrying member. Not only do many feel that film theory is much less central to the identity of the field; within cinema studies itself the disappearance of "film" as a clearly defined aesthetic object anchoring our young discipline is also the cause of some anxiety. Indeed, as of December 2002 the organization became the Society for Cinema and Media Studies, reflecting the apparent displacement of film and the enlargement of the organization to something like moving image or screen studies.

So what becomes of cinema studies if film should disappear? Perhaps this is a question that only film theory can answer.

## 2. The Incredible Shrinking Medium

In May 1999, I took advantage of a bachelor weekend in New York to make the rounds of the new summer movies. Something was clearly afoot. Released earlier that spring, *The Matrix* was dominating the screens. As I settled in to watch previews at a large downtown cineplex, I noticed that nearly every big summer film was following its lead. This was the summer of digital paranoia. In a trend that began with *Dark City* the year before, films like *The Matrix,*

*Thirteenth Floor,* and *eXistenZ* each played with the idea that a digitally created simulation could invisibly and seamlessly replace the solid, messy, analog world of our everyday life. Technology had effectively become nature, wholly replacing our complex and chaotic world—too "smelly" according to the lead Agent in *The Matrix*—with an imaginary simulation in which social control was nearly complete. (A welcome antidote was Abel Ferrara's resolutely no-budget version of William Gibson's *New Rose Hotel,* which recast the Hollywood version of cyberpunk as a low-tech political chamber play whose message was that the future is already here and living in industrial New Jersey.) The digital versus the analog was the heart of narrative conflict in these films, as if cinema were fighting for its very aesthetic existence. The replacement of the analog world by a digital simulation functions here as an allegorical conflict wherein cinema struggles to reassert or redefine its identity in the face of a new representational technology that threatens to overwhelm it. The implicit and explicit references to computer gaming in these films are also significant and premonitory.

This conflict, of course, is entirely disingenuous for reasons that are both economic and aesthetic. Cinema had been down this road before. In response to the explosive growth of television in the 1950s, for example, cinema represented itself as a spectacular artistic and democratic medium in contradistinction to television, whose diminutive image belied its potentially demagogic power. In actuality, many players in the film industry had already prepared their Faustian bargains with the broadcast industries and their competing technologies, and the same is no less true today.[2] Though sincerely felt by some directors and writers, this battle of the media giants was something of a marketing ploy to maintain an idea of cinema's status as a prestige experience and as an "Art." As television took on the role of a mass, popular medium, cinema reserved for itself, at least in the world of product differentiation, the image of an "aesthetic" experience.[3]

2. For an overview of Hollywood's response to the rise of network television, see Tino Balio, ed., *Hollywood in the Age of Television* (Boston: Unwin Hyman, 1990); and Janet Wasko's contribution to Peter Lev, ed., *Transforming the Screen, 1950–1959* (New York: Charles Scribner's Sons, 2003) 127–146.

3. The response to the explosive growth of home video in the 1980s was somewhat different. Here the paradigm film is undoubtedly David Cronenberg's *Videodrome* (1983), in which video paranoia comes in the form of the half-inch cassette as the bearer of infection. Unlike the spectacular CinemaScope and Cinerama films of the 1950s, however, many of the video paranoia horror films were small-screen works that began to feed the direct-to-video market. Moreover, after an initial dip in theater attendance, video developed as a major revenue source for the major studios

This conflict between new and old technologies also has aesthetic precedents in the history of Hollywood cinema. The staging of the digital as simulation functions in the same way as the narrative dream or fantasy in the classic Hollywood musical. By striking an opposition of imaginary and real as two different narrative registers represented within the same film, Hollywood narrative, even in its most outlandish form, asserts all the more stridently its status as "reality." This is a classic case of Freudian *Verneinung*. When this strategy occurs as a narrative representation of technology, it is always a contest between competing versions of the "real" dissembling the fact that each is equally imaginary. Narrative conflict with the digital reasserts the aesthetic value of analog images as somehow more real than digital simulations, not only at the cinema but also in computer gaming and other new media. *The Matrix* is a marvelous example of how Hollywood has always responded ideologically to the appearance of new technologies. Incorporated into the film at the levels of both its technology of representation and its narrative structure, the new arrival is simultaneously demonized and deified, a strategy that lends itself well to marketing and spectacle. In terms of market differentiation, computer-generated imagery codes itself as contemporary, spectacular, and future-oriented; a sign of the new to bolster sagging audience numbers. At the same time, the photographic basis of cinema is coded as "real," the locus of a truthful representation and the authentic aesthetic experience of cinema. Photography becomes the sign of the vanishing referent, which is a way of camouflaging its own imaginary status. So, in the canny conclusion of *The Matrix* we enjoy both the apotheosis of Neo, the digital superhero, and the preservation of the last human city, Zion, a distant utopia hidden away at the Earth's core that functions as the site of the "real."

This allegorical conflict between the digital and the analog also provides a new opportunity for forging an opposition between technology and art. Perhaps the oldest criticism in the history of film theory is that film and photography could not be art because they were technology: an automatic inscription of images without the intervention of a human hand. Through the narrative inscription of technology as the antithesis of art, in which a representation of the photographic process now becomes the signifier, cinema re-

---

and their multinational corporate underwriters and now accounts for a significant portion of a film's profit margin. By the mid-1980s there was even a boom in new theater construction. For a useful overview, see Stephen Prince's *A New Pot of Gold: Hollywood under the Electronic Rainbow, 1980–89* (New York: Charles Scribner's Sons, 2000), especially 79–89.

claims for itself the grounds of "humanistic" expression.[4] This claim is also not new. It is already clearly present in silent cinema but is now narrativized in a new way to give new life to an old concept.

There is yet one more ironic twist to the logic of digital paranoia in fin-de-siècle cinema. As I took in previews for *The Mummy* and *Phantom Menace,* it was clear to me that at the level of representational technologies, the digital had in fact *already* supplanted the analog. Feature films comprised entirely of computer-generated images such as *Toy Story* (1995) or *A Bug's Life* (1998) were not harbingers of a future world, but rather *the* world of cinematic media as experienced today. Computer-generated images are no longer restricted to isolated special effects; they comprise in many sequences the whole of the mise-en-scène to the point where even major characters are in whole or in part computer-generated. In fact, technological transformations of the film actor's body in contemporary cinema are indicative of a sea change that is now nearly complete. One could say that the body of the film actor has always been reworked technologically through the use of special makeup, lighting, filters, editing, and so on. Contemporary cinema, however, is taking this process to new levels. One of the many fascinating elements of digital cinema is not just the thematic idea of cyborg fusions of technology and the body. Digital processes are increasingly used actually to efface and in some cases entirely to rewrite the actor's body. Film "actors" have become Frankenstein hybrids: part human, part synthetic. This strategy first came to popular attention in *Terminator 2* (1991), but newer films have taken the process even farther. In *The Mummy,* Im-Ho-Tep is a constantly mutating digital construction that has more screen time than Arnold Vosloo, the actor who plays him in the live-action sequences; in *Phantom Menace,* the annoying Jar Jar Binks lacks only a synthesized voice to make him an entirely computer-generated creation. Cyberware, a Monterey, California, company that specializes in three-dimensional scanning and digitization of actors, assures that Arnold Schwartzeneger will have a career as a "synthespian" long after he has retired

4. The counterexample, of course, is experimental films influenced by the machine aesthetic prevalent in the European avant-gardes of the 1920s. Ferdinand Léger and Dudley Murphy's *Ballet Mécanique* (1924) is one example, but even more appropriate is Dziga Vertov's *Man with a Movie Camera* (1929), in which machinism represents a specifically filmic aesthetic by exploiting, and making the subject of the film, all the mechanical possibilities of analyzing and reconstituting movement and the relations among movements distributed in space. This was also part and parcel of a more general Soviet theoretical fascination with the mechanical engineering of the actor's body and human vision by the filmic apparatus.

or passed on to the Chateau Marmont in the sky. The digital Agents have already won, it would seem, but they continue to play out the conflict to delay our recognition of the fact. They are even savvy enough to *act* as if they've lost, the better to preserve our sleep, which feeds energy to the system.

The reworking of the actor's body by technological processes is not something entirely new. Yet something is changing. The gradual replacement of the actor's recorded physical presence by computer-generated imagery signals a process of substitution that is occurring across the film industry. The successive stages of the history of this substitution might look something like this.[5]

- 1979: Lucasfilm, Ltd., establishes a computer animation research division to develop special effects for motion pictures.
- 1980s: *Digital image processing and synthesis* become increasingly prevalent in television advertising and music video production. Steven Jobs's Pixar and George Lucas' Industrial Light and Magic emerge as the most innovative producers of digital imaging for motion pictures.
- Late 1980s: *Digital nonlinear editing systems* begin rapidly replacing the mechanical Steenbeck and Moviola tables as the industry editing standard. From 1995 they begin to be perceived as a universal standard.
- Late 1980s: successful trials of digital cameras with resolution approximating that of 35mm film.
- In 1989, James Cameron's *The Abyss* produces the first convincing *digitally animated character* in a live-action film—the "pseudopod." The experiment is raised to a new level in 1991 with *Terminator 2*'s use of a

5. For an interesting historical and aesthetic survey of these issues, see Andrew Darley's *Visual Digital Culture: Surface, Play, and Spectacle in New Media Genres* (New York: Routledge, 2000); as well as the anthologies *Culture, Technology, and Creativity in the Twentieth Century,* ed. Philip Hayward (London: J. Libbey, 1990); and *Future Visions: New Technologies of the Screen,* ed. Philip Hayward and Tana Wollen (London: British Film Institute, 1993). Another significant factor in this history is what *American Cinematographer* referred to already in June 1981 as "the emerging new film/video interface," meaning primarily video-assisted shooting and electronic editing (linear and nonlinear). Initially, the most significant effect was on postproduction. See Prince, *New Pot of Gold* 111–123; as well as Charles Eidsvik's "Machines of the Invisible: Changes in Film Technology in the Age of Video" and Jean-Pierre Geuns's "Through the Looking Glasses: From the Camera Obscura to Video Assist," both in *Film Quarterly: Forty Years—A Selection,* ed. Brian Henderson and Ann Martin (Berkeley: University of California Press, 1999).

character that morphs continually between human actors and computer-generated images, the T-1000 terminator.

- 1990: *Digital sound* is introduced with *Dick Tracy* and *Edward Scissorhands.* By the end of 1994 most studios are releasing prints with digital soundtracks.
- 1993: *Jurassic Park* makes prevalent and popular the possibility of generating *"photographically" believable synthesized images.* This trend continues with increasing success throughout the 1990s.
- 1995: Pixar releases the first fully *synthetic feature film, Toy Story.*
- 1998–2001: Increasing popularity of digital video cameras, whose use for fiction films is popularized in films of the Dogma movement, such as *Festen* (1998) and Mike Figgis' *Time Code* (2000).
- 1998: *Pleasantville* and then *O Brother Where Art Thou?* (2000) are among the first films whose negatives are digitized for treatment in postproduction. By 2004, *digital intermediates* are becoming standard practice.
- June–July 1999: Successful test screenings in New Jersey and Los Angeles of *Star Wars I: The Phantom Menace* using *fully electronic and digital projection.*
- June 2000: *Digital projection and distribution* come together as Twentieth Century–Fox and Cisco Systems collaborate in transmitting a feature film, *Titan A.E.*, over the Internet and then projecting it digitally in an Atlanta movie theater.

The next ten years may witness the almost complete disappearance of celluloid film stock as a recording, distribution, and exhibition medium. For the avid cinephile, it is tempting to think about the history of this substitution as a terrifying remake of *Invasion of the Body Snatchers.* In the course of a single decade, the long privilege of the analog image and the technology of analog image production have been almost completely replaced by digital simulations and digital processes. The celluloid strip with its reassuring physical passage of visible images, the noisy and cumbersome cranking of the mechanical film projector or the Steenbeck editing table, the imposing bulk of the film canister are all disappearing one by one into a virtual space, along with the images they so beautifully recorded and presented.

What is left, then, of cinema as it is replaced, part by part, by digitization? Is this the end of film, and therefore the end of cinema studies? Does cinema studies have a future in the twenty-first century?

## 3. Back to the Future

Periods of intense technological change are always extremely interesting for film theory because the films themselves tend to stage its primary question: *What is cinema?* The emergent digital era poses this question in a new and interesting way because for the first time in the history of film theory the photographic process is challenged as the basis of cinematic representation. If the discipline of cinema studies is anchored to a specific material object a real conundrum emerges with the arrival of digital technologies as a dominant aesthetic and social force. For 150 years the material basis of photography, and then of film, has been defined by a process of the mechanical recording of images through the registration of reflected light on a photosensitive chemical surface. Moreover, most of the key debates on the representational nature of photographic and filmic media—and indeed whether and how they could be defined as an art—were deduced, rightly or wrongly, from the basic photographic/cinematographic process.

As digital processes come more and more to displace analogical ones, what is the potential import for a photographic ontology of film? Unlike analogical representations, which have as their basis a transformation of substance isomorphic with an originating image, virtual representations derive all their powers from numerical manipulation. Timothy Binkley greatly clarifies matters when he reminds us that numbers, and the kinds of symbolization they allow, are the first "virtual reality."[6] The analogical arts are fundamentally arts of intaglio, or worked matter—a literal sculpting by light of hills and valleys in the raw film whose variable density produces a visible image. But the transformation of matter in the electronic and digital arts takes place on a different atomic register and in a different conceptual domain. Where analog media record traces of events, as Binckley puts it, digital media produce tokens of numbers: the constructive tools of Euclidian geometry are replaced by the computational tools of Cartesian geometry.

This transformation in the concept of materiality is the key to understanding some basic distinctions between the analog and digital. Comparing computer-generated images with film reaffirms that photography's principal powers are those of analogy and indexicality. The photograph is a receptive substance literally etched or sculpted by light forming a mold of the object's reflected image. The image has both spatial and temporal powers that rein-

6. "Refiguring Culture," in Hayward and Wollen, *Future Visions* 93.

Frame enlargement from *2001: A Space Odyssey* (MGM, 1968).

force photography's designative function with an existential claim. As Roland Barthes explained, photography is an "emanation of the referent" that testifies *ça-a-été:* this thing was; it had a spatial existence that endured in time.[7] Even film's imaginary worlds, say, the moonscapes of *2001,* are founded by these powers. Computer-generated images, alternatively, are wholly created from algorithmic functions. Analogy exists as a function of spatial recognition, of course, but it has loosed its anchors from both substance and indexicality. And it is not simply that visuality has been given a new mobility wherein any pixel in the electronic image can be moved or its value changed at will. Because the digital arts are without substance and therefore not easily identified as objects, no medium-specific ontology can fix them in place. The digital arts render all expressions as identical since they are all ultimately reducible to the same computational notation. The basis of all representation is virtuality: mathematical abstractions that render all signs as equivalent regardless of their output medium. Digital media are neither visual, nor textual, nor musical—they are simulations.

But here a first important objection can be raised. Is "film" in its most literal sense synonymous with "cinema"? To say that film is disappearing means only that photochemical celluloid is starting to disappear as the medium for registering, distributing, and presenting images. As celluloid, with its satisfying substantiality and visibility available to the naked eye, disappears into a

7. *Camera Lucida,* trans. Richard Howard (New York: Hill and Wang, 1981), especially 80.

virtual and electronic realm, is cinema itself disappearing? When, after a long battle for legitimation in the academy, which has only recently been won and not in all corners of the humanities, cinema studies is finally enjoying unprecedented professional recognition and maturity, has it all been for naught?

One simple response is to say that digital cameras, or even "virtual" cameras creating wholly synthesized spaces on computers, are still based on the same optical geometry as traditional cameras and rely on the same historically and culturally evolved mathematics of depth and light rendering descended from *perspectiva legittima.* Although digital processes have produced many fascinating stylistic innovations, there is a strong sense in which what counts intuitively as an "image" has changed very little for Western cultures for several centuries. Indeed, there is much to be learned from the fact that "photographic" realism remains the Holy Grail of digital imaging. If the digital is such a revolutionary process of image making, why is its technological and aesthetic goal to become perceptually indiscernible from an earlier mode of image production? A certain cultural sense of the "cinematic" and an unreflective notion of "realism" remain in many ways the touchstones for valuing the aesthetic innovations of the digital. Of course, what remains absent from the process of digital representation is what thinkers like André Bazin or Roland Barthes held fundamental to the photographic image: its causal force as a literal spatial and temporal molding of the originating event, preserved in a physical material.

Nonetheless, I think there is a deeper and more philosophical way of discussing "virtuality" in relation to both film and cinema studies. One consistent lesson from the history of film theory is that there has never been a general consensus concerning the answer to the question "What is cinema?" And for this reason the evolving thought on cinema in the twentieth century has persisted in a continual state of identity crisis. Despite its range and complexity, the classical period of film aesthetics can be understood as a genealogy of conflicting debates that sought the identity of film in medium-specific concepts or techniques: the *photogénie* of Louis Delluc and Jean Epstein; Béla Balázs' defense of the close-up; the rhythmic *cinégraphie* dear to French Impressionist filmmakers; the montage debates during the Soviet golden age; Walter Benjamin on mechanical reproducibility and the decline of aura; Siegfried Kracauer's photographic affinities; Bazin's defense of the long take and composition in depth; and so forth. Arguably, this kind of argumentation extends all the way to the anti-illusionist theories of the avant-gardes of the 1960s and 1970s, which wanted to rid the medium of any extraneous literary and narrative codes in order to restore to film the aesthetic purity of its fundamental artistic materials: the elimination of depth to emphasize the flatness of the picture plane; manipulation of focus and other photographic properties to undermine representation and to draw attention to the grain and materiality of the image's surface; the use of discontinuity to restore the autonomy of shot and frame and to draw attention to the transition between images; and so forth.

In its historical efforts to define film as art, and thus to legitimate a new field of aesthetic analysis, never has one field so thoroughly debated, in such contradictory and interesting ways, the nature of its ontological grounding. The perceived necessity of defining the artistic possibilities of a medium by proving its unique ontological grounding in an aesthetic first principle derives from a long tradition in the history of philosophy. Deconstruction has not completely, or perhaps not even partially, purged our culture of the instinct to view and value Art in this way. This same perspective produced a sort of aesthetic inferiority complex in both film theory and cinema studies whereby, if all the above principles were true, cinema could be defined only as a as mongrel medium that would never evolve in an aesthetically pure form. Hence the great paradox of classical film theory: intuitively, film seemed to have a material specificity with claims to self-identity; nonetheless, this specificity was notoriously difficult to pin down. There was something about the spatiality and the temporality of the medium that eluded, indeed confounded, hierarchies of value and concepts of judgment in modern aesthetics.

Therefore, the difficulty of placing film as an object grounding an area of study does not begin with the digital "virtualization" of the image. Indeed one might say that the entire history of the medium, and of the critical thought that has accompanied it, has returned incessantly to film's uncertain status. What accounts for this flux at the very heart of cinema studies, which has always seemed less of a discipline than a constantly shifting terrain for thinking about time-based spatial media? All disciplines evolve and change, of course. But I would argue, and I think this is a positive thing, that film studies has never congealed into a discipline in the same way as English literature or art history. Even today it is far more common to find university cinema studies in a wide variety of interdisciplinary contexts; the fully-fledged Department of Film Studies is rather the exception that proves the rule. There are reasons both economic and political for this situation, but I find the possible philosophical explanations more interesting to explore.

Cinema's overwhelming and enduring status as mostly, though not exclusively, a popular and industrial art has proved exclusionary from a certain snobbish perspective. But there is another, deeper reason why cinema studies has remained the much-loved though bastard child of the humanities. From the standpoint of early modern aesthetic theory, the painting, the sculpture, and the book have a reassuring ontological stability—their status as objects, and therefore potentially *aesthetic* objects, seems self-evident. However, despite the apparent solidity of the celluloid strip rolled with satisfying mass and weight on reels and cores, and despite continuities in the experience of watching projected motion pictures, cinema studies has continually evolved as a field in search of its object.

Why is "film" so difficult to place as an object of aesthetic investigation? Perhaps because it was the first medium to challenge fundamentally the concepts on which the very idea of the aesthetic was founded. Up until the emergence of cinema, most of the fine arts remained readily classifiable and rankable according to Gotthold Ephraim Lessing's 1766 distinction between the arts of succession or time and simultaneity or space. As I argued in *Reading the Figural,* this distinction became the basis for defining an aesthetic ontology that anchored individual arts in self-identical mediums and forms. Moreover, implied in Lessing's distinction is a valuation of the temporal arts for their immateriality and thus their presumed spirituality or closeness to both voice and thought. Among the "new" media, the emergence of cinema, now more than 100 years old, unsettled this philosophical schema even if it did not successfully displace it. In the minds of most people cinema remains a "visual" medium. And more often than not it still defends its aesthetic value by aligning itself with the other visual arts and by asserting its self-identity as an image-making medium. Yet the great paradox of cinema with respect to the conceptual categories of eighteenth- and nineteenth-century aesthetics is that it is a temporal and "immaterial" as well as spatial medium. The hybrid nature of cinematic expression—which combines moving photographic images, sounds, and music as well as speech and writing—has inspired equally cinema's defenders and detractors. For its defenders, especially in the 1910s and 1920s, film represented a grand Hegelian synthesis—the apogee of the arts. Alternatively, from the most conservative point of view cinema can never be an art because it is a mongrel medium that will never rest comfortably within the philosophical history of the aesthetic. The suspicion, or anxiety, that cinema could not be defined as Art derived from its hybrid nature as both an art of space *and* an art of time. Indeed, some of the most compelling contributions of classical film theory recognized and valued this: Erwin

Panofsky's definition of cinema as an art that dynamizes space and spatializes time; Sergei Eisenstein's discussion of the filmic fourth dimension; and André Bazin's account of the cinematographic image in terms of a temporal as well as spatial realism or a unique spatial record of duration. The most philosophically elaborate discussion of this idea would be Gilles Deleuze's concepts of the movement-image and the time-image.

The difficult hybridity of film can be pushed even further. In early modern aesthetics there is a traditional privileging of what Nelson Goodman called the *autographic* arts.[8] These are the arts of signature. From hand-drafted manuscript to easel painting, autographic arts are defined by action—the physical contact of the artist's hand—and by a certain telos: they are concluded as aesthetic objects once the artist's hand has completed her or his work. All autographic arts are therefore unique. There is only one original; any repeated manifestation must be either a copy or a forgery.

Alternatively, Goodman's criteria for *allographic* arts, of which music is his primary example, include the following. They are two-stage arts in which there is a spatial and temporal separation between composition and performance. More important, they are amenable to notation. Here the primary creative work is finished when the notation is complete. All performances are variants on this principal act. Thus musical composition is a kind of writing, as of course is literature or poetry, though painting and sculpture are not. And while the action of printing is allographic, like painting literature is an autographic art for Goodman in that the creative act flows from and terminates with the artist's hand. Repeated printings are simply instantiations, then, that are identical in all relevant aspects with the original notation.

Film shares with music a difficult status in the history of aesthetic evaluation, and Goodman's concepts help us understand why. All two-stage arts are difficult to judge because the author is absent from the performance. No "signature" verifies their authenticity as art, even if the composer conducts his or her own work. The touchstone here is that the temporal and allographic arts lack a tactile substance that serves as the medium for a permanent and inalterable authorial inscription. And in fact, film shares with music a real Dionysian madness as a result of its complex temporality.

8. See his *Languages of Art* (Indianapolis: Bobbs-Merrill, 1968), especially the chapter "Art and Authenticity" 99–123. Goodman in no way assumes hierarchies of value in presenting the distinction between autographic and allographic arts. His concern, rather, is with how the problem of discourse shifts with respect to different forms and strategies of notationality in nonlinguistic art practices.

However, in music the notational act of composition serves as the guarantee of the author's signature. And here film differentiates itself most clearly from music according to Goodman's criteria. Film is obviously a two-stage and perhaps a multistage art, but where do we make the division between composition and performance? Paradoxically, making a photographic image would seem to be, like etching or lithography, both an autographic and two-stage process. From Bazin to Barthes, the photographic act is understood as producing a unique record of a singular duration. But subsequent prints must be struck from an original, thus constituting the second stage of the photographic process. As in lithography, "The prints are the end-products; and although they may differ appreciably from one another, all are instances of the original work. But even the most exact copy produced otherwise than by printing from that plate counts not as an original but as an imitation or forgery" ("Art and Authenticity" 114). Thus, in either photography or cinematography, producing an "original" may not serve as a notational act. Here technological reproducibility raises obvious problems. The original negative of *Citizen Kane* (1941) is lost. Rhetorically, one may wonder if all existing prints are therefore imitations. And this is to set aside the vexed question of who is the author of a film: the screenwriter? the director? the star actor? Do films have a primary notational origin: the script? the storyboard? Is the film *Citizen Kane* simply the performance of Herman Mankiewicz's and Orson Welles's written screenplay? Or is the film the unique preservation of the multiple creative acts performed both before the camera and afterward, in the postproduction processes of editing image and sound? In any case, as in musical composition, all are displaced in space and time from the actual performance of the film.

The digital image extends these problems in another direction. Computer-generated images are not autographic for two reasons: as "synthetic" images they cannot be considered the physical act of the author's hand, nor do they result in an end product. Indeed one of the great creative powers of digital images is their lack of closure, a quality Philip Rosen has characterized as "practically infinite manipulability": they are easily reworked, reappropriated, and recontextualized.[9] Synthesis, sampling, and sequencing are among the fundamental creative acts—or what I will later call, after Stanley Cavell, the automatisms—of the digital arts. In this respect they are the very antithesis of

9. See his *Change Mummified: Cinema, Historicity, Theory* (Minneapolis: University of Minnesota Press, 2001) 319–326.

the autographic arts. Alternatively, they are a paradigm for allographic arts, since any copy is fully identical with the "original." This is so for a specific reason. One can say that the sampling and reworking of a digital image is a new performance of it or even indeed that the new performance is a citation or paraphrase of the "original." But even if films or live music can also cite or paraphrase precedent works, they are not allographic arts in the same way as computer-generated works. Why? Because these digital creations are produced by a rigorous notation: the algorithms, programs, or instruction sets according to which they are computed. While *Toy Story* has as many authors as any big-budget Hollywood movie, paradoxically, it is fully notational in ways that no predigital-era film could be.

It is important to emphasize that Goodman's argument is not an "aesthetic" one, since the criteria of signature and uniqueness are the grounds neither for valuing nor for defining the specificity of art forms. Nonetheless, *autographicality* and *notationality* would seem to function as concepts defining the aesthetic nature of creative acts. The clearest examples of autographic arts imply a unique author whose work is accomplished in a one-stage act. Two-stage arts require aesthetic grounding in a system of ideally inalterable notation. Film does not fully satisfy either criterion. Alternatively, the synthetic image presents a radical case: undoubtedly a two-stage image, it can also be considered fully notational. Reproducing the same program or algorithm will produce an image identical with the "original" if such an original can be said to exist.[10] Unlike other two-stage arts, each performance will be identical instantiations of the same instruction set. Neither music nor dance can make this claim. And paradoxically, by this criterion the synthetic image would be aesthetic in a way the film image is not. (And here is a most terrible conclusion: every art has aesthetic value except film!)

Film's difficult status with respect to concepts of notationality has been a key concept of film theory, especially the structuralist and semiological approaches of the postwar period. And here we can return to the film/cinema distinction with interesting consequences.

10. There is an even more unusual paradox here. As various synesthetic programs like Color Music and Text-to-Midi show, the same algorithm can be used to produce outputs in different media: a set of musical sounds may be transformed as color values or ASCII text as music. In this sense, from the perspective of notation the resultant color or sound is mathematically identical with its "source" even though perceptually their inputs and outputs differ. In Part III I will further explain that such creative automatisms are made possible by a key aspect of information processing—the separation of inputs and outputs.

Film theory gained much from an awkward term when Etienne Souriau designated as *filmophanic* the film perceived as such by the spectator during projection. This effort to make precise the different analytical dimensions of film theory—*profilmic* space in front of the camera, *screen* space (photographic dimension), *film* space (temporal dimension), *spectatorial* or psychological space—derived from a fundamental distinction coined by Gilbert Cohen-Séat in 1946, that of cinematographic and filmic facts.[11] As Christian Metz noted in his commentary on this distinction in *Language and Cinema,* what we culturally define as "film" has a dizzying series of overlapping and often contradictory connotations: a physical object resting in film cans; an object of economic exchange; an aesthetic object defined both singularly and generally. For Metz, Cohen-Séat's distinction had the value of putting film theory on a sound methodological basis, for "filmic facts" isolate film as a localizable signifying discourse with respect to its varying sociological, economic, technological, and industrial contexts.[12] Here film comes into focus as an object of theory as a semiological fact that is distinguishable from the vaster social and historical terrain of cinematic phenomena, some of which intervene *before* production (economic and legislative infrastructure, studio organization, technological invention and innovation, biographies of creative personnel), others *after* the film (audience and critical response, ideological and cultural impact of the film, star mythology), and others *during* the film but *apart from* and *outside of it* (architectural and cultural context of movie viewing, and so on).

Metz's goal here is not only to specify the object of film theory, but also to delimit precisely the object of film semiology. And here, suddenly, is the brilliance and difficulty of his book *Language and Cinema.* In his rereading of Cohen-Séat, Metz distinguishes between *film* as actual or a concrete discursive unity, and *cinema* as an ideal set. This distinction launches us toward another sense of the virtuality of film and film theory. Cohen-Séat calls "cinema" the sum of phenomena surrounding the film while remaining external to it. But film theory cannot do without a certain concept of cinema, or at least a sense of the word "cinema," which in everyday parlance refers also to "the sum of

11. Cohen-Séat develops this argument in his *Essai sur les principes d'une philosophie du cinéma* (Paris: PUF, 1946), especially 54. Souriau's distinctions are outlined in his article "Les grands caractères de l'Univers filmique," in *L'Univers filmique* (Paris: Flammarion, 1953) 11–32. For an overview of both thinkers in English, see Edward Brian Lowry's *The Filmology Movement and Film Study in France* (Ann Arbor: UMI Research Press, 1985).

12. *Language and Cinema,* trans. Donna Jean Umiker-Sebeok (The Hague: Mouton, 1974) 12.

films themselves, or rather the sum of traits which, in the films themselves, are taken to be characteristic of what is sensed to be a certain 'language' . . . There is also the same relationship between cinema and films as between literature and books, painting and paintings, sculpture and sculptures, etc." (*Language* 22). Thus, when one speaks of "cross-cutting" in the climactic sequence of *The Matrix,* in which the action of Neo's final confrontation with the Agents in the simulated world of the Matrix is alternated with an attack by the robotic Sentinels on the rebel ship *Nebuchadnezzar* in the "real" world, one refers to it as a singular filmic figure while also saying that the figure is cinematographic; that is, it has the qualities of belonging to cinema or the semiological/aesthetic resources of cinema. By a curious dialectical turn, cinema in this sense re-inscribes itself within the filmic fact as defined by Cohen-Séat.

Therefore, the semiological distinction between cinema and film requires a vertiginous dialectical circularity between two terms and two sets. Here film and cinema are contrasted as actual and ideal objects that in fact cannot be separated. This is the difference between an *énoncé,* or discrete utterance, and language or *langue,* as a virtual system of differences; or, more simply, the difference between an individual and concrete message and the abstract code that gives it sense. Thus the semiological status of film cannot be established without reference back to a specificity that is, paradoxically, cinematographic. But according to Metz this specificity is defined neither by the criterion of substantial self-similarity (the uniqueness of a medium or a material) nor by an aesthetic ontology. It can be defined only by the set of all possible films or filmic figures that could be derived from the possibilities of cinematic "language," and this language is in a continual state of innovation and change.

So now film theory confronts two kinds of ideal sets. One groups together all the potential messages of a certain perceptual or aesthetic order without necessarily coinciding with either a single and unique code or a homogeneous substance. These are all the actual films that have been or could be made, that is, aesthetic artifacts defined as "cinema" in the same sense that the novels of Henry James could be defined as "literature." But the sense or meaning of individual films would be impossible to analyze without a unity of another kind—that of code. Here Metz makes a definite break not only with classical film theory but also with classical aesthetics. Within the filmic, the cinematographic inscribes itself as a vast virtuality that is nonetheless specific and homogeneous—this is the notion of cinematic codes. The notion of codes could not be constructed without the possibility of regrouping, at least conceptually, "all messages of a certain sensory modality," that is, the totality of films that constitute cinema. But only the messages are concrete and singular; the codes are virtual, and the quality of being cinematic in no way derives from the physical nature of the signifier. A code, then, "is *a constructed rather than inherent unity, and it does not exist prior to analysis* . . . [Codes] are . . . units which aim at formalization. Their homogeneity is not a sensory one, but rather one of logical coherence, of explanatory power, of generative capacity" (*Language* 28; my emphasis).

Thus, the quality of being cinematic, or even of defining, if we still dare, cinematographic specificity, rests on the analysis and definition of a code or codes immanent to the set of all films. But "immanent" does mean originating in either an ontology or the material specificity of the signifier. The materiality of the cinematic signifier, as Metz often insisted, is heterogeneous. Fundamentally, it is composed from five matters of expression: moving photographic images, speech, sound effects, music, and graphic traces. Moreover, any given narrative film will be comprised of a plurality of codes, both cinematic and noncinematic, whose very nature is to be conceptually heterogeneous. Here cinema presents an important lesson in philosophy to modern aesthetics, for it is useless to want to define the specificity of any medium according to criteria of ontological self-identification or substantial self-similarity. Heterogeneous and variable both in its matters of expression and in the plurality of codes that organize them, the set of all films is itself an uncertain territory that is in a state of continual change. It is itself a conceptual virtuality, though populated with concrete objects, that varies unceasingly, and therefore, to extract the codes that give this sense narrative and cultural meaning is a process that is, as Freud would have said, interminable.

The historical variability behind film's virtual life can be posed from yet another perspective, and it may be a less happy one. In his remarkable book *The Death of Cinema: History, Cultural Memory, and the Digital Dark Age*, Paolo Cherchi Usai makes a startling claim that complicates film's virtual life. Cinema is inherently an autodestructive medium. Every art suffers the ravages of time, of course. But structural impermanence is the very condition of cinema's existence. Each passage of frames through a projector—the very machine that gives filmophanic/projected life to the moving image—advances a process of erosion that will eventually reduce the image to nothing. Moreover, what Cherchi Usai calls the "matrix," or the chemical substrate, of film is perhaps the most impermanent and variable substance for the registration of images yet found in the history of art-making: what doesn't explode in flames (nitrate) will slowly dissolve (vinegar syndrome). Digital media have their own forms of entropic decay and obsolescence, of course. Nonetheless, one may say that the material basis of film is a chemically encoded process of entropy. This is one of many ways in which watching film is literally a spectatorship of death.

The history of film and film theory has often fantasized the existence of a Model Image. In Cherchi Usai's terminology this is the perfect or normative image—an eternal and Platonic form perfectly consistent with aesthetic norms of photographic beauty and pleasure. But not only is this Model Image imaginary in the full psychoanalytic as well as philosophical senses of the term; film history would not exist if the Image was permanent and atemporal. The intelligibility of film history, no less than of film theory, relies on the virtuality of the image in the sense that what it documents is the disappearance of its object. As Cherchi Usai puts it: "The ultimate goal of film history is an account of its own disappearance, or its transformation into another entity. In such a case, a narrating presence has the prerogative of resorting to the imagination to describe the phases leading from the hypothetical Model Image to the complete oblivion of what the moving images once represented."[13]

Curiously, from the standpoint of film theory this might be a strange defense of film art from the perspective of the aesthetic. Often criticized in the history of the aesthetic as a medium of mechanical copying, the aesthetic experience of cinema is in essence nonrepeatable. No two prints of the same film will ever be identical—each will always bear its unique traces of destruction with a specific projection history; thus each print is in some respects unique. And, for similar reasons, there will never be identically repeatable viewings of the same print. Thus, Cherchi Usai writes: "The assumption is that the spectator is indifferent to the fact that the moving image is derived from a matrix, and believes in the possibility of seeing it again under the same condition as previously. From that standpoint, as much as in oral literature . . . cinema is not based on reproduction. It is an art of repetition" (*Death of Cinema* 59). And this is true so long as we keep in mind that each repetition is also a difference.

Cherchi Usai is that rarest of animal, a film historian and archivist who is also a philosopher. And once historians begin to think like philosophers (an unlikely event in any case) the impertinent scandal of *The Death of Cinema* will achieve its full force. Moving image "conservation" is impossible, and moving image "restoration" is a contradiction in terms, since time is not re-

13. *The Death of Cinema: History, Cultural Memory and the Digital Dark Age* (London: British Film Institute, 2001) 89.

versible. And there is poetic justice in the fact that film, being among the most temporal, and therefore virtual, of the arts, is also the art on which the entropic quality of time works fastest. In this respect, Cherchi Usai recommends giving up all claims to resurrecting the Model Image.

> Moving image preservation will then be redefined as the science of its gradual loss and the art of coping with the consequences, very much like a physician who has accepted the inevitability of death even while he continues to fight for the patient's life. In monitoring the progress of image decay, the conservator assumes the responsibility of following the process until the image has vanished altogether, or ensures its migration to another kind of visual experience, while interpreting the meaning of the loss for the benefit of future generations. In doing so, the conservator—no less than the viewer—plays a creative role that is in some way comparable to the work of the image maker. The final outcome of the death of cinema is the foundation of an ethics of vision and the transformation of the Model image into the Moral Image, mirroring the imperatives and values connected with the act of viewing. (105)

Film, it would seem, is a very uncertain object. And it is this very instability that makes it so riveting and fascinating for some, and a cultural scandal for others. The solid ontological anchoring of a worked substance is grasped only with difficulty, yielding an art that, so far, leans more than any other on an experience of the Imaginary. On this basis the virtuality of film takes on yet a new sense. In a short but brilliant essay, Raymond Bellour defines film as *le texte introuvable,* or "the unfindable text." The difficulties of film semiology return implicitly here to the questions of notationality raised by Goodman. Literary texts may be cited critically and analytically in the same notation as their source. But film loses what is most specific to it once it is captured in a different analytic medium: the frame enlargement or film still absents the movement that defines its particular form of visuality: "On the one hand, [film] spreads in space like a picture; on the other it plunges into time, like a story which its serialization into writing approximates more or less to the musical work. In this it is peculiarly unquotable, *since the written text cannot restore to it what only the projector can produce;* a movement, the illusion of which guarantees the reality."[14] Writing may capture succession. Yet it fails to reproduce film's peculiar quality of an automated, ineluctable movement.

14. "The Unattainable Text," *Screen* 16.3 (Autumn 1975) 25; my emphasis.

Here the curious paradox of film is that its materiality cannot be grasped because it *resists writing*. And one of the curious consequences of structuralist film theory and narratology is their demonstration of film narration as a complex, highly elaborated, and codified system that nonetheless escapes notation.

By the same token, the imbrication of spatiality with temporality in film, and the fact that it cannot be anchored in a system of notationality, lead to another idea: that of Metz's definition of film as the "Imaginary signifier." The passage in film semiology from the structuralist to the psychoanalytic conception of the signifier pushed Metz towards a redefinition of film as a sensory modality that is also a psychical structuring. Rather than a haptic object or a stable self-identical form, the film viewer is always in pursuit of an absent, indeed an *absenting*, object. In Metz's elegant description, psychologically the spectator is always in pursuit of a double absence: the hallucinatory projection of an absent referent in space as well as the slipping away of images in time. The inherent virtuality of the image is a fundamental condition of cinema viewing where the ontological insecurity of film as an aesthetic object is posed as both a spatial uncertainty and a temporal instability.

So, even the filmophanic definition, which defines the singularity of film as a phenomenological event—the attended film projection—finds itself split by a certain virtuality. And in this respect, I still hold that the experience of the imaginary signifier is something of a psychological constant in theatrical film viewing. Instead of an "aesthetic" analysis, cinematic specificity becomes the location of a variable constant, the instantiation of a certain form of desire that is at once semiological, psychological, technological, and cultural. Here film theory reconnects usefully with the historical argument above. Throughout the twentieth century, the technological processes of film production have innovated constantly, its narrative forms have evolved continuously, and its modes of distribution and exhibition have also varied widely. But what has persisted is a certain mode of psychological investment—a modality of desire if you will. Film theory, and the history of film theory, remains important for the range of concepts and methods it has developed for defining the "cinematic," no matter how variable the concept, and for evaluating both the spectatorial experience (perceptual, cognitive, affective) and the range of cultural meanings that devolve from films.

Now that the Society for Cinema Studies has changed its name to the Society for Cinema and Media Studies, one might be tempted to conclude that this is a case of "If you can't beat 'em, join 'em." Or, more conservatively, one could imagine an organization of archivists and antiquarians content with rehearsing and refining their understanding of a medium which had a good run but which is now simply "history."

While historically many important debates in film theory have based themselves in a certain materiality, it is nonetheless a historical actuality that film has no persistent identity. Rather, its (variable) specificity lies elsewhere: a twofold virtuality defined by a vertiginous spatialization of time and temporalization of space as well as a peculiar perceptual and psychological instability wherein the spectator pursues a doubly absent object. Consequently, cinema studies can claim no ontological ground as a discipline—that is, if we continue to insist that the self-identity of an art be defined by medium specificity, or what I have called the criterion of substantial self-similarity. In fact the ontological ungroundedness of film from the standpoint of aesthetic philosophy offers an important object lesson for every discipline that seeks a stable frame or substance. That specificity, no matter how mobile, derives from and is legitimated by the wealth of its concepts. In this respect, institutional cinema studies has recently neglected to its peril the importance of theory and the history of theory: the invention, critique, and reassessment of the fundamental concepts that underlie the kinds of questions we ask—whether historical, sociological, or aesthetic—and the kinds of answers those questions allow.

So, cinema studies can stake no permanent claims on its disciplinary territories; its borders are in fact continually shifting. Stating the matter in its most specific terms: there is no medium-based ontology that grounds film as an aesthetic medium and serves as an anchor for its claims to exist as a humanistic discipline. Now the same could be said for both the College Art Association and every section of the Modern Language Association. And it would be hard to find a humanities professor these days who wouldn't be willing to take the default deconstructive position that the claim for self-identity in their respective disciplines is just an illusion based on a faulty assumption (that is, until the time comes to argue for a new post!). At the same time, the study of literature and of the history of art still enjoy a cultural prestige that is hardly secured for the study of film, much less for the study of digital and interactive media. The enduring quality of the book as an "interface," for example, as well as the social forms of its use, enjoy a history whose *durée* is long enough to be forgotten by many as *having* a history, and an embattled one. And this perceived permanence contributes to the ideological solidity of an idea of literature and its persistent cultural capital.

Contrariwise, the history of film and cinema has been lived in a mere three or four generations in which the medium's aesthetic and social forms have evolved rapidly and varied considerably. However, the impermanence and mutability of cinema studies as a field should be seen as one of its great strengths: the self-consciousness of film theory about the uncertain ontological status of the medium and the conflictual nature of the debates that have defined the genealogy of film study mark it still as one of the most intellectually daring areas of intellectual inquiry of the last century. And this, I believe, is one of the persistent attractions of film for intellectuals.

I will return to these ideas at the end of Part III, as well as to the still-unanswered question of cinema studies in relation to the "new" media. But before turning to these questions, we must try to answer another: What *was* cinema?

# II

## WHAT *WAS* CINEMA?

It may be felt that I make too great a mystery of these objects. My feeling is rather that we have forgotten how mysterious these things are, and in general, how *different* different things are from one another, as though we had forgotten how to value them. This is in fact something movies teach us.

—Stanley Cavell, *The World Viewed*

Within the entrails of the dead planet, a tired old mechanism quivers. Tubes radiating a pale, vibrant glow awoke. Slowly, as though reluctantly, a switch, in neutral, changed position.

—Jean-Luc Godard, *Histoire(s) du cinéma: Puissance de la parole*

## 4. Film Begets Video

One of the great ironies of my generation of film studies scholars is that we gained acceptance for a new field of research by defending an object that no longer exists. Indeed we have spent our careers witnessing its disappearance. The question is not whether cinema will die, but rather just how long ago it ceased to be. By "cinema" I mean the projection of a photographically recorded filmstrip in a theatrical setting. In the 1970s, it was still possible to believe in film as an autonomous aesthetic object because the physical print itself had to be chased down in commercial theaters, repertory houses, and film societies. Film history was a pursuit founded on scarcity, for any film not still in its commercial run was difficult to see, and the only way to see a film was to see it projected. Those of us who ran film societies could talk for hours about the location, provenance, and comparative conditions of various prints with a level of connoisseurship rivaling that of the most demanding art historian. The materiality of the cinematic experience was tangible.

I mark my personal experience of the end of cinema around 1989. It was some time in this year that on entering my local video store in Hamden, Connecticut, I saw that Pasolini's entire *oeuvre* was available on videocassette. Five years earlier, I might have prioritized my life around a trip to New York to fill in the one or two Pasolini films I hadn't seen, or to review *en bloc* a group of his films. For when would I have the chance again? That evening, I'm sure I passed on Pasolini and moved on to other things, for opportunity and time were no longer precious commodities. There was time. For film scholars, only a few short years marked the transition from scarcity to an embarrassment of riches, though at a price: *film had become video.*

As Robert C. Allen has recently argued, Hollywood is no longer primarily in the "movie business." And this is so not just because the major studios have become absorbed into multinational entertainment conglomerates.[1] Rather,

1. "'Please Rewind the Tape, Daddy': Writing the Last Chapter of the History of Hollywood Cinema," unpublished lecture. Also see Robert C. Allen, "Home Alone Together: Hollywood and the 'Family Film,'" in *Identifying Hollywood's Audiences: Cultural Identity and the Movies,* ed. Melvyn Stokes and Richard Maltby (London: British Film Institute, 1999) 109–134. As Stephen Prince observes: "In 1987, home video revenues were $7.5 billion compared with $4 billion box office. In 1989, the differential increased to over $11 billion for video against a $5 billion box office. Wall Street took notice and by mid-decade began using home video revenues as a basis for appraising studio stock values" (*A New Pot of Gold: Hollywood under the Electronic Rainbow, 1980–89* [New York: Charles Scribner's Sons, 2000] 97). By the end of the decade, network television revenues had also declined from 11 percent of total to just 1 percent. The advent of DVDs

domestic box-office sales, and consequently the manufacture of motion pictures to be experienced in a theatrical setting, no longer represent the studios' central economic activity. By the end of the 1980s, sales and rentals of videocassettes had surpassed U.S. box-office receipts. In 2004, video sales and rentals produced 63 percent of studio feature-film revenues as opposed to 21 percent from box-office receipts. In 1998, video game sales equaled theater receipts for the first time and, with revenue growth at about 25 percent per annum, now consistently outpace ticket sales.

What has become of cinema in this scenario? Theatrical screening of films is a marketing device to enhance video/DVD sales and to promote and sustain franchises in toys, games, and related sources of revenue. This is the dark side of the virtual life of film: "filmed entertainment" is just another element in the software chain of diversified media giants, though an important one, since it feeds significantly expanding nontheatrical markets. The basic economy of the entertainment industry emits through the cathode ray tube rather than reflecting from the white screen. For some time, the global audience's primary experience of motion pictures has been fundamentally that of the videocassette and broadcast television. Computer gaming and Internet-based activity consume much more leisure time than going to the movies. The projected print has lost its primary economic importance, and consequently the cultural stature of film has been transformed along with the phenomenology of film viewing.

All that was chemical and photographic is disappearing into the electronic and digital. When Allen refers to the 1990s as "Hollywood's last decade," he wants to be taken literally. Hollywood's main economic focus is no longer exhibition revenues derived from producing "films" to be screened in movie theaters. In addition, the nature of "film" itself has been transformed in the same time frame as digital processes replace photographic ones in every stage of recording, editing, and now distributing and exhibiting motion pictures. These simple facts converge in two inescapable conclusions for film scholars. First, we are witnessing a marked *decentering of the theatrical film experience,* which already has profound consequences for the phenomenology of movie

---

has accelerated this trend. Adams Media Research reports that in 2003 consumers spent $14.4 billion on movies for the home, almost $5 billion more than they spent on cinema tickets or video rentals. The same report notes that DVD sales doubled from 1999 to 2003, and that consumers continued to buy DVDs at triple the rate that they consumed videocassettes. See Wilson Rothman, "Movie Buffs Don't Rent DVDs. They Buy. Lots," *International Herald Tribune* (28–29 February 2004) 9.

spectatorship. Second, this decentering follows from the *displacement of a "medium"* wherein every phase of the film process is being replaced with digital technologies. The experience of cinema and the experience of film are becoming increasingly rare.

## 5. The Death of Cinema and the Birth of Film Studies

Phenomenologically, our social and cultural experience of watching movies has been irreversibly transformed by television, video, the computer, and computer networking. Has the medium of motion pictures also changed? And if so, what are the consequences for the study of film? The enormous popularity of *Jurassic Park* (1993) and the effect it had on mainstream filmmakers marked a turning point in this respect wherein the relative positioning of the photographic and the digital was reversed. From this moment forward, the major creative forces in the industry began to think of the photographic process as an obstacle to creativity, as something to be overcome, rather than as the very medium of cinematic creation. In a previous era of cinematic creation, the physical world both inspired and resisted the imagination; in the age of digital synthesis, physical reality has entirely yielded to the imagination. In this state of affairs, celluloid filmstock continues to persist primarily as a distribution medium because of the installed base of projection equipment in movie theaters and worries about piracy. But this may not continue for long.

As I argued in Part I, periods of technological change are always interesting for film theory because the films themselves tend to stage its primary question: *What is cinema?* Paradoxically, the emergence of professional film studies is coincident with what may now be understood as a long period of economic decline for the cinema, first in competition from broadcast television (1955–1975), and then from video and DVD (1986–present). The social and economic history of this rivalry is complex, of course, and outside my purview here. But perhaps the drive to understand film and cinema was fueled in direct proportion to its economic displacement and physical disappearance? In just the same way, my generation might owe a certain historical attitude toward film to the functioning of broadcast television as a film museum. The model here would be the serial presentation of *Citizen Kane* as the "Million Dollar Movie" on WOR-TV in New York, surely one factor in making it the best-known and most-studied film for several generations of American film schol-

Frame enlargement from *Jurassic Park* (MCA/Universal, 1993).

ars. For many of us, television was our first repertory theater, and to television we owe strategies of programming by genre and close analysis based on repetitive viewing. Similarly, no one will deny that videotapes and DVDs are precious analytical and pedagogical tools that most of us would hate to do without. Moreover, it seems clear that the popularity of videotape has eroded one kind of cinephilia while promoting another: *le rat de cinémathèque,* a pursuer of imaginary experiences, has become the video collector and hoarder or home archivist. As the luminous electronic screen replaces the black box of the movie theater, and the DVD replaces the film print, the disappearance of cinema makes it precious to us. What we always believed was the most modern art is suddenly becoming antiquarian. The birth of film studies is concomitant with the death of cinema. Can any other discipline characterize its history as rising on the decline of its object?

From the standpoint of film theory, there are two ways of looking at this question. Neither is without additional ironies and paradoxes. On one hand, the displacement of the film print and of theatrical film viewing might encourage us to refine and appreciate with ever greater precision what film is. Very soon, going to the cinema may no longer mean watching film. The sight of 35mm film well projected on the big screen, and indeed movies made to be experienced sensually in just this way, are suddenly becoming precious. Despite my fascination with the digital, recently my aesthetic and intellectual passion has been much more greatly stirred by films like Terence Malick's *The Thin Red Line* (1998) and Béla Tarr's *Werkmeister Harmonies* (2002). I am certain there is more philosophically to this fascination than the nostalgia of a middle-aged film scholar for a certain kind of art cinema.

On the other hand, does it matter at all that the days of photochemical art are numbered? With respect to digital technologies, cinema is reinventing itself—just as it has done in previous periods of technological transition—by producing stylistic innovations while respecting narrative continuities. In short, *Attack of the Clones* (2002) and *The Two Towers* (2002) are perfectly recognizable in most respects as classic Hollywood cinema despite their innovations in visual style. Here the transfer to a different creative medium—that of computer synthesis—seems to make little difference. While film may disappear, cinema nonetheless persists. And in fact digital filmmaking may inspire exciting new forms of cinema not yet imagined.

For similar reasons, grounding our discipline on an idea of either *film* or *cinema* studies may delimit too rigidly the boundaries of our inquiries. As Noël Carroll has argued, using the idiom "moving images" is preferable to using the word "film" because "what we call film and, for that matter, film history will, in generations to come, be seen as part of a larger continuous history that will no longer be restricted to things made only in the so-called medium of film but, as well, will apply to things made in the media of video, TV, computer-generated imagery, and we know not what. It will be a history of motion pictures or moving pictures, as we now say in ordinary language, or as I recommend we call it, a history of 'moving images,' of which the age of film, strictly speaking, is likely to be only a phase."[2] Written in 1996, this state of affairs has largely come to be, and I think that it is a good thing. In the same time frame, Carroll has made a very good case against medium-specificity arguments, or the idea that there is something ontologically unique about photographic and cinematic images. From a different perspective, I have argued that photography and film are the progenitors of the "virtual arts," and that there are as many continuities as discontinuities between old and new media. In this respect, what we call "film" is an unstable or variable object unanchored by familiar aesthetic criteria of self-identity.

While I strongly hold this position, I will now confess to my more anxious side, for I have not yet convinced myself that the question is closed. At the beginning of the twenty-first century we have come full circle again. And as the

2. *Theorizing the Moving Image* (Cambridge: Cambridge University Press, 1996) xiii.

photographic medium threatens to disappear forever on the scrapheap of technology, suddenly the main questions of classical film theory seem worth revisiting, despite the healthy skepticism of someone like Carroll. As film disappears into the electronic and virtual realm of numerical manipulation we are suddenly aware that something *was* cinema. The history of film theory has produced more than ninety years of debate on the question "What is cinema?" Yet suddenly we feel compelled to ask the question again, but in the past tense. For cinema professionals, a distinct qualitative change is being felt in very tangible ways, if difficult to define precisely. Only the transition to sound generated a comparable critical discourse of enthusiasm and loss in equal measure. In retrospect, however, the key difference was that the medium of the movies was not transformed. Previously occurring in a separate performance space, sound was initially incorporated as part of the photographic medium. But the emergence of digital filmmaking and, more radically, of digital image synthesis might mean that the very nature of the medium is changing—in short, becoming something that is no longer *film* in the ordinary sense of the term. This means that we need some new philosophical answers to some old theoretical questions:

- What is a medium?
- Is "film" in the conventional sense fundamentally tied to photography as a medium?
- When filmmaking and viewing become fully digital arts, will a certain experience of cinema be irretrievably lost?

In what ways does the emergence of digital filmmaking encourage us to rephrase these questions and try to answer them in new ways?

## 6. A Medium in All Things

Let's provisionally accept the premise of classical film theory that the photographic process is the basis of the film medium. By what criteria can photography be defined as a medium? I offer this definition for the sake of argument: *The material basis of photography, as well as film, is a process of mechanically recording an image through the automatic registration of reflected light on a photosensitive chemical surface. This image is analogical, defined as a transformation of substance isomorphic with the originating image regardless of scale.* As I will clarify later, analogy also indicates a specific kind of causality—a transformation that is continuous within a given unit of time, forming a discrete spatial image in direct contact with a profilmic event. Before the digital era, this was always the adventure of photography.

In photochemical photography, analogy also means that the time of exposure effects a transformation of substance in which time, light, and density are directly proportional. Film adds to this definition the reproduction of movement and duration in photographing equidistant frames of equal size projected at a uniform rate of speed. Moreover, the act of projecting may be fundamental to the visual experience of film, which is, after all, successive variations in the quality of light (brightness, color, contrast) passing through spatially and visually distinct frames.

I would like to call "film" any image recorded and projected according to these criteria. This definition is formal, but later it will also inspire qualitative commentary.

Both analog video and digital recordings depart from this definition in ways significant enough that it is desirable to ask whether the analogical and the digital present significant differences as "media." In Part III I will use this observation to test my intuition that although a movie like *Shrek* (2001) was distributed theatrically on film, this is not a medium for which it has a particular affinity. In fact the creative medium of digitally synthesized artifacts like *Final Fantasy: The Spirits Within* (2001) and *Monsters, Inc.* (2001) does not seem to be film in this sense.

This conjecture means, first, that a medium should be distinguished from its physical support and channel of transmission, even if they share the same substance or material. Videotape (analog or digital), MPEG-2 encoding, broadcast television, and the Internet may all function as distribution channels in which essentially the same artifact (say, Fritz Lang's *M*) can be viewed. Assuming optimum conditions, despite changes in scale, differences in contrast, croppings of the frame, and small variations in rates of projection, the differences in form between film and video versions of *M* may be no more (or less) significant than variations among existing 16 and 35mm prints. The basic distinction between film and video or analog and digital as carriers of information may not be enough to clarify the questions "What is a medium?" and "Does it matter?" For motion pictures like *Shrek* or *Star Wars 2: Attack of the Clones*, celluloid functions only as a distribution medium, a way of presenting movies widely in existing theaters even if *these* artifacts might be preferably seen with electronic and digital projection.

This observation opens another parenthesis: *Do moving-image media have special affinities with specific viewing environments?* For the moment, I would also still insist on holding on to the specificity of theatrical film viewing, because for me, intuitively, electronic images and screens are not "cinema"; that is, they cannot produce the social and psychological conditions of a certain pleasurable spectating. Conversely, digital images do not seem to "want" mechanical/celluloid projection. Their intrinsic sensual properties are not realized, and are perhaps even inhibited, when presented on celluloid filmstock.

What this means is that a medium should not be considered as a "material" in any literal or simple sense. "Film" may be distinguishable from "motion pictures," and indeed it may increasingly be the case that motion pictures are not films. By what right, then, can we distinguish film as a medium? Noël Carroll has argued, to a certain extent persuasively, that we cannot, and there are some interesting lessons to be learned from his observations.

In ordinary language, when we speak of the medium of an art form, we usually want to know in what consists a painting, a sculpture, a play, or a photograph, or what leads us to characterize a work of art as such. And even within the genre of moving images we may want to know in what consists a film or a video. In its simplest intuitive definition, a medium is something the artist transforms in the making of art. Yet our commonsensical notions of a medium or of media are powerfully contradictory. We easily speak of different media, or we characterize an artist as working in a medium. The connotations of the noun "medium" are broad and varied, however. For example, the *Oxford English Dictionary (OED)* suggests two meanings that are often used interchangeably in an artistic context:

> 4. a. Any intervening substance through which . . . impressions are conveyed to the senses . . . Often *fig.*
>
> 5. a. An intermediate agency, means, instrument or channel. Also, intermediation, instrumentality: in phrase *by* or *through the medium of. spec.* of newspapers, radio, television, etc., as vehicles of mass communication.

Is a medium a substance, an instrument, or simply a channel? Or is it a variable combination of these and other qualities? In the passage quoted above, Noël Carroll himself easily refers to things like film, television, or video. Yet in a series of interesting articles, he has argued strenuously that there is no logically justifiable way of specifying what these things are, because the different senses of "medium" are incompatible or contradictory.[3] In this respect, he challenges what he calls "the doctrine of medium specificity" in both film theory and the philosophy of art.

Carroll characterizes the doctrine of medium specificity in three principal arguments. It is not exactly clear who adheres to this doctrine and is thus the subject of his criticisms. Nonetheless, Carroll's logical exposition of the doctrine offers some interesting observations on the difficulties of defining the concept of artistic media. They may be summarized as follows:

1. The first proposes a "purist program" stating "that if the medium in question is to be truly regarded as an art, then it must have some range of autonomous effects" ("Medium Specificity Arguments" 3). I call this *the criterion of self-identity.*
2. That arts may and should be differentiated in terms of the uniqueness of a medium. This means isolating either an essence or a function that may resolve all subsidiary aesthetic questions asked of the medium. Carroll further clarifies this point by distinguishing an internal component and a comparative component. The internal component addresses intrinsic properties, or how a medium identifies itself by establishing "the range of effects that accord with the special limitations and possibilities of the medium in question . . . The internal component examines the relation between the medium and the artform embodied in it. Each medium has a distinctive character, conceived of in terms of limitations and possibilities, which sets the boundary for stylistic exploration in the artform embodied in the medium" ("Medium Specificity Arguments" 8). Alternatively, the comparison component is extrinsic, evaluating what the medium does best relative to other media in some univocal sense. In either case, the self-identity of the medium is grounded in the identification of what I call *aesthetic a prioris* that define the distinctiveness of creative options within the assumed medium.
3. And finally, the assertion that art forms can be analyzed in terms of the possession of a unique, determinate medium has directive implica-

3. See in particular the essays collected in Part I of *Theorizing the Moving Image,* including "Medium Specificity Arguments and the Self-Consciously Invented Arts," "The Specificity of Media in the Arts," and "Defining the Moving Image," as well as a later essay, "Forget the Medium!" in *Screen-Based Art,* ed. Annette W. Balkema and Henk Slager (Amsterdam: Rodopi B. V., 2000) 55–62.

> tions about what artists should and should not do. I call this *the injunctive argument.*

In film theory, the doctrine of medium specificity would therefore assert "that each artform has a distinctive medium; that the material cause, so to speak, of an artform—its medium—is also its essence (in the sense of its telos); that the essence of an artform—its medium—indicates, limits or dictates the style and/or content of the artform; and, finally, that film possesses such an essence" ("Defining the Moving Image" 50).

Carroll's objections to medium-specificity arguments are fundamentally twofold: that a medium directs its uses, and consequently that the evolution of art practiced in a given medium is directed by a telos, or ever more nearly perfect instantiations of the medium's essential qualities. Or in other words, he objects both to defining a medium as a univocal and atemporal material cause, and to grounding injunctive judgments in this cause. When this is the case, theoretical arguments about a medium's essential properties are expressed as qualitative directives or injunctions regarding uses to which a medium may or may not be put. Gotthold Ephraim Lessing is no doubt the aesthetic progenitor of these kinds of qualitative arguments wherein a philosopher differentiates media according to fundamental properties (succession or simultaneity) and then adjudicates proper and improper uses of a medium. These injunctions often take the form of an "excellence requirement" and a "differentiation requirement." The excellence requirement invokes the criterion of self-identity as the need to identify those aesthetic a prioris that exemplify the medium in terms of what it does best, both uniquely and in comparison with other media. Thus, a medium will evolve by seeking out those uses and effects that conform mostly closely to its material essence. The differentiation requirement enjoins each art form to express those qualities that best distinguish it from the other arts. This is an injunction against hybrid forms as well as a strategy for seeking out and refining the essential properties of a medium by comparing its likenesses to and differences from other arts. However, such injunctions are counterintuitive, as most modern arts involve mixed media that more often than not have divergent and nonconverging potentials. "Obviously," Carroll concludes, "what is meant by the phrase 'artistic medium' is highly ambiguous, referring sometimes to the physical materials out of which artworks are constructed, sometimes to the implements that are used to do the constructing and sometimes to the formal elements of design that are available to artists in a given practice . . . Be that as it may, it should be clear that most artforms cannot be identified on the basis of a single medium, since most art forms correlate with more than one medium" ("Defining the Moving Image" 51).

In this manner Carroll argues, as I have done, that one of the great interests of film is how it functions as a hybrid medium. It has no single leading component; rather it is comprised of multiple components irreducible, one would think, to a single essence, and thus remains open to a plethora of diverse and even incompatible styles and formal approaches. These arguments may be taken as criticisms. But Carroll's comments may also encourage us to think of a medium as comprised of distinct components, which could in fact be physical, instrumental, and/or formal. Nothing here would disallow specifying media with a strong kinship (film, video, and digital imaging) as having a variable distinctiveness containing overlapping as well as divergent elements or qualities.

However, it is not so much the notion that there *are* media that incenses Carroll, as the ideas that the material structure of a medium determines its "essence" and that this essence, once defined, should limit the uses to which a medium can be put. The injunctive dimension of medium-specificity arguments, when there is one, seems to function as an unreasonable limit on artistic inventiveness. And Carroll is right to argue that what are often represented as violations of the medium are in fact violations of preferred styles or practices. This observation leads him to opt for a pragmatic view of art based not on the logic of artistic materials, but on what artists do or make of those materials: "In short, the purposes of a given art—indeed, of a given style, movement, or genre—will determine what aspects of the physical medium are important. The physical medium does not select a unique purpose, or even a delimited range of purposes, for an art form" ("Specificity of Media in the Arts" 28).

Now, in this statement and elsewhere, Carroll implicitly allows some idea of "medium," although it is unclear in what this idea consists. Throughout the essays he has devoted to the topic, Carroll writes as if we can take for granted that painting, dance, theater, film, and video are relatively distinctive art forms, and that part of their distinctiveness derives from the material components from which they are created. But from the standpoint of Carroll's aesthetic pragmatism, the things that are of interest to philosophical definition or aesthetic judgments are only the individual practices created for the medium in question. For this reason a medium cannot act as a determinate or directive force limiting future possibilities of stylistic innovation. And indeed Carroll is probably right to argue that most medium-specificity arguments are less "ontologies" than "briefs in favor of certain styles, genres and artistic movements" ("Medium Specificity Arguments" 19) inspired by physical aspects of the medium in question. Still, in ordinary language we call these things painting, dance, theater, film, or video. There must be some sense of medium directing these intuitions.

So, when Carroll makes a statement like "remember that all media have more than one constituent component" ("Specificity of Media in the Arts" 28), he seems to allow that a medium can be defined, perhaps by enumerating its fundamental components. In a footnote to the "The Specificity of Media in the Arts," he admits that media might be individuated on the basis of their physical structures, while arguing that it may be undesirable to do so. It is preferable to try to understand media as cultural and historical constructions. But here is an interesting point about the "self-consciously invented arts," as Carroll puts it, though I believe it may count for every medium. Carroll argues, quite rightly, that the recording and presentation technology of film (thus the physical structure of the medium) has evolved continually with respect to the desire to achieve new aesthetic purposes or effects: "our stylistic aims, needs, and purposes lead to changes in the very physical structure of media . . . The physical structure of a medium does not remain static. It is modified as a result of the needs and imperatives of our existing and emerging styles, genres, and art movements. Those often literally shape the medium, rather than the medium dictating style" ("Specificity of Media in the Arts" 36, n. 13).

All media evolve in time, then, but not toward a predetermined essence. Rather, they are adapted to various external purposes—creative innovation, for example, or market differentiation, as in the adoption of widescreen processes in the 1950s. This is an important point, which I characterize now as the *historical objection.* However, recognizing the evolution of the physical structure of the medium of film is only an argument against defining media in terms of having an essence, defined either by the criterion of substantial self-similarity or by the enumeration of their aesthetic a prioris. In no way does it obviate the possibility or desirability of defining the variable specificity of moving-image media.

Carroll would prefer, however, to disallow medium-specificity arguments because he finds them to be invariably essentialist. Essentialism is defined here in three principal ways. The strongest form of the medium-specificity doctrine may be represented as follows: "that the various media (that artforms are embodied in) have unique features—ostensibly identifiable in advance of, or independently of, the uses to which the medium is put—and, furthermore, these unique features determine the proper domain of effects of the art form in question" ("Specificity of Media in the Arts" 34). This is what I have called the criterion of self-identity, wherein essence comprises a self-realizing teleology. Second, any subsequent conditions generated from this primary criterion will be both necessary and jointly sufficient. Finally, a less logically strict definition is what Carroll calls Grecian or Platonic essentialism, whereby a theorist hypothetically presents a necessary condition for an art form because it is found useful for understanding that art form. Essentialism is philosophically undesirable, however, first of all because most art forms are demonstrably not self-identical either formally or substantively; and second, because the concept of medium is correlated in an often confused way with material, instrumental, and formal definitions; and finally, because the presumed physical structures of media are historically variable and highly responsive to inventive purposes that are not foreseeable.

For these reasons, Carroll renounces any distinctive definition of film, video, or digital imaging. The best that can be done is to define certain practices (the sight gag, suspense editing, the film metaphor) in piecemeal fashion or, alternatively, to pose a general category of artistic expression—moving images—in which criteria of medium specificity are irrelevant. This latter position is instructive for my purpose here. To present a nonessentialist definition of moving images, Carroll proposes five necessary though not jointly sufficient conditions. Therefore, something ($x$) is a moving picture:

1. *Only if* x *is a detached display,* that is, a visual array presenting an image whose space is discontinuous with the spectator's bodily orientation.
2. *Only if* x *belongs to a class of things from which the impression of movement is technically possible.*
3. *Only if performance tokens of* x *are generated by a template that is a token;* that is, the individual projection of a given "movie" is inseparable from its presentation template (celluloid strip, videotape, MPEG-2 file). Nonetheless, the movie will also continue to exist as long as some token of it does, regardless of the physical basis of the template.
4. *Only if performance tokens of* x *are not artworks in their own right.* The performance of a play is an autonomous and unique interpretation that may be judged as an artwork in its own right. But a movie "performance" is only the repeatable display of a record (film projection,

playing a videotape), which is why Carroll insists "that motion pictures are not objects of artistic evaluation, whereas theatrical performances are . . . [Motion] pictures are not a performing art—i.e., they are not something whose performance is itself an art" ("Defining the Moving Image" 69). Another way of saying this is that for Carroll all aspects of movie creation (scenario writing, acting, direction, editing, etc.) are integrated into a final record from which they are not detachable. And we evaluate not the recording, but rather the artistic activities embodied and fixed within it.

5. *Only if* x *is two-dimensional.*

Why does this definition preclude the notion of a medium? Perhaps it does not. It proscribes only essentialist definitions that imply aesthetic injunctions because their principal arguments present necessary conditions requiring joint sufficiency. Alternatively, Carroll's criteria for defining "moving images" might help describe the variable specificity of moving-image media. Ironically, these statements encourage us to discern the relative distinctiveness of various moving-image media by qualifying the nature of their adherence to these conditions. Film and video use different kinds of detached displays, for example, and their conveyance of an impression of movement is rendered technically possible through different recording and presentation technologies. Carroll's characterization of "moving images," moreover, is only a logical definition—it clarifies nothing concerning sensory or cognitive differences between, say, film and video in their analogical rendering of images and in their conveyance of an impression of movement. Nor can it aid us in evaluating the experiential differences in watching film and video or distinguishing their perceptual, cognitive, and contextual differences as well as similarities. In short, his critique discourages thick perceptual and psychological descriptions that might help in understanding the distinctiveness of different moving-image media. Carroll's definition is technically consistent but aesthetically uninteresting. It may clarify how a film can be transferred to analog video or DVD without losing its status as a motion picture, but it offers nothing for comprehending what significant aesthetic or perceptual transformations might also take place. Indeed the definition implies that those transformations are insignificant, at least for understanding what motion pictures are.

This conclusion is paradoxical, since Carroll's own conditions encourage attention to the physical nature of motion picture recording and projection or playback. And this position is consistent with an ordinary-language understanding of the concept of a medium. Here conditions 3 and 4 present their real interest. For they would seem to imply that motion pictures *require* a medium in the sense of a material of recording and conveyance. While Carroll emphasizes the concept of performance as a key criterion for distinguishing motion pictures from other art forms, the concept of templates leads in another direction.

According to his own definition, any record of a motion picture requires a template. Carroll assumes the neutrality of the template as the ability to generate invariant tokens, regardless of the physical structure of the template. (This would count for the origin of the artifact as well as its presentation.) In other words, he assumes the essential similarity of all tokens of a given type regardless of the physical nature of the template. For the type "Fritz Lang's *M*" to persist, it must have a template, that is, a medium. If all celluloid copies of *M* were destroyed, we would certainly be grateful to have a DVD. But we might also continue to wonder if it were a *film,* and consequential aesthetic questions would be raised by this reflection. After taking great pains to disallow any criteria for comprehending what identifies a medium, he persists in using the concept as if everyone recognized intuitively what a medium is and does, or of what it is capable. We are left either with an implicit definition of a medium as a physical structure that is entirely impassive and neutral with respect to aesthetic purposes, or an explicit categorization of such a high level of generalization as to blur any potential distinctiveness.

While I am sympathetic to Carroll's "antiessentialism" and to his pragmatic view of art making, his critique leaves little room for understanding what the concept of a medium might entail, even as the object of his critique. Carroll finds little value in distinguishing, say, film from video or digital synthesis. All qualify as "moving images" according to his definition. In my previous example, *M* remains the same "motion picture" regardless of the template that serves as its channel of transmission—celluloid, analog video, or digital versatile disk. Any qualitative noise or distortions introduced by the channel would seem to be irrelevant. Alternatively, artists care very much about the material they work with, and spectators, too, make strong intuitive aesthetic judgments about the differences between film, video, and digital presentations. Are the material components of making and watching moving images really irrelevant to various kinds of aesthetic judgments we may want to make about them? We may want to ask, even if the answer may sometimes lack philosophical clarity, how and why powerful artistic, perceptual, and psychological effects in film are lost in the transfer to another "medium." And this might lead us to attribute, nonetheless, a variable specificity to different moving-image media. We may still want to characterize *M* as a film rather than as a moving picture, and in this case we will want to know what film is and what cultural values we have assigned to it historically. What is gained from Carroll's definition for the comparative component (distinguishing moving pictures from neighboring art forms) may also entail a loss in the capacity for discerning differences among motion picture media.

There is much to be learned from Carroll's criticisms. But it should still be possible to invoke the concept of a medium in ways that are not reducible to arguments concerning essence, teleology, and injunction. Much can be said about medium specificity that is nuanced historically and without legislating what artists should or should not do. Moreover, Carroll's own characterization of the doctrine of medium specificity is an idealization, or worse, a philosophical caricature. One is hard put to find an author, movement, or tendency in the history of classical film theory that exemplifies this doctrine in an unequivocal way.

Carroll's critique, no matter how persuasive in certain of its aspects, might risk throwing the baby out with the bathwater. It is certainly true that the identity of film is, and has been for some time, unraveling in all directions into moving images. But Carroll's logic of generalization is insensitive to differences and to potential qualities in recognition of which one may want to preserve an idea of medium flexible enough to comprehend how media may individuate themselves while nonetheless preserving certain properties in common. For this reason, media are plural not only because they are various or admit historically to qualitatively different styles and practices, but also because the self-identity of a medium may accord less with a homogeneous substance than with a set of component properties or conceptual options. I am happy to admit as many hybridizations of media as artists can invent in their actual practice. But what makes a hybrid cannot be understood if the individual properties being combined cannot be distinguished. If we cannot be precise about the range and nature of these options, we cannot understand, as either artists or philosophers, what media might do, how they may evolve with respect to one another, or how we might work with a medium or even invent a new one, even if that recognition occurs only after the fact.

## 7. Automatisms and Art

Let us say, then, that the medium of an art form combines multiple elements or components that can be material, instrumental, and/or formal. These elements may be variable, and a medium may be defined without presuming an integral identity or essence uniting these elements into a whole. But a medium is also that which *mediates*—its stands between us and the world as representation *(Vorstellung)*, or it confronts us in a way that returns our perceptions to us in the form of thoughtfulness. We need to go beyond a formal definition and try to understand how a medium inspires or provokes sensual, that is to say, aesthetic experience. A medium is not simply a passive material or substance; it is equally form, concept, or idea. Or, more provocatively, a medium is a terrain where works of art establish their modes of existence, and pose questions of existence to us.

In contemporary philosophy, the most challenging reconsideration of the concept of medium in relation to photography and film is undoubtedly Stanley Cavell's *The World Viewed.* Here Cavell argues that the creation of a medium is the creation of "automatisms." Although the subtitle of his book is *Reflections on an Ontology of Film,* Cavell's idea of ontology in no way assumes an essentialism or teleology. It refers, rather, to a mode of existence for art and to our relationships with given art forms. This mode of existence is not static, however. A medium, if it is a living one, is continually in a state of self-transformation. Cavell's conception of aesthetic creation is quite original. In his view, media are not given a priori. "[The] task is no longer to produce another instance of an art," he writes, "but a new medium within it."[4] In this perspective, automatisms are both the material of aesthetic creation *and* the result of artistic practice. Automatisms in this sense are forms, conventions, or genres that arise creatively out of the existing materials and material conditions of given art practices. These in turn serve as potential materials or forms for future practices. Cavell calls these materials "elements," or fundamental acts constituting the specific possibilities and necessities of a given medium; in so doing, they remake the meaning of the medium in each artistic act. What constitutes these elements is unknowable prior to the creative acts of artists and the analytical observations of critics—this is why they are considered potentialities or virtualities expressed in the history of a medium and its uses.

Why characterize these elements as "automatisms"? They are certainly inspired by the instrumental automatisms of photography and film, that is, the self-acting processes of mechanical reproduction. I will return to this point later. However, an unremarked assumption in Cavell's concept is how automatisms act as variable limits to subjectivity and creative agency. Insofar

4. *The World Viewed: Reflections on the Ontology of Film,* enl. ed. (Cambridge, Mass.: Harvard University Press, 1979) 103.

as they function as potentialities of thought, action, or creation, automatisms circumscribe what subjectivity is or can be and how it is conditioned conceptually, though these conditions are neither inflexible nor invariable. Certainly Cavell values the inventiveness of artists and indeed credits them to a great degree with the creation of media. It is fundamentally through a practice or actual artistic acts that media are recognized and assume an identity, no matter how variable. Yet this practice does not occur in perfect freedom. Automatisms circumscribe practice, setting the conditions for creative agency and the artistic process.

In this respect, several layers of sense may be uncovered within the concept. For example, the *OED* gives five primary definitions for the term "automatism":

1. The quality of being automatic, or of acting mechanically only; involuntary action.
2. Mechanical, unthinking routine.
3. The faculty of independently originating action or motion.
4. Any psychic phenomenon that appears spontaneously in consciousness; any action performed subconsciously or unconsciously, undirected by the mind or will of the normal personality; also the mental state in which these phenomena occur.
5. *spec.* A technique in surrealist painting . . .

The instrumental qualities of cameras, the fact that they set into play a number of imaging processes at the request of, but also independently of, human action, will be as central to Cavell's arguments about photography and film as they were to André Bazin's. The Surrealist sense, which acknowledges that every creative act has its collective and unconscious dimensions, is also certainly important. However, on a more quotidian level, every practice has automatisms in the sense of working distractedly from routine or unquestioningly following norms and conventions. Call these habits or even codes if you will, but no act of creation occurs in perfect freedom. Nor would the singularity of each creative act be recognizable and comprehensible without a basis for understanding the encounters between automatism and artistic will.

Creation is never free, then, nor can originality be identified without the background of repetitive automatism. This necessity is not necessarily a bad thing. The mastery of a medium may include the renewal and extension of long and venerable histories of collective artistic automatisms, that is, traditions. For example, Cavell writes that "in mastering a tradition, one masters a range of automatisms upon which the tradition maintains itself, and in deploying them one's work is assured a place in that tradition" (*The World Viewed* 104). Indeed, this is one of Cavell's ways of evaluating and valuing work produced within the Hollywood studio system.

This argument inspires a final point. Having an Idea in art generates automatisms in the form of multiple expressive variations. In encountering automatisms as limits, artists invent new creative strategies as ways of overcoming or transforming them. But once these strategies are incorporated as elements of style, they in turn may function automatically as an aesthetic idea or strategy generating new variants on or instantiations of its concept. Automatisms are iterative; they function in series. When a new medium is discovered, says Cavell, "it generates new instances: not merely makes them possible, but calls for them, as if to attest that what has been discovered is more than a single work could convey" (*The World Viewed* 107).

Therefore, automatisms are iterative, but in two interacting ways. They proliferate purposes or uses independent of an individual artistic agency and so function as limits; in this sense they are transsubjective and perpetuate repetitiveness, similarity, or continuity. But in responding creatively to these limits artists create new styles or purposes for a medium (differences), and these in turn may proliferate into individual or collective practices as new automatisms. But note that creation is not the struggle to liberate oneself from automatisms. This is an impossible task. The emphasis, rather, is how automatisms forge the autonomy of the work of art or of the medium in which it emerges. "[The] point of this effort," Cavell explains, "is to free me not merely from my confinement in automatisms that I can no longer acknowledge as mine . . . but to free the object from me, to give new ground for its *autonomy*" (*The World Viewed* 108). Especially in modern art, automatisms provoke a sense of autopoiesis, such that "the notion of automatism codes the experience of the work of art as 'happening of itself'" (107). Unlike classical art, wherein automatisms function as the renewal and extension of tradition, the modernist artwork provokes in each of its instances the sense of being self-actualizing, of standing alone. It is as if in each act of art making the possibility of producing art, and of having an aesthetic experience, has to be reasserted without any promise of success. In this way, the modern work of art embodies an existential condition expressive of our own current mode of existence: in the absence of tradition, whether moral or epistemological, the self is provoked to a state of continual self-actualization or invention. I will deepen this argument later. The main point here is that in the contemporary situation, we recognize art only retrospectively, as having happened, which is why it provokes the sense of happening of itself, that is, as automatism.

In this sense, artistic activity consists not in discovering the essence of a medium, but rather in exploring and perhaps renewing or even reinventing its powers of expression. Therefore, the existence of an art is neither defined nor guaranteed by the nature of its physical materials or structural properties, but rather by the forms of expressiveness it enables, or which can be discovered in it. This is an attitude curiously close to Spinoza's own conception of automatism in the *Ethics.* Here automatism expresses what it means to have an Idea. An Idea is an expression not of thought, but of our powers of thinking, which itself occurs in a medium that Spinoza calls signs. Ideas are not separable from an autonomous sequence or sequencing of ideas in thought that Spinoza calls *concatenatio.* This concatenation of signs unites form and material, constituting thought as a spiritual automaton. Neither thought nor creation occurs without a medium. A medium in this sense is not a passive or recalcitrant substance subject to artistic will. It is itself expressive as *potentiae,* or powers, of thought, action, or creation. But these powers are variable and conditional. In exploring their potential we discover the conditions of possibility of a medium; in exceeding or exhausting them we may in fact create a new medium, and new powers of thought and creation. Nonetheless, the conditions of possibility for these acts are always unknowable in advance, which is why it is wise, like Cavell and Carroll, to adapt a pragmatic perspective when asking in what art making consists. By the same token, the frontier that marks the creation of a new medium from an old one is often indistinct and highly mobile.

Cavell implicitly replies here to several of Carroll's objections to the use of the concept of medium. If media are not given a priori, the creative process is free of injunctions or determinate purposes, although, importantly, they do not function without limits. Furthermore, in characterizing a medium as the creation of automatisms, Cavell more often than not invokes the plural form, suggesting that a medium is not a univocal substance or self-identical form, but rather is comprised of multiple elements that can be material, instrumental, and/or formal, all of which may develop independently of one another in uneven rhythms. Finally, these elements are historically variable, both singly and collectively. They evolve in relation to actual artistic practices and independently of any abstract teleology or ideology. A creative act by definition transforms its medium or may even create a new medium. But this variability does not mean that no form or identity may be attributed to a medium, nor is the physical situation of a medium entirely without importance.

## 8. Automatism and Photography

> On n'a pas besoin de faire du cinéma . . . dès que la caméra tourne le cinéma se fait tout seul.
>
> —Jean Eustache, program notes for *Numéro zéro*

To reinvoke my initial questions, then, what is photography according to Cavell, and how does it contribute to thinking about the medium of film? How may the concept of automatisms inform this thinking? Here the automatic quality of automatisms must be probed more deeply.

In their most basic definition, automatisms refer to the fundamental elements of photography and film. An element is "fundamental" in the degree to which the elimination of one or more of these components inspires doubt as to whether the resulting artifact *is* a photograph or a film. Thinking in this way is also to ask: To what do we attribute the power of photography or film—to their hold on our perceptions? For Cavell, this is a question neither of representation nor of meaning, but rather of ontology. And the question of ontology is inseparable from that of medium.

Cavell defines the material condition of film as "*a succession of automatic world projections*" (*The World Viewed* 72). This is a provocative definition. Comprehending all its ramifications means understanding how the parts of this definition interrelate as a whole, attending to its key concepts. This involves considering automatisms of image making (the photographic process), of movement or succession, and finally of perception (the projected or screened world). By what reasoning do we say that taking a photograph is automatic or that it is comprised of automatisms? What kind of picturing does photography propose that is distinct from painting, for example? Why are photographs of the world? How does photography's "worlding" place us subjectively with respect to a depicted physical reality and with respect to the aesthetic world presented by photographs and films?

While every medium can be characterized by its automatisms, Cavell's concept is inspired in the first instance by mechanical reproducibility in photography and film. "Automatic" is qualified first as an instrumental fact of photography in that, as Bazin put it, "For the first time, between the originating object and its reproduction there intervenes only the instrumentality of a nonliving agent. For the first time an image of the world is formed automatically, without the creative intervention of man."[5] Photography was arguably one of the first media whose fundamental processes had the quality of being "[self-acting] under conditions fixed for it, going of itself" *(OED)*. In other words, the instrumental conditions of picturing were changed by photography in that the process of image making itself devolves to a number of automated or self-actualizing processes: the organization of reflected light by the lens, the registration of duration by the shutter, and the reaction of photosensitive chemicals to light. I find it useful to refer, then, to the photographic *act* as a pragmatic and existential process, combining the actions of the photographer or cinematographer with those of the camera itself. While any number of automatisms are formal and imaginative, others are mechanical, such that, as Jean Eustache once remarked, "once the camera starts to turn, cinema makes itself."[6] If this impression is correct, what processes contribute to this self-making? What qualitative features do photography or film presuppose prior to or independently of individual creative "characterizations" of the medium?

Any working photographer will allow that the range of possible and desired effects in photographic images derives from a thorough knowledge of the mechanics of cameras, the optics of lenses, and the chemistry of raw stock, papers, development, and printing—in short, of the "medium" in its common instrumental and material senses. Instrumentality and chemistry are not identical with photography's automatisms, but they do help us understand in what those automatisms consist conceptually. In contrast to painting, photography is the conversion of light into matter as the result of several automatic processes. The photographer chooses a lens of a given focal length, a shutter speed, and an *f*-stop; but once the shutter is released the image is formed automatically in a chemical reaction to light reflected from a physical situation localizable in space and time. The aleatory and nonquantifiable pattern of silver halide grains reacts to the pattern and intensity of light resolved by the

5. "Ontology of the Photographic Image," in *What Is Cinema? Vol. I*, trans. Hugh Gray (Berkeley: University of California Press, 1967) 13.

6. Program notes for *Numéro zero*, published online by Agence du Cinéma Indépendant pour Sa Diffusion, www.lacid.org/films/fichesfilm/fiche.php3?film=348; my trans.

lens in a given unit of time. Before and after exposure, all kinds of "painterly" effects can be suggested. But the basic fact remains that the primary sense of every photograph is that it is *a spatial record of duration* fixed in a photochemical reaction to reflected light in a process deriving from the mechanical operation of cameras and lenses.[7] Capturing a cone of light involves opening a window on time. The capacity of the lens to resolve reflected light into an image on a plane surface, and the photochemical reaction to light in a fixed duration, involve variables that may be set by the photographer. But once the shutter snaps, the recording process is out of her or his hands, and the aesthetic result is temporarily unknowable. Before the digital era, this was always the adventure of photography. Note also that the multiple instrumental components defining photography's automatisms cannot be neutral or value-free. Photographic lenses could be designed for or adapted to a variety of perspectival systems. But the manufacturing norm used for constructing photographic lenses derives from the optical geometry of linear perspective. This norm embodies a mathematical concept and a cultural purpose that is reproduced—automatically—in every image recorded with those lenses. Therefore, part of the instrumental structure of the medium expresses a historically and culturally determined aesthetic purpose that is relatively independent of individual intentions. Automatisms are cultural as well as "mechanical."

To sum up provisionally, the material basis of photography as well as film is a process of mechanically recording an image through the automatic registration of reflected light onto a photosensitive chemical surface. The time of exposure effects a transformation of substance in which time, light, and density are directly proportional. The resulting image is analogical, defined as a direct and continuous transformation of substance isomorphic with the originating image regardless of scale. Analogy also indicates a specific kind of causality—a transformation that is continuous within a given unit of time, forming a discrete spatial image.

Since the 1970s, there has been considerable debate concerning the automatic qualities of photography's automatisms. But I would argue, nonetheless, that the following conceptual features of photography are unavoidably confronted as automatisms in Cavell's sense. Each one of these automatisms qualifies the character of photographic causality:

7. This element already suggests one distinctive difference of digital cameras, that is, their immediate, interactive feedback. The image is immediately accessible. Unlike the real-time causation of analog video, it is a product of a *computation* time, which I will discuss in Part III. Hence the notorious and frustrating phenomenon of "shutter lag" in digital and computer-assisted cameras.

1. Be produced by an or a variety of automated procedures. (The operations of lens, shutter, and photochemical receptivity to light are the instrumental conditions for these automatisms in photography.)
2. Have the quality of *isomorphism*—constancy of form regardless of scale in a counterfactually dependent relation; that is, any change in the record must necessarily reflect a change in the event recorded.
3. In addition, photographs are *analogical* in that representations so produced are *continuous and indivisible;* that is, "the axis or dimension that is measured has no apparent indivisible unit from which it is composed."[8]

Or, to put it somewhat differently, in analogical transcriptions inputs and outputs are continuous. This also means that discrete semantic units may be expressed only in the singularity of "takes" (beginning and ending the transcription) or through the combination of takes (editing or montage in a general sense). These characteristics are not unique to photography as an analogical art. Indeed, all analogical transcriptions, whether of image or of sound, may be characterized by this set of qualities, which I call *automatic analogical causation.*

Though subject to all manner of manipulation and transformation, including historical innovations and evolution in the technical processes themselves, these elements serve as limits to subjective decisions and acts—they lend an objective, or, as Bazin would have it, inhuman, quality to the production of images. In this they serve as what I will tentatively call the instrumental or primary automatisms of the photographic act, in that subtracting one or more of these elements from the photographic process encourages us to question whether the artifacts so produced should be characterized as "photographs," or whether, in fact, a new medium is being created.

Man Ray's "Rayographs" provide a provocative example. While Carroll might define these images as photographs, in the absence of a mechanical camera, it is likely that neither Bazin nor Cavell would. Ray created a new automatism for imprinting images on photographic paper; yet in the absence of camera and lens, there may be interesting reasons not to characterize these images as "photography," as Man Ray himself did not.[9] On one hand, in subtracting the camera the Rayograph returns the photochemical image close to

8. Isaac Victor Kerlov and Judson Rosebush, *Computer Graphics for Designers and Artists* (New York: Van Nostrand Reinhold, 1986) 14.

9. Man Ray and the critics of his time more often than not compared these images to painting or even poetry, a sort of autographism in light. And there is good evidence that the images were meant as a Dadaist provocation against photography and its characteristics of mechanical

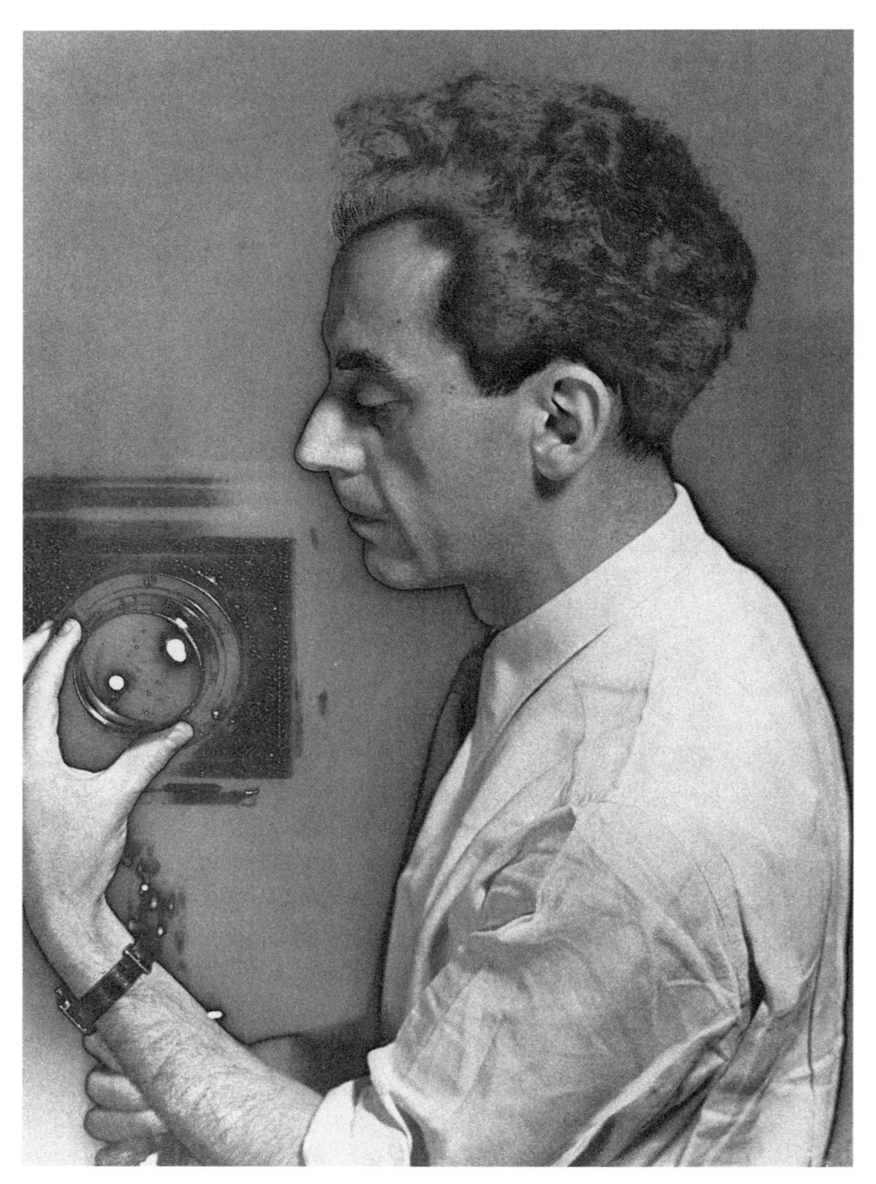

Man Ray, Self-portrait with camera (1931). 

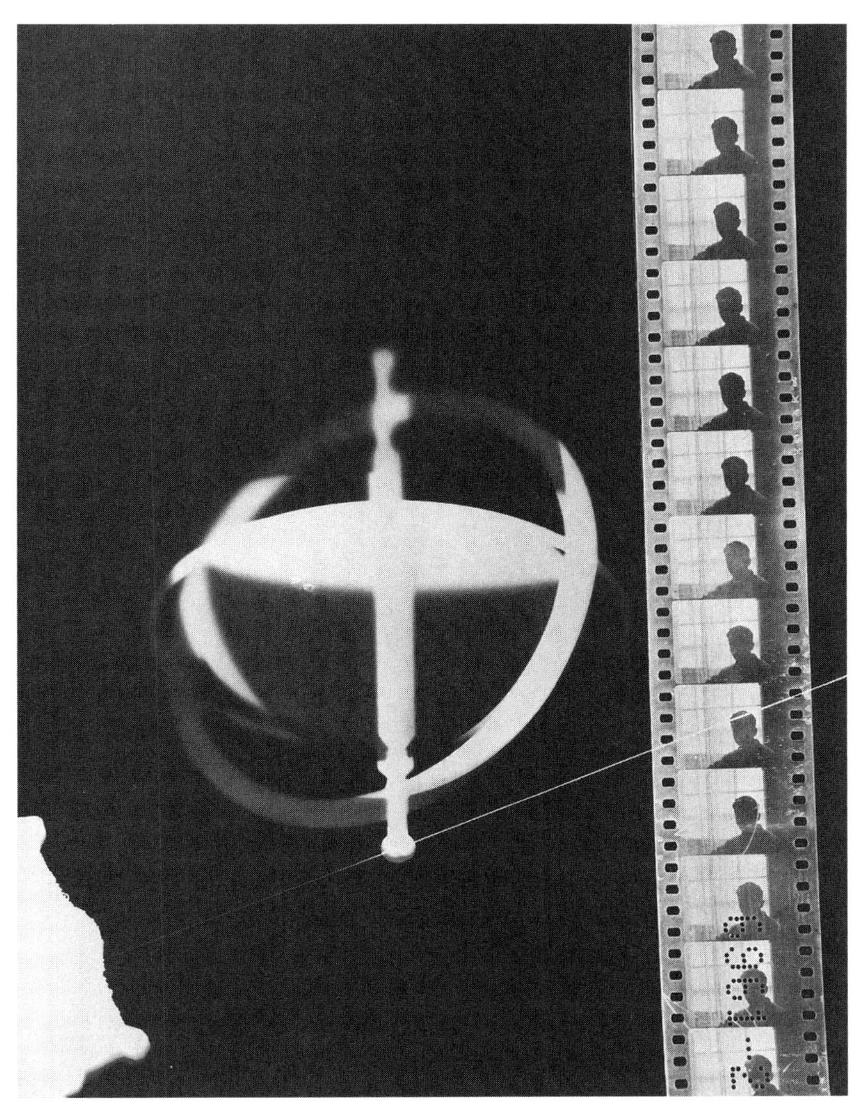

Rayography: Film strip and sphere (Man Ray, 1922). Copyright © Man Ray Trust / Artists Rights Society (ARS), NY/ADAGP, Paris.

its roots in lithography, that is, as direct contact with a photoreceptive material that forms an image with *subtracted* light rather than reflected light. On the other, in deemphasizing photography's representational powers it foregrounds others—indexicality, for example. Photographs may be transformed by hand, but they are not handmade.

## 9. Succession and the Film Strip

The idea of *succession* suggests another important element. The material basis for the reproduction of movement begins with the sequence of self-contained still frames recorded on the film strip; from this derives the ineluctable linear drive of filmic temporality. Organizations of shot and sequence also ultimately find their powers in this principle of succession. Movement is thus as much an automated process as the photographic registration of individual frames, which is why qualities of space, time, and movement are inseparable in film. (As I will explain in Part III, they are interrelated in different ways in analog and digital video images.) As photographs, these frames are given as substantial visible wholes; they exist as blocks of duration in themselves (photograms) before resolving, through the automation of movement, into a screen duration marked off in shots, whose existence is counterfactually dependent on the profilmic event so recorded. In film, the automated quality of succession means that, under normal conditions, depicted movement is homeomorphic with photographed movement. Because movement is recorded as a succession of spatial segments of a quantitative nature, it may be altered (fast or slow motion) without altering the isomorphism of image. Discreteness occurs only at the level of photograms and shot transitions.

Noël Carroll has critiqued so-called realist theories by objecting to their characterization of the unity of the frame in this way, his counterexamples being photomontages and process shots of various kinds.[10] But there is a way in

reproducibility. See Emmanuelle de l'Ecotais, *Man Ray: Rayographies* (Paris: Editions Léo Scheer, 2002) 11–27. For complementary discussions, see Philippe Dubois, *L'acte photographique* (Brussels: Editions Labor, 1983) 66–68.

10. "Concerning Uniqueness Claims for Photographic and Cinematographic Representation," in *Theorizing the Moving Image* 37–48. In my view, Carroll mischaracterizes or miscomprehends the causal arguments he critiques as presupposing identity relations between the image and what it depicts. Below I will show that neither resemblance nor (spatial) representation accounts for photography's hold on our perception in either Bazin's or Cavell's accounts. Kendall L. Walton responds implicitly to Carroll's objections in a somewhat different way in his essay "Transparent Pictures: On the Nature of Photographic Realism," *Critical Inquiry* 11 (December 1984) 246–277.

which the intraframe or spatial montage of process shots should be thought of no differently from sequential or temporal editing. Returning to a time when all special effects were photographic, one could insist that each element of the composite shot has a physical world referent, even if the whole adds up to a diegetic, metaphorical, or imaginary world. Each photographic element of a photomontage has a similar referentiality even if the whole is to be read as another kind of composite. In this respect, composite photography and photomontage differ little from other kinds of editing. If we accept the substantial unity of the basic photographic elements, then in every case it is a matter of assessing these composites as examples of montage. Or, one would have to follow Carroll to the letter and say that there is no apparent spatial unity to a one-minute take because it is comprised in actuality of 1,440 still frames. In which case, there is no film, only photography.

It also bears noting here that the instrumental conditions for producing succession vary greatly in film and electronic media, and within electronic media between analogical and digital video, to the extent that Babette Mangolte has wondered, "Why is it so difficult for a digital image to communicate duration?"[11] (I will examine this question more deeply later.) The particular quality of automated movement in theatrical film projection also excludes the potential for interactivity, even the limited interactivity of video viewing—an important automatism available to more recent moving-image media. Thus, succession means that fundamentally every film is an animated film as the automated reconstitution of movement from a succession of still images. In contrast to the stillness of photography, Vivian Sobchack thus characterizes succession as "the transformation of moment to momentum that constitutes the ontology of the cinematic, and the latent background of every film."[12] Understood in this way, the automatism of succession overturns Lev Manovich's assertion that digital synthesis returns pride of place to the "minor

11. "Afterward: A Matter of Time. Analog versus Digital, the Perennial Question of Shifting Technology and Its Implications for an Experimental Filmmaker's Odyssey," in *Camera Obscura, Camera Lucida,* ed. Richard Allen and Malcolm Turvey (Amsterdam: Amsterdam University Press, 2003) 263.

12. "The Scene of the Screen: Envisioning Cinematic and Electronic Presence," in *Materialities of Communication,* ed. H. U. Gumbrecht and K. L. Pfeffer (Stanford: Stanford University Press, 1994) 95. Lev Manovich's assertion in *The Language of New Media* that there is a tension between photographic and graphical practice in the history of cinema is not at issue here. Later I will explain that this is not a spatial or stylistic distinction, as Manovich implies, but rather a temporal and causal distinction wherein filmic and digital practice confront each other as distinct ontologies. I will also show that my position does not vary greatly from Cavell's own discussion of "animation" in *The World Viewed* 167–174.

genre" of graphical film with another line of reasoning: every film is an animated film. Animation, in the sense of reconstituting movement from a series of still images, is at the heart of all analogical moving-image practices. Any distinctions between them would only want to account for the different ways of producing succession.

## 10. Ways of Worldmaking

> Film takes our very distance and powerlessness over the world as the condition of the world's natural appearance. It promises the exhibition of the world in itself. This is its promise of candor: that what it reveals is entirely what is revealed to it, that nothing revealed by the world in its presence is lost.
>
> —Stanley Cavell, *The World Viewed*

The combination of the instrumental automatisms of photography and uninterrupted linear automated movement in film contributes strongly to our sense of the relative specificity of cinematic experience as the projection of an "autonomous" world. This is so not only because the human hand is once removed from its making, but also because we are phenomenologically screened from this world—we are present to a world from which we are absent. Obviously I agree with Cavell (and, *inter alia,* Bazin, Siegfried Kracauer, and Roland Barthes) that photographs are *of* the world in some fundamental sense. But why is it that we seem to invest in the power of movies to project a *world* and not just a series of images? Here Cavell's Heideggerian inspiration coincides remarkably with Christian Metz's and Jean-Louis Baudry's more psychoanalytically inflected arguments, though with important differences. For in the projection process, film gives us not just moving images but also a condition of viewing or spectating, as well as the desire for a specific kind of sight: "the magical reproduction of the world by enabling us to view it unseen" (*The World Viewed* 101). Cavell makes some interesting claims concerning the phenomenology of this projected world. The most important include the causal relation between photography or film and physical reality, and cinema's framing of perception as a "moving image of skepticism" (188). One derives from the photographic act itself, the other from philosophy.

Among the most commented-on passages in *The World Viewed* is Cavell's assertion early in the book of our confidence that a photograph, whether still or moving, is not a painting. Further on, Cavell presents a yet more provocative, qualitative distinction: "A painting *is* a world; a photograph is *of* the world" (24). In this difference inheres their ontological distinctiveness. We may attribute qualities of image or representation to both paintings and photographs, but a deeper examination shows that they present very different modes of existence to our acts of viewing. In speaking of modes of existence, I am less interested in how paintings and photographs function as "representations" than in how they indicate their states of being, or how they disclose (or not) their genesis in past acts of making. Indeed if photographs provoke in us an "ontological restlessness," in Cavell's fine phrase, this may be because in spite of their uncanny isomorphism photographs are not "representations" at all. The more we think about photographs, the more difficult it is to place them ontologically and to understand how they bridge the world and our perception. Photographs, in fact, confront us with conundrums of being, of our place in the world and of our perceptual relation to the world and to the past. And, as Roland Barthes also insisted in *Camera Lucida,* his last and one of his most compelling books, only a qualitative self-examination of what photographs provoke in us, can deepen our comprehension of this experience.

Why is it that in ordinary usage we are inclined to say that we *make* pictures and *take* photographs? Perhaps because the instrumental conditions of painting and photography as picture making differ substantially. Paintings and photographs have differing modalities for registering events. Both document the process of their making, but they do so through processes that differ in nature. In this can be distinguished their very different modes of existence. An event is a state of affairs—actions localizable in physical time and space—and what interests me is how they cause paintings or photographs to come into existence. Since neither painting nor photography is a "live" medium registering and relaying events in real time, we can further specify that they indicate *past* states of affairs. The difficulty arises in characterizing the nature of the past to which they refer and how this indicativeness manifests itself.

Let us say that the primary sense of the photograph is not to represent objects, but rather *to transcribe historical events.* This transcription is inseparable from the automated processes of a time-bound fixing of reflected light spatially organized by a lens. In other words, as an automated instrument, the camera is designed to register and preserve a profilmic event to which it was once present. The photograph has no sense apart from this function. The photochemical reaction to reflected light takes place continuously throughout the photogram in a given unit of time, which then persists as a trace or index, preserving the framed event as a record of spatial duration fixed in a homogeneous substance. As a result of its particular circumstances of production, this index is very much a historical document. Moreover, it is getting harder and harder to remember that in the photochemical era, subsequent alterations of the exposed negative were difficult, requiring considerable expertise in complex darkroom procedures.

Because the photographic act captures images in an automated and time-bound process, the photographic image is counterfactually dependent on a profilmic event from which it is displaced in space and in time; that is, any change in the record must necessarily reflect a change in the recorded event. But at the same time, photography's mode of presence is to evoke an unbridgeable gulf of time surging before us in the form of an absent cause. Every photograph is indebted to a past world; in viewing photographs we redeem this debt in the form of a detached looking. From this derive photography's phenomenological peculiarities, or what Cavell calls photography's *strangeness.* Photographs as well as filmed images present a mode of existence split by qualities of presence and absence, present and past, now and then, a here before us now encompassing a there displaced in time. In this they present a peculiar kind of virtuality that consists in making past time spatially present.

Painting presents no such ontological splits, because it is another kind of historical record altogether. The only state of affairs that concerns it or to which it refers is fully present to us and disclosed on the surface of the canvas in an act of self-indication. For Cavell, one of the great discoveries of postwar American painting, exemplified in Jackson Pollock's use of the all-over line, was the acknowledgment of one of the most primitive facts of a painting's existence: "not exactly that a painting is flat, but that its flatness, together with its being of a limited extent, means that it is *totally there,* wholly open to you, absolutely in front of your senses, of your eyes, as no other art form is" (*The World Viewed* 109).

That a painting is *totally there* means that it functions aesthetically in the modality of presence, of being completely present in space and in time and self-disclosing to sight, even if we ourselves fail to see. Its only causal relation to a past state of affairs relates to the layering of paint on canvas by the artist's hand. Although these layerings are records of past actions, to ordinary perception they give few indications of the *when* of their appearances, nor do they necessarily encourage us to attribute causality to them. In other words, to the untrained eye they present little or no historical evidence. Whether historical or nonobjective, created from life or from imagination, a painterly image is built up over time through the action of the artist's hand; this process is interactive and fully autographic in Nelson Goodman's sense of the term. So-called action painting has something to teach us here in that what every painting documents is less an originating image or referent in the world than the actions of the artist's hand and brush in building up an image over time. This is why the edges of the canvas function as a compositional limit. Compositionally, a painting has edges, but it does not have a frame. What is called the "frame" of painting can function pictorially in any number of ways, including ways we might call photographic. (An easy-to-comprehend example would be Chuck Close's painterly "copies" of Polaroids.) But once completed, the painting is a static object within this limit, defining its immanent or object-al status. If our eyes are attentive to causal processes, what we see on the surface of a completed canvas is not a representation of a physical world referent, if the image even has one, but a complex history of hand-directed actions having evolved over time. Indeed the reflexive act of modernism is, precisely, to foreground the causality of autographic gesture in painting.

The camera may share with painting any number of automatisms, for example, the available perspectival geometries for projecting three-dimensional objects onto plane surfaces. But whether we know that a painting has a past referent or not still differs from the knowledge that photographs invariably refer to historical events localizable in a specific space and time. From this derives another one of their fundamental automatisms. A painting is an ontologically complete object independent of any external state of affairs. But a photograph, even a nonrepresentational one, is rarely held as such. All photographs are "made" in many senses of the term, but the photographic act is fundamentally *documentation*. Photographs are valued as spatial records of past time. In this consists their aesthetic distinctiveness as a spatial art. Visual detail enhances this power and encourages us to value it more. But paradoxically, it can neither fully nor primarily account for photography's historical power.

As Bazin already suggested, the criterion of spatial recognition in no way affects the power or strangeness of this causality. As Cavell explains in his 1985 essay "What Photography Calls Thinking," part of this strangeness derives from the way picturing or representation is usually associated with semblance or the making of likenesses, that is, as "one thing standing for another, disconnected, thing, or one forming a likeness of another."[13] In this respect, "A representation emphasizes the identity of its subject, hence it may be called a

13. Reprinted in William Rothman, ed., *Cavell on Film* (Albany: State University of New York Press, 2005) 118.

likeness; a photograph emphasizes the existence of its subject, recording it; hence it is that it may be called a transcription" ("Thinking" 118). Counterintuitive as it may be, this means that a photograph is not a representation—it is less concerned with likenesses in space than with existences in time. (Alternatively, this does not mean that photography puts us in some direct contact with the world.) In contradistinction to painting, for example, photographs constituted a new mode of picturing, changing our notions of representation as well as ways of picturing and comprehending the world. Thus Cavell contrasts visual representation with visual *transcription,* and so emphasizes the causal role of the object in relation to the photograph. A painted portrait is a representation in which the artist makes a likeness, after her or his own vision of the subject represented. A photographic "portrait," however, is first an assertion of existence: that the subject, human or not, was present to the camera in past space-time. Further, in its intractable existence, the photographic subject resists the artistic imagination in its being-for-itself. It is this resistance that the inhuman instrumentality of the camera registers as much as anything else. The photographer's subjectivity is always in a state of confrontation with these intractable automatisms, and although she or he may create different ways of photographically "characterizing" their subject, or subsequently alter the image in all manner of ways, none of these activities will substantially affect the photograph's mode of existence as transcription or documentation.[14] In contradistinction to the disclosure of autographic gesture in painting, then, photographs disclose another kind of ontological unveiling: "that objects participate in the photographic presence of themselves; they participate in the re-creation of themselves on film; they are essential in the making of their appearances. Objects projected on screen are inherently reflexive, they occur as self-referential, reflecting upon their physical origins. Their presence refers to their absence, their location in another place" (*The World Viewed* xvi).

To say that photographs transcribe or document rather than represent presents further interesting consequences. It may be more accurate to say, as Noël Carroll has suggested, that documentation has become the culturally predominant sense in which photographs are contextualized and given cultural sense, but that is certainly not the only aesthetic use to which they are put. However, there are good reasons why we treat these images, justly or unjustly, as docu-

14. See, for example, Joel Snyder and Neil Walsh Allen, "Photography, Vision, and Representation," *Critical Inquiry* 2.1 (1975) 149–150.

ments. To take Carroll's own example, in a photograph of a square inch of white wall, the referent may be unrecognizable as such. Carroll finds it absurd to characterize such an image as a "representation," and he is correct, but for the wrong reasons. This image may be purposely out of focus, solarized, colorized, or what have you. But it remains in its origins a document of a historically specific space and duration, automatically recorded, for reasons I have explained above. The referent may not be recognizable, but as a result of our experiences of the camera's peculiar causal automatisms, its existence will always be assumed. Many abstract films and photographs even rely on this prior knowledge for their effects. Thus films of unrecognizable or nearly unrecognizable images such as Peter Gidal's *Room Film* (1973) remain *films,* while Stan Brakhage's *Mothlight* (1963) is rather a motion sculpture animated by the projection apparatus, as is the more difficult case of Peter Kubelka's *Arnulf Rainer* (1958–1960), a cameraless film involving metrical combinations of clear and black leader. Scratch films remain for me painterly objects animated by projectors, while something like Paul Sharits' *S:TREAM:S:S:ECTION:S:SECTION:S:S:ECTIONED* (1968–1970) is a hybrid painterly/filmic object, interesting in one way for its exploration of the overlapping borders of these two worlds. These cameraless artifacts are often a way of exploring the other fundamental automatism of film, namely, succession as the basis of automated movement. And in subtracting the camera while retaining the projector and filmstrip, they probe that indistinct border separating film from other kinds of moving images.[15]

My deeper point, however, is that the cultural presence of photography since the mid-nineteenth century has made us keenly aware of its automated functions. Thus our sense of the peculiar causality of photographs—the difficulty of detaching them conceptually from a past state of affairs—requires no visual evidence other than that of the presence of the photograph itself. In other words, the recognition or identification of space is not a necessary condition for the attribution of the causal quality of transcription in photographs. Contrariwise, to assume that a painterly image has a past referent to which the artist was present requires that the identification or recognition of spatial features which the artist may have observed be corroborated with ex-

15. *Arnulf Rainer* and *Mothlight* further complicate these questions, since, undoubtedly, contact printing or a kind of rephotography was used to strike projected prints of the films. In a reflexive gesture, which follows in reverse Chuck Close's automatism of making and enlarging a Polaroid self-portrait and then reproducing it as a painting, the camera reappears here to document and release the original autographic creative act.

*The Battle of Waterloo* (ca. 1820), artist unknown, oil on canvas.

Alexander Gardner, *A Harvest of Death* (Gettysburg, July 1863). From *Gardner's Photographic Sketch Book of the War* (Washington, D.C.: Philp and Solomons, 1855–1856), plate 36. Collections of the Library of Congress.

ternal historical evidence. Think of Carroll's own example of the battle of Waterloo, painted or sketched by a direct observer of the event. If we take a historical rather than aesthetic interest in this painting, questions will be raised about the artist's interpretation of the event. Are the uniforms correct? Have liberties been taken with the number of troops present or how they were spatially deployed strategically? Are casualties represented, and are their number and types of injuries accurate? Indeed it would be difficult to take any painting or sketch of this event as anything but a subjective interpretation or an imaginative likeness, regardless of the artist's efforts to be "objective."[16] We may want such evidence from photographs, but ordinarily we do not ask for it. Rightly or wrongly, we assume that the photograph itself functions as a primary historical document. (As I will explain in Part III, one of the ethical dimensions of the proliferation of digital images is to make a casualty of this power.) Indeed, such questions are rarely raised by Mathew Brady's photographs of the Civil War, for example, because we assume the past presence of the camera at the events it records. One may and should ask for corroboration of the information that photographs convey, as in Alexander Gardner's posing of Civil War dead for aesthetic effect. But even here it seems both epistemologically and morally objectionable to challenge the prior existence of the physical reality so manipulated or arranged, nor do such arrangements prevent or inhibit us from searching for other kinds of historical information. Causation almost always trumps intention in these cases, and for specific reasons. The photographic act consists primarily in witnessing or testimony, with all the ethical dilemmas that such acts presume. And if photography differs from historical painting, the fundamental sense of this difference is temporal. Photographic causation implies not only the camera's presence at the events it relates, but also its implication in the duration of those events—that the photographic act registers the duration of the events it conveys and indeed conveys duration as much as anything else. It presents the common duration wherein camera and event were commonly held.

To put it most simply, the presence or absence of the camera invokes the

16. "Uniqueness Claims" 44. Carroll's example is in fact specious and misleading. He invokes an "imaginary" painting, not an actual one, and he does not assume that the painter was a direct witness to the battle, yet bases his counterargument on a commitment to historical accuracy replete enough that one could extrapolate beyond the frame to events assumed to have happened there. But who could have had this knowledge, and where would it have come from? The painterly representation is an interpretation that could be supported by documentation. But as a result of processes of automatic analogical causation, the photographed record, if one existed, would be a witness to history with documentary value, no matter how incomplete or limited in perspective.

presence or absence of the world, or, more concretely, that prior state of affairs called profilmic space. (This is also true of digital cameras, of course. But the common element, indeed the only common element, is the lens; hence the current gallery coinage of "lens-based imaging" to distinguish digital capture from photographs in a strict sense. I will examine in Part III whether the very different processes of photochemical reactions and the transcoding function of charge-coupled devices make a difference as well.) This is why in "ordinary perception" we take the frame of a photograph as a provisional limit, a sampling of profilmic space, if you will, and the edges of a painting as the borders of the object itself. Similarly, despite all self-consciousness about the possibility of altering or falsifying photographs, they will still be taken, and questioned, as historical documents in a way that historical paintings or sketches or, better, the sketchings of court artists will not be, even if the artist was present as witness to the events depicted. The compositional framing of a dramatic or historical painting may be inspired by a photographic framing. But the photographic frame will always limit the range of subjective inventiveness and intentionality in the way that a canvas does not. And, contrariwise, the historical presence of a camera in an actual space and time that it records automatically as an impassive witness will also be assumed. The presence of the operator is not even required here, as in surveillance images. Moreover, the artist may alter the basic photographic image as much as she or he likes with either handcrafted or automated processes. But these activities do not change the fact that the altered material begins as a historical document, and indeed our understanding of such altered photographs very often relies on this understanding.

## 11. A World Past

> The camera has been praised for extending the senses; it may, as the world goes, deserve more praise for confining them, leaving room for thought.
>
> —Stanley Cavell, *The World Viewed*

The concept of automatism in its broader senses informs Cavell's notions of filmic ontology in fascinating ways. In raising the concept of ontology, Cavell certainly refers to a set of conditions *("a succession of automatic world projections")* that leads us to intuit a thing as being a film rather than possibly something else (a theatrical presentation, a video, etc.). In this sense he defines "world" as "the ontological facts of photography and its subjects" (*The World Viewed* 73). But this intuition derives less from a formal definition of the object than from the experience of our quotidian encounters with it. While the subtitle of *The World Viewed* is *An Ontology of Film,* this indicates neither an essence of the medium nor an attempt to find its timeless and integral being or teleological direction. It expresses, rather, our being or being-in-the-world, not necessarily as film spectators, but rather as a condition expressed in photography and cinema as such. This is a manifestation of a mind recognizing something that has already happened to itself; namely, the "fall into skepticism, together with its efforts to recover itself, events recorded variously in Descartes and Hume and Kant and Emerson and Nietzsche and Heidegger and Wittgenstein" ("What Photography Calls Thinking" 116). Philosophy has prepared the way for photography, then, and the shift in picturing it inspires. Again, like Roland Barthes in *Camera Lucida,* Cavell is less interested in how photographs represent, picture, or mean, than in how they place us subjectively. Thus *projection,* or "the phenomenological facts of viewing" (*The World Viewed* 73), is coextensive with the subjective condition of modernity, imagined here as a filmic way of encountering the world.

If photographs interest us subjectively, if their mode of existence calls for thinking in a certain way, it is because their conceptual structure provokes certain conundrums of being or to being—thus Cavell's characterization of photography as making us "ontologically restless." It is important to follow his wording closely: "A photograph does not present us with 'likenesses' of things; it presents us, *we want to say,* with the things themselves. But wanting to say that may well make us ontologically restless" (*The World Viewed* 17; my emphasis). Wanting to say that we are present to the objects themselves does not mean we believe or even wish to assert this. For the fundamental perplexity of photographs does not derive simply from the problem of representation, as I have already demonstrated, but rather from the curious sentiment that things absent in time can be present in space, a paradox of presence and absence that ordinary language has trouble resolving. And there is another, equally powerful side to this puzzle: that film presents to me a world from which I am absent, from which I am necessarily screened by its temporal absence, yet with which I hope to reconnect or rejoin. Here Cavell, alone with Gilles Deleuze in recent scholarship, proposes not just an ontology but an ethics of cinema.

Part of the strangeness of photographs, according to Cavell, is that "we are not accustomed to seeing things that are invisible, or not present to us, not present with us; or we are not accustomed to acknowledging that we do (except in dreams). Yet this seems, ontologically, to be what is happening when we look at a photograph: we see things that are not present" (*The World Viewed* 18). Although these things are present to us as picturings, they are usually no longer present either spatially or historically—they have receded from us both geographically and temporally. The frame of the photograph, then, solicits a divided perception, and this division is both spatial and temporal as well as historical—the present perceptual conviction of a past existence in time.

It bears reemphasis that, rightly or wrongly, our conviction of past presence in photographs is independent of being able to recognize or identify space in the image. If mimesis there be in photography, it is not spatial. Rather, it is the confounding perception that things absent in time can be present in space. Think of the puzzling image of the "duck-rabbit," evoked by Wittgenstein and others—this is a paradox of spatial recognition, of identifying linguistically two contradictory things as being presented by the same space. The photograph, however, is a paradox of temporal perception. The advent of photography in the nineteenth century confounded a culture that habitually associated sight or views with spatial (and temporal) presence. The fact of perceiving implied the co-presence in space of the observer and observed; perception meant here identification by sight, even if the original sensation was acoustic or olfactory. Sight and space were indelibly associated. This is partially what Walter Benjamin meant by the concept of aura and its subsequent decline in photographic culture.

The ontological strangeness of photography does not derive only from the picturing of objects absent in space. If this were the case, the criterion of spatial recognition, or representability, would be more important. Real-time displays such as surveillance video or even live television are much less uncanny than photographs. Here co-presence in time fills up, as it were, absences in space. Like other forms of observation at a distance, this absence is felt as a gap that could be overcome. So stranger still for the modern sensibility was the uneasy sense of an image that gave it *time,* or the very idea that time could be given as a *perception.* To see at a distance in space was commonplace by the nineteenth century. But to see at a distance in time was so confounding that it took nearly a hundred years to comprehend it. (Siegfried Kracauer's 1927 essay on photography is perhaps the first deep philosophical exploration of this idea.) Photographic picturing presents us existences in which we are inclined to believe, but in a temporal distance that is unbridgeable. This is why in its deepest sense photographic perception is historical rather than actual.

This sense of historical distance from what is pictured is not explicitly part of Cavell's argument. Yet, this belief in past existence, that we could be present to photographed objects if it were not for time, contributes strongly to feeling ourselves screened from the world thus presented, to our being held before it in a state of anonymous and invisible viewing. Part of Cavell's originality, though, is recognizing that not only is the spectator held in a distance from the photographed world, but this world, too, is screened from the viewer. What we feel in photographs is equally *our* absence from the view presented, that this view is screened for us, and from us, in time. The experience invoked here is in no way an identification of image and nature, as in the writings of Bazin, nor is it exactly physical reality, as Siegfried Kracauer would have it in his late works. Neither physical reality nor profilmic space accounts for the referentiality of photographs, but rather *space past.* Space is inescapably and complexly temporal in photography in a way that painting is not. Photographs do not just picture the already-happened; in making existential claims on our acts of viewing, they picture *history.* And in doing so, they encourage us to reflect on our own ontological situatedness in space-time.

Through his concept of ontology, then, Cavell argues that photographs and films express not only a variable mode of existence for themselves (the medium defined by its automatisms), but also *our* current, and perhaps changing, mode of existence. In other words, the condition of viewing in photography and film expresses the situation of the modern subject. But they also express a displacement of the subject, or even a kind of de-subjectivization or the dissolution of this subject in the anticipation of something else. This happens, first, by relieving us of the burden of perception by automating it *("a succession of automatic world pictures").* Photography and film "overcome" subjectivity not only in removing the human agent from the task of reproduction, but also in relieving it from the task or responsibility for perceiving in giving it a series of automated views. This is another way of saying that film's automatism is also our automatism; or, to reinvoke Spinoza, that in the modern era our spiritual automatisms have had a cinematic character. The quality of succession not only automates movement in the film image; it is at the heart of the mechanical nature of cinema. It catches us up in a peculiar temporality, a passing present of uniform instants over which we have little control. In so doing it not only produces a world in movement; it relieves us from the burdens of perception in the production and projection of manufactured views.

"Photographs are not *hand*-made," Cavell writes; "they are manufactured. And what is manufactured is an image of the world. The inescapable fact of mechanism or automatism in the making of these images is that feature Bazin points to as '[satisfying], once and for all and in its very essence, our obsession with realism'" (*The World Viewed* 20). This realism, however, insofar as Cavell uses the term, has nothing to do with the making or apprehension of likenesses. It is a matter of metaphysical contact with the world from which we have become separated: "So far as photography satisfied a wish, it satisfied a wish not confined to painters, but the human wish, intensifying since the Reformation, to escape subjectivity and metaphysical isolation—a wish for the power to reach this world, having for so long tried, at last hopelessly, to manifest fidelity to another" (21). In this manner, for Cavell cinema appears in response to a long and complex trajectory in the history of philosophy. The rediscovery of Pyrrhonism, or classical skepticism, during the Renaissance, and the decline of theological dogmatism in the wake of the Reformation and Enlightenment philosophy, had three consequences for the emerging subject of modernity. That God was in all of us gave society and collectivity a reason from which the modern subject of scientific empiricism became detached. Confined to itself or within itself, the individual subject then bore responsibility for the epistemological and moral consequences of this isolation. And since God was no longer in the world to give it meaning, whatever meaning nature could give to the individual had to be found in its isolated perceptions. Finally, the individual was equally wrested from nature in her or his perceptions, since humanity and nature no longer shared the same metaphysical context.

Cinema responds to this dilemma as a kind of machine for metaphysics with a distinct place in the complex history of skeptical thought. In one way, in conveying the impression that all we can know of the world is that we have perceptions of it, film embodies the modern skeptical attitude. This is why, for Cavell, film responds to a specific and profound desire: to view the world as it was, but anonymously and unseen. Here the screen functions as neither medium nor support, but rather as a barrier as much conceptual as physical—it is a philosophical situation embodied in photography and film themselves comprising our present (but perhaps passing) ontology as a self divided from the world by the window of perception. The history of skepticism is complex, however, and this desire also expresses a longing to maintain or regain contact with this world *through* our perceptions of it. "What we wish to see in this way is the world itself—that is to say, everything," Cavell concludes. "Nothing less than that is what modern philosophy has told us (whether for Kant's reasons, or for Locke's, or Hume's) is metaphysically beyond our reach or (as Hegel or Marx or Kierkegaard or Nietzsche might rather put it) beyond our reach metaphysically" (*The World Viewed* 101–102). A strange desire, indeed. For in feeling that our hold on the world was confined to our perceptions of it, we began to invent machines for perceiving the whole of the world.

The comparison with painting is again informative. What separates painting and photography in the history of philosophy as it were, is the fall into and return from skepticism. "[What] painting wanted," Cavell argues,

> in wanting connection with reality, was a sense of *presentness*—not exactly a conviction of the world's presence to us, but our presence to it. At some point the unhinging of our consciousness from the world interposed our subjectivity between us and our presentness to the world. Then our subjectivity became what is present to us, individuality became isolation. The route to conviction in reality was through the acknowledgment of that endless presence of self . . . To maintain conviction in our connection with reality, to maintain our presentness, painting accepts the recession of the world. Photography maintains the presentness of the world by accepting our absence from it. The reality in a photograph is present to me while I am not present to it; and a world I know, and see, but to which I am nevertheless not present (through no fault of my subjectivity), is a world past. (*The World Viewed* 22–23)

A world past. It is not just physical reality or profilmic space that constitutes the referentiality of photographs, but, more importantly, a physical presence strongly indicative of space past. "Before" representation, or being taken to represent, this space expresses a causal and counterfactually dependent relation with the past as a unique and nonrepeatable duration; hence Roland Barthes's suggestion that the space of the photograph is copiable and thus repeatable, while its temporal expression is singular—"What the Photograph reproduces to infinity has occurred only once: the Photograph mechanically repeats what could never be repeated existentially."[17] To recognize the ontological presentness of painting, that it is fully disclosed before us in time and space, meant acknowledging its autonomous state of being as well as our own autonomy in confronting it. The deeper lesson of photography for philosophy is understanding not only how the skeptical attitude is expressed in photographic looking, but also how photography returns the world to us while nonetheless holding perception at a distance.

That we wish to see everything in this way means that film responds to a moral condition, a way of being-in-the-world that film manages to express for

17. *Camera Lucida*, trans. Richard Howard (New York: Hill and Wang, 1981) 4.

us as a generalized, cultural perception. For Cavell, the "reality" of film is the actuality of this metaphysical dilemma; there is no other relation of photography or film to reality. The succession of automated world projections is our condition of perceiving as such to the extent that we are modern subjects; or, as Cavell puts it, film is a moving image of skepticism. The skeptical attitude, of which photography is one manifestation, expresses a realization "of human distance from the world, or some withdrawal of the world, which philosophy interprets as a limitation in our capacity for knowing the world . . . It is perhaps the principal theme of *The World Viewed* that the advent of photography expresses this distance as the modern fate to relate to the world by viewing it, taking views of it, as from behind the self" ("What Photography Calls Thinking" 116–117). As spiritual automata, what film produces is an ontological condition for the human subject,

> [not] by literally presenting us with the world, but by permitting us to view it unseen. This is not a wish for power over creation (as Pygmalion's was), but a wish not to need power, not to have to bear its burdens . . . In viewing films, the sense of invisibility is an expression of modern privacy or anonymity. It is as though the world's projection explains our forms of unknownness and of our inability to know. The explanation is not so much that the world is passing us by, as that we are displaced from our natural habitation within it, placed at a distance from it. The screen overcomes our fixed distance; it makes displacement appear as our natural condition. (*The World Viewed* 40–41)

These conundrums of presence and absence, of temporal displacement, of the automated projection of screened views, emblematize the ontological position of modernity as skepticism, of being held at a distance from the world such that our terms of existence, our "reality" as such, is the modality of detached viewing. Filmic automatism thus reprises a metaphysical condition that Cavell implicitly relates to Leibniz's monadism. The situation of film viewing responds to what is, already, the situation or situating of the modern subject as closed within its self-consciousness:

> Our condition has become one in which our natural mode of perception is to view, feeling unseen. We do not so much look at the world as look *out* at it, from behind the self . . . Viewing a movie makes this condition automatic, takes the responsibility for it out of our hands. Hence movies

> seem more natural than reality. Not because they are escapes into fantasy, but because they are reliefs from private fantasy and its responsibilities; from the fact that the world is *already* drawn by fantasy. And not because they are dreams, but because they permit the self to be wakened, so that we may stop withdrawing our longings further inside ourselves. Movies convince us of the world's reality in the only way we have to be convinced . . . by taking views of it. (*The World Viewed* 102)

The last phrase is important for understanding how the phenomenology of film projection expresses for Cavell both the metaphysical isolation of the modern subject and its possible overcoming. Film presents to us not only the visible world or the world as visible, but also our conditions of viewing in just this way. As such, it is not the perfect image of skepticism, nor is it a mechanism whose cultural pervasiveness holds us in a position of skepticism. Photography and film mechanically reproduce the subjective conditions and paradoxes of skepticism in the form of a possible philosophical solution. For Cavell, they pose both the condition of skepticism and a possible road of departure, the route back to our conviction in reality. In contrast again to the psychoanalytic phenomenology of Christian Metz and Jean-Louis Baudry in the 1970s, which explored our unconscious submission to the projection of automated views, Cavell emphasizes how our epistemological situation of having "world-views" is held before us *as a perception.* And this occurs for the very reason that these world projections are automated—they are not produced by us but for us by a cultural mechanism or instrumentality. That skepticism should reproduce itself in a technology for seeing might mean that it is no longer the ontological air we breathe, but a passing phase of our philosophical culture. If the reality that film holds before us is that of our own perceptual condition, then it opens the possibility of once again being present to self or acknowledging how we may again become present to ourselves. This is why Cavell emphasizes that "reproducing the world is the *only* thing film does automatically" (*The World Viewed* 103). For these reasons, film may already be the emblem of skepticism in decline. The irony of this recognition now is that modernity may no longer characterize our modes of being or of looking. The possibility of recognizing photography's deep connectedness with a way of being in the world is becoming more and more evident as that mode of existence is passing into something else, and as photography itself is on the wane. The question now is what comes afterward. For skepticism in decline may be related to film in decline. Electronic and digital imaging may be responding to or provoking a new epistemological situation whose ontologies and ethical consequences remain as yet unexamined.

For Cavell, art becomes modern when in the absence of a validating tradition it is provoked to a state of continual self-questioning and self-invention. Similarly, the subject became modern when, its anchors being cast loose from moral and epistemological dogma, expressions of doubt and its overcoming became questions of the self in relation to its perceptions. No longer assured of its place in the world or in relation to the world, the subject is provoked to new strategies of self-actualization and self-invention. The modern ethical dilemma, then, is how to regain contact with this world, to overcome our distance from it and restore its knownness to us. We wish for the condition of viewing as such because this is our way of establishing and maintaining our connection to the world—by having views of it. And in having views in just this way, one that requests conviction in the prior existence of this world even if it is present to us only in images, brings us out of our private reflections and encourages us to consider again the world as such. To say that film presents a moving image of skepticism, then, means neither that there is no reality to perceive, nor that we have renounced having anything to say about that reality because we are irretrievably detached from it. Nor does it imply that this condition of viewing is a fiction, an illusion of reality that we could overcome with another kind of filmmaking or another more critical philosophy. To assert any of the above would be a parody of skepticism. Cavell is after something else:

> Film is a moving image of skepticism: not only is there a reasonable possibility, it is a fact that here our normal senses are satisfied of reality while reality does not exist—even, alarmingly, *because* it does not exist, because viewing it is all it takes. Our vision is doubtless otherwise satisfiable than by the viewing of reality. But to deny, on skeptical grounds, just *this* satisfaction—to deny that it is ever reality which film projects and screens—is a farce of skepticism. It seems to remember that skepticism concludes against our conviction in the existence of the external world, but it seems to forget that skepticism begins in an effort to justify that conviction. The basis of film's drama, or the latent anxiety in viewing its drama, lies in its persistent demonstration that we do not know what our conviction in reality turns upon. (*The World Viewed* 188–189)

At least perceptually . . .

Cinema provokes in us a divided, ambiguous, or ambivalent perception, not unlike Metz's "I know very well, but all the same . . ."[18] Yet the philosophical consequences of Cavell's arguments go much deeper. Metz's psychoanalytical observation is basically a sociological one that, contrary to his earlier phenomenology, demands we test cinema's projections as illusory. Cavell is responding to a moral or ethical dilemma that requires us to reflect upon the epistemological grounds or groundlessness of these convictions. One reason that "we do not know what our conviction in reality turns upon" is that we continue to demand (and often distrust) visual evidence when what maintains our conviction is in fact a *temporal* perception. But this unknownness of the grounds of our conviction in these ephemeral images—a world suspended in variable patterns of light—is itself a hopeful quality. For while cinema's automatism relieves us from the burdens of perception, it also holds open before us our own agency in acts of perception, and sustains our epistemological inquisitiveness regarding those acts and their consequences. And so Cavell concludes:

> The moral of film's image of skepticism is not that reality is a dream and not that reality confines our dreams. In screening reality, film screens its givenness from us; it holds reality from us, it holds reality before us, i.e., withholds reality before us. We are tantalized at once by our subjection to it and by its subjection to our views of it. But while reality is the bearer of our intentions it is possible . . . to refuse to allow it to dictate what shall be said about it . . . Flanked by its claims to speak for us, it is still open to us in moments to withhold it before ourselves and may gladly grant that we are somewhat spoken for. To know how far reality is open to our dreams would be to know how far reality is confined by our dreams of it. (*The World Viewed* 189)

Perhaps the long dream or fantasy from which the self begins to be awakened through filmic perception is that of the division of humanity from nature, or of a Being speaking with a different voice from that of nature. In this respect, there is one last feature of Cavell's filmic ontology that has received little commentary, and it suggests another important dimension of our uneasy

18. "The Imaginary Signifier," in *The Imaginary Signifier: Psychoanalysis and the Cinema,* trans. Celia Britton, Annwyl Williams, Ben Brewster, and Alfred Guzzetti (Bloomington: Indiana University Press, 1982) 76.

conviction in these images in which our subjectivity is at once sustained and displaced. In this automated perception, humans and things share the same qualitative state of being. Or, as Cavell puts it, "human beings are not ontologically favored over the rest of nature" (*The World Viewed* 37). In their automatic manufacture of an image of the world, film and photography displace us from yet reconnect us to this world, not by disfavoring or alienating humanity, but by casting humanity and nature in a common frame and reintegrating them in a common duration. In our views of the world, we are presented a situation wherein humanity is returned to (visible) nature in sharing the same duration with it. And, according to Cavell, there are moral consequences in failing to grasp this fact: "Then if in relation to objects capable of such self-manifestation human beings are reduced in significance, or crushed by the fact of beauty left vacant, perhaps this is because in trying to take dominion over the world, or in aestheticizing it (temptations inherent in the making of film, or of any art), they are refusing their participation with it" (xvi). In response to the skeptical attitude, which sets the perceiving subject at a distance from nature, in film humanity and nature are of one substance and held in a common duration—they are expressed as having a common Being. They partake of the same ontological substance, and in addition have the same epistemological nature. For "reality" here is not what is, or the accuracy or not of what is pictured, but our condition of being in the world.

Cavell's uses of the terms "ontology" and "reality" in relation to film have nothing to do with the correspondence of an image and its referent. Our sense of the "reality" of film comes not through representation or even the representativeness of its projected images, but rather through the way in which this projecting world confronts us with our own metaphysical condition. And so Cavell concludes:

> Film's easy power over the world *will* be accounted for, one way or another, consciously or not. By my account, film's presenting of the world by absenting us from it appears as confirmation of something already true of our stage of existence. Its displacement of the world confirms, even explains, our prior estrangement from it. The "sense of reality" provided on film is the sense of *that* reality, one from which we already sense a distance. Otherwise, the thing it provides a sense of would not, for us, count as reality. (*The World Viewed* 226)

What is important here is that the "automatic world projections" of filmic perception already promote a partial response to the skeptical attitude. We may not know in what our conviction in reality consists, or how it persists. But the wish to view the world (that is to say, everything) by viewing it unseen recapitulates the phases of skepticism: to assert that the external world is divided from us in perception is a way of beginning to justify our conviction in the existence of that world.

## 12. An Ethics of Time

> Memory is the most faithful of films.
>
> —André Bazin, *What Is Cinema?*

In the epilogue to his 1960 *Theory of Film: The Redemption of Physical Reality*, Siegfried Kracauer asks a surprising question: "What is the good of film experience?"[19] In reconsidering Cavell here (or Bazin, Metz, or Barthes), aesthetic questions of medium specificity have continually turned into ethical questions. This is the deep value of the kind of ontological evaluation that Cavell and Barthes exemplify. We may be interested in what photography and film are, but we are also equally or indeed more concerned by what we have valued qualitatively in the experience of contemplating them, or indeed by what we ourselves become in watching films. Throughout the history of film theory, film aesthetics has concerned itself primarily with the analysis of space. Here, I want to suggest that what most powerfully affects us in film is an ethics of time.

This idea is already suggested in Cavell's assertion that "a world I know, and see, but to which I am nevertheless not present (through no fault of my subjectivity), is a world past." Among film's possible automatisms, the most fundamental involve the expression of temporality. Film's virtual life is sustained by its relationships with time. The powers of analogy are not those of representation or of a spatial mimesis, but rather of duration. If photography and film are the matrix from which time-based spatial media evolve, then an ontological examination of the medium, no matter how variable or unfinished, leads to the surprising conclusion that what we have valued in film are our confrontations with time and time's passing.

In rereading Cavell, I have tried to tease out the multiple senses or dimensions through which we experience this past world today, especially in film

19. (New York: Oxford University Press, 1960) 285.

studies. This recognition of a passing ontology, or an ontology past, yields two possible conclusions. First, the very fading of analogical images encourages a surprising return to classical film theory as an area of thought that Cavell already engages in a complex dialogue. Understanding what we valued in photographic causality makes contemporary once again the concerns of classical film theory, both for clarifying what is new about digital media and for understanding what we have valued in the previous analogical forms of media. What is passing in film's expression of ontology is a certain relation to time or duration and a causality that Philip Rosen has characterized in *Change Mummified* as the "indexical trace."[20] In both fiction and nonfiction cinema, the aesthetics and the ethics of film are closely linked to historical powers of documenting and witnessing wherein the camera confronts the prior existence of things and people in time and in space, preserved in their common duration. The renewed interest of film theory in indexicality is characteristic of how, in the era of digital simulation, we are becoming resensitized to the powers of photography and cinema, especially since this experience is now practically lost—it is already *historical.*

This world past is also a philosophical world, one in which, for Cavell, film emblematized the epistemological situation of skepticism in decline as a reinvention, or continual reinventing, of the conditions of the modern subject. The curious temporality expressed by the concept of automatism affects not only the ontology of modern art, but also that of the modern subject. "Modernism" in this sense is not a period or phase of art history, but rather a mode of experience: how we experience or inhabit duration as the passing of present time. In this respect, modernism in art characterizes a style of questioning that, rather than seeking essences, stable forms, or identities, expresses the constant doubt that we don't know what art *is,* and so the artist must continually recreate new conditions of existence for it. And if film is the most modern of arts, this is because it presents to us, or perhaps sustains us temporally in, just this mode of epistemological questioning and self-(re)evaluation.

Now, in trying to understand film or photography's waning before electronic and digital images, the following responses might be appropriate: describing their different technological processes, comparing their underlying psychological processes (the basic cognitive and perceptual mechanisms by which image and movement are conveyed and understood), or evaluating aesthetic variations in the perhaps measurable quantitative differences underly-

20. *Change Mummified: Cinema, Historicity, Theory* (Minneapolis: University of Minnesota Press, 2001) 20–21.

ing our qualitative judgments of digital and analog images. Undoubtedly, all these exercises in media theory are useful, and much research remains to be done. However, the phenomenological emphasis of classical film theory opens another path, hence my second concluding theme. This is a philosophical perspective that asks: In what ways do photographs and films call us to a qualitative self-examination? How and why do they spark ontological questions by raising for us conundrums of being, of our placement with respect to ourselves and the world? In this manner, revisiting classical film theory today is also a way of revivifying a kind of questioning that explores our sensuous contact with images and recharacterizes their (visible and outward) perceptual density in a way that also leads us inward—a self-examination of our relation to time, memory, and history.

As Philippe Dubois astutely argues, while photographic indexicality designates and attests, it does not necessarily *signify*.[21] Nor does it presuppose relations of identity with the objects it records. In their different ways, both Roland Barthes and Stanley Cavell insist upon the ontological gulf that divides us perceptually, in space and in time, from photographs, and the photograph itself from the state of affairs it has automatically transcribed. Photography and film's phenomenological claims on us lie elsewhere than in spatial qualities of mimesis or resemblance. The causal or indexical powers of photography and film have sense for us, but their *meaning* is always incomplete, open-ended, and ambiguous. This reticence of meaning is not effected by augmenting the amount of "information" contained in an image; no increase of spatial resolution, achieved chemically or digitally, can rebalance this equation. Causally powerful, yet semantically ambiguous, the indexical arts fuel other powers internal to us. In *Camera Lucida* Roland Barthes characterized these powers as the metonymic force of the photograph—an inward process of self-investigation and memory triggered by the *punctum*. But this metonymy is not free. Guided by the causal force of photography, it provokes a historical

21. *L'acte photographique* 70. Deeply indebted to Peirce's philosophical pragmatism as well as to Rosalind Krauss's path-breaking reevaluation of indexicality in modernist and postmodernist photography, Dubois provides the following definition: "the photograph, like every index, derives from a physical connection with its referent: it constitutes a singular trace, attesting to the existence of its object and designating it by right of its powers of metonymic extension. Therefore, the photograph is by nature a pragmatic object, inseparable from its referential situation. This implies neither that the photograph necessarily resembles (is mimetic) nor is it a priori meaningful (carrying signification in itself)—even if, evidently, effects of analogy and meaning, more or less coded, often end up intervening after the fact. These are the generic traits of the index" (93); my translation.

imagination, one that seeks out a relationship to the past and to memory in recognition of the causal connections linking photographs to past states of affairs.

Following a similar line of thought, and in response to his own question, Kracauer suggests that the sensuous examination of the surface of things in film produces simultaneously an interior examination of the self in memory. The perceptual density and indeterminacy of things in their native duration, when framed and reproduced in the alienated form of the photographic image, provoke a nonchronological investigation of memory in the form of *mémoire involontaire.* (In fact, Kracauer often insisted that the experience of film or photography is essentially Proustian.) Film is philosophical because its peculiar form of empiricism—attention to things themselves in their duration—can produce dense phenomenological investigations, not only of things but of ourselves in our phenomenological activity.

In the 1950s, for Kracauer this task was particularly urgent because modernity's terms of existence had changed. In the postwar environment, the appeal of reason and claims for universal values were eroded by two major historical forces: the decline of grand, binding beliefs (whether moral, religious, or ideological) and the steady increase in the prestige of science and technology. Paul Valéry disparaged cinema as an emblem of technological reason, complaining that film's mechanical copying of external life blocked attentiveness to our inward, spiritual life. In Kracauer's view, however, this was the plaint of a nineteenth-century culture in its confrontation with a twentieth-century medium. The steady decline of rationality emblematized by Hitler's rise to power and the spread of European fascism and, in the immediate postwar period, the catastrophic recognition of the attempted annihilation of European Jewry and the future possibility of global nuclear annihilation had overwhelmed the spiritual commitments of the nineteenth century and their special claims to reason. "If ideology is disintegrating," Kracauer wrote,

> the essences of inner life can no longer be had for the asking . . . Conversely, if under the impact of science the material components of our world gain momentum, the preference which film shows for them may be more legitimate than he [Valéry] is willing to admit. Perhaps, contrary to what Valéry assumes, there is no short-cut to the evasive contents of inner life whose perennial presence he takes for granted? Perhaps the way to them, if way there is, leads through the experience of surface reality? Perhaps film is a gate rather than a dead end or mere diversion? (*Theory of Film* 287)

Through these questions, Kracauer's materialist aesthetics both confirm and respond proleptically to Cavell's characterization of cinema as a moving image of skepticism. Where Cavell stresses the division that the subject longs to overcome in its perceptions of the world, Kracauer characterizes film and photography as refamiliarizing us, or putting us again in spiritual contact with this world—what Kracauer called "physical reality." What we register and seek to overcome or redeem in looking at photographs and films is a temporal alienation, a felt displacement in relation to things and their histories, whether natural or social, not only because they are in the past, but because we ourselves are subjectively immersed in passing time or the flow of life. Thus, the material content of physical reality is not simply nature, but rather what phenomenology calls the *Lebenswelt:* the global accumulation of the events, actions, activities, and contingencies of everyday life, an asubjective world overwhelming individual perception and consciousness. Film and photography aid us in this overcoming because their semantic reticence or ambiguity, their "fringe of indeterminate meanings" in Kracauer's parlance, ignites a circuit flowing between an external, surface perception of things and an inward movement characterized by memory and subjective reverie. This is an interior wandering sparked by external sensations, what Kracauer called "psychophysical correspondences," whereby we animate objects on the screen through often involuntary self-explorations, investing them with the force of our memories. For Kracauer, then, the psychology of film spectatorship is marked by a peculiar ebb and flow, from exteriority to interiority and back again. These currents are sustained in film's particular relationship to duration. The temporality of the projected film sustains us in a given duration that parallels the flux of becoming characteristic of the *Lebenswelt,* or flow of everyday life. In this way film transcribes not only objects, but also the duration wherein they exist and persist. And this duration not only pulls us into the thicket of things; it also propels us simultaneously inward to voyage through nonchronological layers of memory.

The decline of philosophical or theological certainty liberates us from the eternal as well as from the absolute. Alternatively, the rise of science as the new universal image of nature introduces an image of change, but only at the cost of nature's quantitative reduction to measurable causal processes. In either case, qualitative time is lost to us. How may we then refind an experience of lost time or duration? Perhaps the gateway to our present inner life, what we value in our current mode of existence, is through the experience of surface reality in the matrix of its duration? Perhaps film's particular attentiveness to the external life that surrounds us leads back to and enriches a mental or psychological life that is bereft of anchors in unchallenged universals? Kracauer's cinematic ethics, then, can be read as a prescient reevaluation of particularity and contingency in relation to the external world and also as the condition of an emerging (post)modern subjectivity. Falling between what Kracauer called the last things—Art, Religion, and Philosophy, with their penchants for totality and absolutes—the experience of film returns to us the forms and shapes of time as change in its singularity, contingency, and open-endedness.

Photography and film are temporal arts before they are spatial arts; this is the key to understanding how and why we value them. As I have argued throughout Part II, fundamentally a photograph is an automatic transcription of a past state of affairs. Photographs may be made to serve many other functions, and they may serve as material for all kinds of sense-making. But in a deep sense, before transforming them as signs, fictions, or works of art, we approach them as historical documents. As I will further explain in Part III, automatic analogical causation produces in us a conviction of past existences in time, so much so that Cavell's characterization of the photographic philosopher as skeptic must be counterbalanced with another perspective—Siegfried Kracauer's sense of the photographer as historian.[22] From another perspective, Cavell's cinematic conditions of viewing—making things absent in time present in space; the state of viewing as an invisible and anonymous onlooker; the power of a skepticism that examines our conviction in the world as the condition of our perceptual distance from it—could well be understood as a kind of historiographic sensibility. Indeed, where skepticism starts with our perceptual disconnectedness from the world, a historiographic sensibility may find, in those same conditions, a comprehensive relation with the world and its past, however provisional.

Like photography, film transcribes before it represents while producing images in and as movement. As such, films compound the temporal sense of photographs such that what is visible or perceptible in the image is not fixable as a spatial relation in a conventional sense. It is, rather, a movement disjoined from space, which psychologically moves the viewer as the double pursuit of an image both lost to time past and passing in time present. In both photography and film, the virtual is always overrunning the actual: on one hand, there is the hallucinatory projection of events lost to the (virtual) past in the present

22. A key theme throughout Kracauer's writings on photography and film, these arguments are brought to the foreground in his last book, *History, or the Last Things before the Last* (New York: Oxford University Press, 1969). See also my *Reading the Figural* (Durham, N.C.: Duke University Press, 2001), chap. 5.

perceptual image; on the other, the irreversible succession of passing presents where space in movement appears and disappears into the virtual time of memory. Like all the other analogical arts, in film the existential powers of duration are sustained in a process of continuous causality wherein their apparent self-making preserves the past in a way that excites memory. All of film's powers as an art of duration are indebted to this analogical causation through which we attribute a past (and passing) existence to the present image, an existence which is no longer actual nor visible, but which works through the image as a virtual force. After the spatial presentation of past time, and the passing of space in time as succession, there is third quality of duration expressed through film as a photographic art. This is one of the deepest paradoxes of film experience—the recurring desire to relive in the present a nonrepeatable past. Many prints may be struck from a photograph or film, but the act of transcription (an automated transformation of space by time in a direct causal relation of limited duration) happens only once. The past thus preserved in a photographic or filmic image is a nonrepeatable event. Yet through photography and film, we wish repeatedly to re-view this past in a new present moment, to reconnect the past it presents to the moment that is now ours, but passing.

*The World Viewed* was first published in 1971. Along with Siegfried Kracauer's *Theory of Film,* it is the last great work of classical film theory. And like all the best endgames, these books are already products of the future as much as the past—not just retrospective looks, but, as or more powerfully, openings onto a barely imagined future. If *The World Viewed* already envisions in photography and film the passing of skepticism in philosophy, it also aids us in remembering the powers of film, already waning before a televisual and videographic or electronic sensibility. By the same token, there are reasons why classical film theory now seems less historical than actual, and why it powerfully engages us in the transition to a new millennium and, perhaps, to a new medium. Film study now reconsiders the impact of André Bazin, Roland Barthes, Siegfried Kracauer, the early Cavell, and, even farther back, the work of Erwin Panofsky, Béla Balázs, and Jean Epstein, as if to resurrect our most powerful ancestors to remind us of the complexity and density of a phenomenological experience that our video-charged sensibilities have already forgotten. And here is one last paradox of time: that we come to recognize and value the automatisms of a given art too early or too late, either at the point of their astonishing novelty, or in tardy recognition of their displacement by new forms and new automatisms.

The two camera set-ups of *Numéro zéro* (Jean Eustache, 1971).

Also in 1971, before his first feature was released to theaters, Jean Eustache shot a long film that he called, significantly, *Numéro zéro.* Shown only once in abridged form on French television, the film disappeared for more than thirty years before being rediscovered and returned to its original form for a 2003 release in France. For me it is uncannily important that this work should reappear so long after it was shot, as if to remind us what cinema *was* and wherein film's powers lay in the predigital era.

One hundred and ten minutes long, *Numéro zéro* examines a particular filmic automatism: the utopia of filming continuous duration. The film was shot in the apartment where Eustache lived with his grandmother, Odette Robert, who raised him through most of his youth. Odette Robert recounts her life across six generations of French history. After a brief silent prologue filmed by a collaborator, Adolfo Arreitta, in which Odette and Eustache's son are seen shopping on a nearby street, the entire film is recorded in one "take" filmed from two static camera positions: one framing Odette on the right with Eustache in the foreground left, his back to the camera; the other a tighter shot of Odette.

In the course of the film, Eustache marks the slate in what seems to be the middle of the shot. In this manner we come to realize that the run times of the two cameras are staggered so that the magazine of one can be changed while the other continues to film. There are ten magazines to be used continuously, one after the other. The film ends when the raw stock is used up and filming is no longer possible. Herein lies the impossible gesture of *Numéro zéro*—to recount history in such a way that no "time" will be lost; time, that is, as equivalent to the continuous exposure of film.

*Numéro zéro* is a film of passing time and the powers of time's passing. The recorded space of the film itself multiplies signs of elapsed time. Eustache and Odette drink whiskey: the bottle and glasses gradually empty; the bowl of ice gradually melts. Eustache smokes a cigar, Odette her precious Gauloises—the ashtrays fill. It is afternoon, and the sun sets; the quality of light in the room gradually changes. At regular intervals Odette pauses as Eustache marks the slate, one through nine. (The tenth magazine is used for the silent prologue.) Through the window in the background, the light gradually changes and softens.

The quality of Odette's speech is equally important. Her flow of speech is also an index of elapsing time. She recounts confidently but rapidly in a near-continuous stream. She pauses on cue for the slate, and then continues without missing a beat, or a memory. One feels that it is filmic speech somehow, reproducing memory at a continuous pace and in a continuous duration. In this way, *Numéro zéro* documents film's affinity for two types of duration. On one hand, there is memory or historical testimony, whose medium is speech. Odette's testimony presents a disjunct chronology, whose discontinuous leaps in time are as complex and orderly as in any early film by Alain Resnais. Most important here is the historical uniqueness of Odette's witnessing, expressed as the film's evocation of a nonrepeatable past redoubled in the act of the filming, itself structured as a nonrepeatable event. On the other, there is "real time," that is, continuous duration recorded uninterrupted by two cameras in a way that preserves the singularity of the passing present. In the course of the film Odette is interrupted in midsentence as the phone rings. Visibly surprised, Eustache nonetheless answers and is elated to discover that the call is from Dutch television wanting to buy one of his films. This unforeseen disruption of the course of filming is one more expression of the film's impossible *parti pris:* that no event should be lost, no matter how transitory or happenstance.

Eustache considered the film a deeply personal project and did not envision showing it to a general public. On completion, the full version was shown only once, to eight friends (one of whom was Jean-Marie Straub, who later "rediscovered" the film) in Eustache's apartment on the rue Mollet in the eighteenth arrondissement. Odette died three years after the film was shot; Eustache took his own life in 1981. But the question remains: Why is this film important now? Because it expresses so clearly yet complexly, in its aesthetic structure, film's profound affinity with historical documentation and testimony. In this respect, *Numéro zéro* is much closer to Claude Lanzmann's *Shoah* (1985) than it is to something like Andy Warhol's *Empire* (1964). This conceit or folly of wanting to film uninterrupted duration is a way of showing that (real) time is neither homogeneous nor continuous. Certainly, the film documents a presence and a memory conveyed through voice; but it also documents passing time as embedded in a space—the precious conservation of time and memory in small and fragile fragments of space that time will always overwhelm, for both Odette and Eustache are dead. Producing (invisible) memory in a visual medium, the actual perceptible space of the film is also continuously passing into the virtuality of the past in general. It produces duration for us, and it includes us in a duration equivalent to that of the events so transcribed. *Numéro zéro* presents an experience of time not unlike that characterized by Roland Barthes in his analysis of Alexander Gardner's 1865 portrait of Lewis Payne awaiting execution for the attempted assassination of William H. Seward. Forgiving Barthes his doubts regarding film, less important here than the experience of the *punctum* is how film augments photographic duration as the expression of time's passing. This is not only the intuition of a past to which we remain directly connected through automated analogical causation, but also the anticipation of a future that will continually become the past. "I read at the same time," Barthes writes of the photograph of Lewis Payne, "*This will be* and *this has been;* I observe with horror an anterior future of which death is the stake. By giving me the absolute past of the pose (aorist), the photograph tells me death in the future . . . I shudder, like Winnicott's psychotic patient, *over a catastrophe which has already occurred.* Whether or not the subject is already dead, every photograph is this catastrophe" (*Camera Lucida* 96).

We may regret the passing of the analogical arts. But I do not want to sound a nostalgic note, for this transformation is not a catastrophe and we cannot know what will become in time. Neither can we judge what will be new about digital cinema and potentially valued in digital imaging without a sense of what we have already forgotten in the videographic and electronic century in which we already live. A film like *Numéro zéro* presents not only a world past, but also a passing world: a relation to duration and pastness, which may no longer be as accessible to us, or may no longer reflect or express our current mode of existence and our longing for a future existence. And one wonders if Barthes fails here before the ethical demands of the photograph. (Can he answer the question: What is the good of film experience?) Indeed, photography and film confront us with the vertigo of duration and time's passing. And even if our own mortality is inevitable, death is not the future of every passing present. Barthes's morbidity should be pushed in another direction. Here the photograph may be read as preserving our connectedness to the past and provoking thought about its hold on us in the present. Moreover, if we are attentive to this present, we may find embedded within it a future that remains before us, open and undetermined.

There are philosophical reasons why the idea of a medium is difficult to grasp and to comprehend. In Cavell's definition, the very concept of a medium, in its vertiginous variability, insistently raises for us the question of the new, or what constitutes our modernity. In this respect, the current situation of digital moving images will not be exempt from the difficulties wherein the creativity of media expresses the temporality of the modern—the perplexity of a present time that remains mysterious to us because we cannot yet understand what it is becoming or will become. (Understanding the modern always comes after the fact; we grasp it in the course of its becoming our immediate past.) That which perplexes is often new, presenting itself to our perception before we are yet able to recognize or accept it as an image or to ask what it is an image of. The modernity of art has also been less a question of its form than a mode of existence presenting itself as a question, which is why for Cavell the function of modern art is to challenge continually not only our conceptions of what art is, but how and with what it is made. It is not the discovery and exploration of the material basis of a given medium that constitute its modernity, but rather the constant doubt that we don't know what painting, photography, or cinema is, and must therefore continually recreate new conditions of existence for them. What characterizes a medium as modern is our awareness that it occupies a continuous state of self-transformation and invention that runs ahead of our perceptions and ideas. Hence the uncertain historical interval, itself without a clear or focused image, that moving-image scholars now inhabit—we stand between the questions "What *was* cinema?" and "What will digital cinema *become*?"

When Cavell writes in *The World Viewed* that "reproducing the world is the *only* thing film does automatically," we can see that the definition of a medium by its automatisms is larger than the simple fact of its technologies or instrumentalisms. A medium is always plural, not singular. It should not be simply identified with a substance or material, and its creative manifestations change and vary over time. This way of thinking does not mean, however, that one may not attribute any form of identity to a medium. Nor is the substance or instrumentalities of a medium entirely without importance. Here automatism takes on a new sense. It is *technique* as well as *technology*, where style and *technē* interact in complicated and sometimes contradictory ways. Although there may be infinite creative variations for expressing space, movement, and duration "filmically," all these elements of style are contained in a power or potential defined by photographic automatisms of analogical transcription, succession, and projection. The invention of film was not the invention of cinema. The fact that spatial movement could be automatically recorded and projected did not in itself permit the creation of cinema. It did make it possible, however, and set the conditions for artistic creation from spatial movement given as the projection of an automated succession of still photographic images. Therefore, part of the physical structure of the medium expresses a historically and culturally determined aesthetic purpose that is relatively independent of individual intentions.

More broadly, Cavell's concept of automatism encourages us to rethink the notion of a medium as a horizon of potentialities. Neither an essence nor a substance or instrumentality, as defined by its automatisms, a medium may appear in response to technological processes and in that sense be conditioned by them. But in my new characterization of the concept, in their virtual life automatisms are equally sensitive to the historical variability of their technological elements and to the responsiveness of those elements to often unforeseen aesthetic purposes. Every art form may be characterized by multiple automatisms, although, for certain periods of short or long duration, some automatisms may predominate and so become primary (for example, the perspectival automatisms embodied in the design of lenses, a persistence represented by the term "lens-based practice"; or, more complexly, the transcriptive automatisms of automatic analogical causation in image or sound recording). An automatism serves as a limit, both technological and conceptual, and thus inspires repetition. Yet it also inspires difference and the creation of the new, whether in the form of a tradition that extracts small variations from persistent similarities, or in the form of the modern that seeks invention and difference of potential in a series of creative acts that challenge present notions of the media. A question raised insistently in the vocabulary of being, the Idea of art most often unravels into multiple and contradictory becomings. This is one reason why Stanley Cavell has characterized the condition of modern art as a perpetual self-questioning.[23]

A medium, then, is nothing more nor less than a set of potentialities from which creative acts may unfold. These potentialities, the powers of the medium as it were, are conditioned by multiple elements or components that can be material, instrumental, and/or formal. Moreover, these elements may vary, individually and in combination with one another, such that a medium may be defined without a presumption that any integral identity or an essence unites these elements into a whole or resolves them into a unique substance. In this definition of creative media, concepts precede materials, but only in the sense that concepts are inspired by potentialities that these materials are capable of expressing. The creative Idea, as I have defined it, inspires the creation of automatisms that, on one level, belong to these potentialities in that they give life to the Idea, they selectively enable its expression. (In film, these potentialities are conditioned by the technological envelopes formed by lenses, the particular causal process set in play by shutters and photosensitive chemicals, succession defined as the seriality of sequential self-contained frames, and the ontological situation of projection.) Here a second level is comprised—the Idea becomes actually expressed in the unfolding of a form, a form expressed through the creation of automatisms. A medium is less a substance or material than a horizon or territory populated by automatisms. What is most provocative, and productive, about Cavell's concept of artistic automatisms is how acts of creation are characterized as a sort of machinism. Obviously, the technological arts—whether photographic, videographic, or digital—exem-

23. For a fascinating reassessment of Cavell's concepts of automatism and medium, especially in the context of postmodernism, see Rosalind Krauss, *"A Voyage on the North Sea": Art in the Age of the Post-Medium Condition* (New York: Thames and Hudson, 1999).

plify in many ways the automatic character of automatisms. But this is not to say that machines create art or that artists function like automata. Rather, I want to account for the peculiar pressure of *technē* in any art as well as the interaction of *technē* and technology, wherein Ideas are expressed as creations both of and in a medium. No more succinct description of automatisms can be found than Sol Lewitt's quip that "the Idea is the machine that makes the art."[24] The medium is the means by which the Idea is expressed and through which it gives form to process. Through an Idea one recognizes the unrealized powers of a medium, a virtual life lying within the horizons delimited by its constitutive elements, whether simple or complex. In this the materialism of all art making is understood. The creation of automatisms brings the medium into existence, making it actual and present; or rather, automatisms are the expressive means through which the artwork presents itself and establishes its conditions of existence in space and in time.

As film disappears into digital movies, then, a new medium may be created, not in the substitution of one form or substance for another, but rather through a staggered displacement of elements. The electronic image has not come into being *ex nihilo* from the invention of digital information processing, but through a series of displacements in the relationship between the formative and constitutive elements of moving-image media: how an image is formed, preserved, placed into movement, expresses time, and is presented on detached displays. We may be confident in our ordinary sense that film, analogical video, and digital video are relatively distinct media, without assuming that a medium is defined essentially by substantial self-similarity. Every medium consists of a variable combination of elements. In this respect, moving-image media are related more by a logic of Wittgensteinian family resemblances than by clear and essential differences.

If, as Roger Scruton has suggested, the arts may be evaluated along a continuum running from causality to intentionality, what fades in film is the historical dimension of photographic causality as the assertion of past existences in time.[25] The digital image is more and more responsive to our imaginative intentions, and less and less anchored to the prior existence of things and people. In the twenty-first century, Méliès will have won over Lumiére, though with a new set of technologies and strategies. Cinema will increasingly become

24. Quoted in Sam Hunter and John Jacobus, *Modern Art: Painting, Sculpture, and Architecture* (New York: Abrams, 1992) 326.

25. "Photography and Representation," *Critical Inquiry* 7.3 (1981) 577–603.

the art of synthesizing imaginary worlds, numerical worlds in which the sight of physical reality becomes increasingly scarce. And what will it mean that the sight of these synthetic worlds is "'photographically' real"? Perhaps it is a good thing that our faith in images is so shaken. And this state of affairs presents us with a second question: If our fascination with film relates to a recognition of a fading or past state of (cultural) being or being-in-the-world, what new automatisms and ontologies do we confront in the emergence of digital media? These are the principal themes of Part III.

# III

## A NEW LANDSCAPE (WITHOUT IMAGE)

Je pense à quelque chose. Quand je pense à quelque chose, en fait, je pense à autre chose toujours . . . Par exemple, je vois un paysage nouveau pour moi. Mais il est nouveau pour moi parce que je le compare en pensée à un autre paysage. Ancien celui-là, que je connaissais.

—Jean-Luc Godard, *Eloge de l'amour*

## 13. An Elegy for Film

Film is facing an uncertain future. The cinephiles of the new millennium now occupy a curious temporal state, not unlike the protagonist of Jean-Luc Godard's 2003 *Eloge de l'amour.* "In Praise of Love" is the English translation of the title of Godard's film, but the sense of the French word *éloge* is more ambiguous. Combining the senses of "elegy" and "eulogy," this cinematic song of praise addresses an object that is either gone or presently passing out of existence.

Godard's film, and its protagonist Edgar, are simultaneously nostalgic and future-seeking, backward and forward looking, as befits contemplation of an art form undergoing a stark historical mutation. This temporal ambiguity is also expressed by the two-part structure of the work: an elliptical narrative present shot in fine-grained 35mm black-and-white, followed by a more linear past conveyed in color-saturated video. In a first viewing, one wonders why video is used to evoke memory and the past and black-and-white film the present. This logic is as complex as it is subtle. As in so many of his films, Godard is encouraging us to look again, to reconsider how and what we see through film or through video. And in so doing, the projected work encourages a deep phenomenological examination concerning film in our time that is lost or sharply reduced when watching *Eloge de l'amour* on DVD. Curiously, the conceptual force of Godard's aesthetic choices is not completely lost when presented digitally; nonetheless, the perceptual density of the evidence of our senses is sharply attenuated. In even this well-mastered DVD, not only is resolution lost in the black-and-white sections, but the video images appear less color saturated and somehow more "natural." In the DVD version, the edges of two extremes are reduced to a happy medium: video color finds its home on the television monitor, while film is uprooted to a land where it will always rest an uneasy immigrant. Perhaps Godard's last exercise in medium specificity, *Eloge de l'amour* is a praise song for the 35mm matrix. Video may be the future of cinema, but, ironically, the color palette achieved in the second part of the movie is best accomplished when video is printed on film. And so, while the black-and-white scenes suggest a present that may be passing out of existence—the disappearance of film as a medium—the color sequences may never again achieve their impressionistic vibrancy and luminosity when and if these video images are no longer presentable through 35mm projection.

The narrative of *Eloge de l'amour* allegorizes the present virtual life of film. The protagonist, Edgar, seeks to create a work from the life of Simone Weill, though it is unclear what form this work will take: a cantata? an opera? a novel? a play? a film? Edgar's project is less a work than a potentiality searching for a form and a medium; it has a purely virtual existence. This virtual project is doubled by the search for the woman to voice the work—found but unrecognized as such in the video past to come, ineffable in the filmed present. The video section presents something like the search for a form or forms for memory, wherein "Spielberg Associates" seek to purchase the past of the woman's grandparents, who were resistance leaders during the Occupation. But just as this strand of the story runs parallel to Edgar's search without intersecting it, the woman's possible presence in the project rests unrecognized as much as the future form of the work itself. Seen but unrecognized in the past, she is present but evanescent in the black-and-white "present" of the film. Here she is portrayed either in shadow or in the background, or as indexes of an off-screen presence. Sometimes an unseen voice—out of focus, off-screen or out-of-frame—she ends as a story recounted by others. After her death, nothing remains but the ambiguous contents of the small valise she has left behind. Our hero is offered one of her personal effects, a book, *Le voyage d'Edgar,* and herein lies the unsettled temporal space presented by the film. We will never see Edgar's project or know the form it may ultimately take, if any. We are in the middle of a voyage whose endpoint is uncertain and whose beginning is already forgotten. In the passage from filmic to videographic time, the (video) future is already in the past, the present strives to preserve an aesthetic memory of what film was, and we the viewers struggle to envision the work to come, which is always just beyond our reach.

In this way, *Eloge de l'amour* marks the current fate of film as an indiscernible point of passage—the present realization of an already unattainable past. This transition is expressed as a continually changing landscape. Near the end of the color sequences, Edgar is on a train from Brittany to Paris. We watch a deeply saturated seascape with a setting sun as Edgar voices off-frame: "I think of something. When I think of something, in fact, I think of something else . . . For example, I see a landscape new to me. But it is new to me because I compare it in thought with another landscape. Very old that one, that I used to know."

I once thought that one of the most rewarding tasks of a film teacher was to restore for students the historical and phenomenological experience of watching silent films. But I have recently come to realize, with some personal alarm, that during the past twenty years we have all lost in some degree the capacity to involve ourselves deeply and sensually in the 35mm image, well projected in

Frame enlargements from *Eloge de l'amour* (Avventura Films, 2003).

a movie theater. Film is no longer a modern medium; it is completely historical. And indeed, the task now is to ask students to imagine an era, not so long past, when the default perceptual norms were not videographic, when there were no expectations of interactivity with the image, and when screens were found principally in movie theaters. Theatrical cinema is, no doubt, the ancient land to which Godard refers, no less than the *nouvelle vague*'s presentation of modernity in remaking the black-and-white 35mm image of Hollywood cinema of the 1940s. And so Godard asks us once again to compare the two landscapes, film and video, the passing present and the emerging future, not only to recover a perceptual past that is quickly being lost to us, but also to realize that the aesthetic future of the electronic image may be tied to film, though in ways we have not yet anticipated or fully understood.

Film, I have argued, is a historical medium par excellence. But it is also now becoming “history”; that is, it is quite likely that film is no longer modern or constitutive of our modernity. For the time being, theatrical cinema is our passing present, our disappearing ontology. But this also means that it is not yet completely past, and that the emergent future may remain, for some time to come, cinematic. To imagine a conclusion, then, I want to explore two overarching themes: first, to present some criteria for evaluating the transformation from film to digital in the moving image and for indicating what aesthetic roles film might still play in contemporary image practice; and second, to argue that a certain conception of film theory still provides the core concepts with which this transition may be understood and evaluated.

## 14. The ~~New~~ “Media”

Part II of this book began with the observation that a certain idea of cinema is already dead, its phenomenology transformed by television and video. Under pressure from video and computational processes, contemporary cinema is currently in a state of self-transformation, and its future is difficult to foresee. A new territory has unfolded on electronic and digital screens, and this is a landscape “without image” for two reasons. The first reason is historical. The future of the electronic and digital arts is only thinly drawn and barely recognizable in the present. The problem here is not the novelty or “newness” of the digital and the electronic. Rather, we do not possess a historical image of these forms because we do not yet completely understand what concepts condition their possible genealogies. Nor do we have a sense of how they inform our present understanding of what history means for us, or in what sense they constitute our modernity as lived today.

The second reason is ontological. These forms are also without image in the sense that what appears on electronic and digital screens does not fully conform to the criteria by which in the past we have come to recognize something as a created, aesthetic image. Here we confront a new kind of ontological perplexity—how to place or situate ourselves, in space and in time, in relation to an image that does not seem to be "one." On electronic screens, we are uncertain that what appears before is *an* "image," and in its powers of mutability and velocity of transmission, we are equally uncertain that this perception has a singular or stable existence either in the present or in relation to the past. But more on this later.

For these reasons, it is difficult to comprehend in what the "medium" of computational processes consists and, in fact, what makes them "new." The designation "new media" is misleading for a number of reasons. First, it encompasses too wide a variety of computationally processed artifacts: CD-ROMs; HTML authoring; interactive game design and programming; image and sound capture or synthesis, manipulation, and editing; text-processing and desktop publishing; human-computer interface design; computer-aided design; and all the varieties of computer-mediated communication.

The term "digital cinema" poses similar problems. Many commentators confuse the very different creative processes of digital capture or acquisition, computer synthesis, digital postproduction, and digital distribution, not to mention the many interesting questions raised by the transition to digital sound production. A theatrical movie today may combine one or more of these processes with more-traditional photographic capture, though it is increasingly rare to find a moving image entirely unaffected by digital practices. At what point does something become "digital cinema"? Must the raw material be captured on high-definition video? Would the presence of digital sound and the transferral of all picture elements to a digital intermediate count? Or would the mastering and release of an analogical film on an interactive DVD transform it into a digital movie? All these cases involve not so much the creation of a new medium or media as a reprocessing of existing print and visual artifacts into digital forms. From this perspective, there are no "*new* media"; there are only simulation and information processing used in reformatting old media as digital information.

So-called new media may not be so new for another reason. Lev Manovich's book *The Language of New Media* takes a salutary perspective in noting that contemporary computational practices appear as the convergence of two parallel histories, both beginning in the 1830s: on one hand, daguerreotypy as the beginnings of photography and other time-based spatial media; on the other, Charles Babbage and Lady Ada Lovelace's early experiments in analytical computing.[1] For Manovich, new media are nothing less or more than the synthesis of these two histories in the translation of all existing media into numerical data manipulable by computers and accessed via electronic screens. Manovich calls this "transcoding," a process wherein all previous cultural forms become subject to the computer's ontology, epistemology, and pragmatics. Cinema and its prehistory are as much the progenitors of new media as computers and their prehistory; one cannot be understood without the other.

Manovich's book and recent articles are comforting to film theorists, since he places so much emphasis on the importance of cinema as a "cultural interface." As a result of its century-long success as an immersive and broadly accessible cultural form, cinema dominates our cultural understanding of in what moving screened images consist. Further, this idea of cinema serves as a template for the design of a great variety of digital interactive media.

Manovich is correct, I think, to insist that in their sibling rivalry with cinema the forms and operations of interactive media have emerged through a process of creating a new digital "language" and cultural interface as the remediation of an older, analogical and photographic one. Nevertheless, a number of historical cautions should be raised around this story. First, despite his fascination with cinema, Manovich's understanding of its history and theory lacks depth and complexity. In this respect, he sets in place a retroactive teleology from which all time-based image practices are evaluated from the point of view of film. Alternatively, it is worthwhile to confront the hubris of film history with the broader context of media archaeology. The recent work of William Uricchio, among others, has uncovered a third trajectory, wherein the prehistory of television and electronic or scanned images—with their powers of temporal simultaneity, point-to-point communication, and real-time interaction—predates that of film and runs parallel to it.[2] Two con-

1. (Cambridge, Mass.: MIT Press, 2001) 19–26.

2. See, among other important texts, William Uricchio, "There's More to the Camera Obscura than Meets the Eye," in *Arrêt sur image et fragmentation du temps / Stop Motion, Fragmentation of Time,* ed. M. B. François Albera and André Gaudreault (Lausanne: Cinema Editions Payot, 2002) 103–120; idem, "Storage, Simultaneity, and the Media Technologies of Modernity," in *Allegories of Communication: Intermedial Concerns from Cinema to the Digital,* ed. J. O. Fullerton and J. Fullerton (Eastleigh: John Libbey, 2004) 123–138.

clusions might be drawn from this acknowledgment. One would be that Manovich brings the histories of cinema and computational processes too closely together; his fascination with cinema obscures important differences as well as similarities between the photographic and electronic arts. And, ironically, while he develops many useful concepts for specifying the forms and operations of digital interactivity, despite the centrality of cinema to his argument it is unclear what cinema and photography will become in the aftermath of their computational transcoding. A second conclusion might be more disturbing for the *cinéfilles* and *cinéfils* of contemporary film study. (*Hommage à* Serge Daney.) The long view and the larger historical context of media archaeology suggest that the history of cinema has been only a long digression in the more culturally significant merging of the history of electronic screens with the history of computational processes.

In any case, a more complex and nuanced historical context is needed for us to begin to comprehend how a photographic ontology, in Cavell's sense of the term, is being displaced by a digital ontology. For it is not yet given that we have the tools for understanding what a computational "medium" might be or what would make it new, modern, or actual in relation to the photographic and the cinematographic. Especially in popular criticism, there is considerable historiographical confusion concerning what makes new media new. In the last ten years, the emergence and popularization of digital technologies have provoked four historical attitudes, all of which obfuscate the complexity of our current relationships with analogical and digital media. Perhaps the most common is what Thomas Elsaesser characterizes as "business as usual."[3] This perspective acknowledges no historical change at all: film disappears, but cinema continues because the dominance of the digital image and digital postproduction processes has had little to no impact on the narrational norms characteristic of theatrical fiction films. Or, in a similar vein, one eliminates all distinctiveness by forgetting the question of medium and collapsing all time-based spatial expression under the supergenre of the moving image.

Philip Rosen makes the larger claim that popular discourses wanting to account for the novelty of new media tend to displace or deny historical self-consciousness about their origins or genealogies through a variety of rhetorical strategies. Thus, the creation of the idea of "new media," whatever such a vague designation might imply, models the history of digital inventiveness as

3. "The New New Hollywood: Cinema beyond Distance and Proximity," in *Moving Images, Culture and the Mind*, ed. I. Bondebjerg (Luton: University of Luton Press, 2000) 189.

the temporal displacement or replacement of analogical media. These strategies involve the metaphor of conquest (the analogical is supplanted by the digital); the presumption of a radical break on the technological time-line, which posits a linear chronology disavowing a relationship to the (analogical) past; and, finally, the casting of digital technologies in the form of the forecast.[4] Here the newness of new media is presented as a form of rational extrapolation whereby technologies or products still in the lab or on the drawing boards become exemplary of an inevitable shift that lies just ahead of us.

Our historical distance from the *Wired* 1990s, short as it is in 2007, already provides an ironic perspective from which to comprehend these historical excesses. However, we are still searching for historical tools for understanding and evaluating the novel situations that confront us on screens reflective or electronic. Nor have we yet overcome a radical division in which one either mourns the passing of film as an *art argentique* or celebrates the emergence of the digital as technological destiny. Clearly, though, the possible disappearance of photography and film into computationally based practices informs new attitudes to time and to history that require careful attention. As I related in Part II, not only has film become history, but through the work of Rosen and others film studies has raised new and interesting questions that examine the indexical arts in relation to historical knowing by evaluating their expressive powers of causation, duration, and past-relatedness. Moreover, film studies' confrontation with the digital and the electronic, combined with the displacement of the theatrical model of spectatorship, has made us more attentive to the history of cinema studies itself, of its methods and questions in relation to an ever-changing object. (I will address this last point more expansively in *An Elegy for Theory.*)

Nevertheless, today most so-called new media are inevitably imagined from a cinematic metaphor. Undoubtedly, the art of cinema is renewing and refashioning itself through the incorporation of digital processes, while a certain idea of cinema informs and insinuates itself into the development of interactive entertainments. Here, the arts of analogy are not displaced by digital technologies; rather, an idea of cinema persists or subsists within the new media as their predominant cultural and aesthetic model for engaging the vision and imagination of viewers. But this also means that it is difficult to envision what kinds of aesthetic experiences computational processes will innovate once

4. *Change Mummified: Cinema, Historicity, Theory* (Minneapolis: University of Minnesota Press, 2001) 301–349.

they have unleashed themselves from the cinematic metaphor and begin to explore their autonomous creative powers, if indeed they eventually do so.

I am closer now to explaining why ~~new~~ is under erasure and "media" is in scare quotes. Phil Rosen has wisely warned us to be attentive to the "hybrid historicity" of the digital arts, both with respect to the past processes from which they emerge and which they in fact prolong, and with respect to the senses of time and history to which they may give rise. Our contemporary sense of the moving image has evolved from three interwoven strands of the virtual arts that engage with one another in uneven historical rhythms—photography and film, electronic imaging and transmission, and computational processes—and we need concepts that can bring these strands together while recognizing the complexity of their relationships and differences. This book is not and cannot be a study of "new media," although I will have occasion to make some remarks on digital media in general. I am more concerned here with problems of imagining "digital *cinema*," and the paradoxes to be confronted in that particular combination of words. This is a matter of evaluating what the moving image is becoming, and indeed, has (un)become in the era of digital capture and synthesis. By focusing resolutely on the current destiny of photography and film in their transformation by computational processes, the future emerging from this passing present may yet be better understood.

There is debate or discussion today because we are confronted with something new in the image, something that disturbs the perceptual defaults of the chemically based analogical image. We confront something that looks like photography, and continues to serve many of its cultural functions. Yet a felt change is occurring, or perhaps has occurred, in our phenomenological relationship with these images. A subtle shifting of gears is taking place in our current ontology, in our relation to the world and to others, as mediated through technologically produced images. What we find to be uncanny and unsettling, I would suggest, is the spatial similarity of digital images to the now antecedent practices of photography and film. The ontological strangeness provoked by digital imaging is not the same as that of photography, yet many continuities bridge the two kinds of practice and our cultural relationship to them. As a result, photography and film remain the baseline for evaluating a certain kind of perceptual experience, although (and this is the temporality of all ontological questioning) we find ourselves pushed to examine something new in this experience that has already happened to us. The examination of the new, the actual, and the contemporary is the recovery of a transition already past, and so we must revisit some familiar questions of classical film theory in a new context.

In the sections that follow, I will map out the conceptual difficulty of imagining what cinema becomes in the digital era by examining arguments concerning "perceptual realism," the function of analogism and indexicality in digital capture and synthesis, and the relative distinctiveness of analogical transcription with respect to digital conversion as causal processes. In addition, the current conjunction of electronic displays with computational processes will present two historical difficulties for envisioning the place of contemporary cinema studies in the study of digital imaging. On one hand, this conjunction indicates yet another dislocation of "film" and the continuity of its ontological expressiveness. (And this is less a disappearance than a displacement into new and surprising contexts.) On the other, computational processes put conceptual pressure on our ordinary senses of the nature and qualities of a medium or media, or indeed, of the "image" itself. The process of transcoding is now advanced enough that any notion of aesthetic specificity—of image, sound, music, or text—has completely dissolved into computers and computational processes. Where before there may have been photography, cinema, or video, there are now only computers and the kinds of capture, synthesis, and processing they allow or encourage.

The presumed newness of digital practices refers less, then, to the creation of a new medium than to a large-scale historical process wherein existing textual and spatial media are transcoded into digital form so as to be manipulable by computational processes and communicable through information networks. Just as the nature and extent of the historical novelty of "new media" must be reexamined, so also must we ask: Can information processing be considered a creative medium? Can the computer as a simulation machine or information processor give rise to creative automatisms?

## 15. Paradoxes of Perceptual Realism

In Part II, I presented some of the fundamental elements or automatisms that distinguish film as a photographic medium, while accepting the complex set of family resemblances through which the photographic is connected to, yet distinct from, videographic expression within the larger category of moving-image practices. Conditioned by the logic of automatic analogical causation, these automatisms of photographic transcription, succession, and projection are also automatic or automated as mechanically occurring processes. More so even than photography and film, the digital arts, if there are any, are characterized by automated procedures. Select, cut, copy, paste, sort, rip, sample, filter: these and other actions are designed to be self-actualizing in response to specified commands. It remains to be seen, however, whether and if these procedures produce *automatisms,* that is, whether the computer's algorithmic processes have indeed made possible the creation of a new kind of medium or media.

Other questions arise from the perspective of digital cinema. Have computational processes changed the nature of the image as we ordinarily characterize it? Have the components of the image changed along with the possibilities of their combination in time? Can digital cinema express duration and past-relatedness with the same force as film, or does it even want to? In any case, to discover or acknowledge the existence or creation of digital automatisms will be to know whether the computer can be a medium and, as such, can produce art, and how it has changed the creative process in cinema.

This difficult problem cuts to the heart of whether digital cinema may or may not be characterized as *film,* for example whether something like Alexandr Sokurov's *Russian Ark* (2002), captured directly to hard disk, is of the same species as Jean Eustache's *Numéro zéro.* There is little difficulty in accepting both as belonging to the supergenre of moving-image media. The information constitutive of both objects is captured in movement by optical lenses, presented on detached displays in two dimensions, and so forth. If only the overarching conditions of moving-image media are applied, the possible borders between film and digital cinema will completely overlap. However, I have made the case that there are criteria for marking distinct aesthetic differences between photographic transcription and digital capture, and strong reasons for wanting to characterize film as a medium. I will expand these reasons here, not only to comprehend better the relative specificity of film as it becomes historical before our eyes, but also to imagine and to understand what is becoming, and will become, digital cinema.

In either case, the distinctiveness of filmic processes and digital capture or synthesis is clouded by three conceptual difficulties endemic to our cultural understanding of digital imaging and its evolution. The first, as I have already suggested, refers to the still-unexamined question of whether the computer is a medium, and thus whether one can make art from digitized information and computational processes. Since we have already relinquished the criterion of substantial self-similarity (that a medium consists only of stone or metal or paint or silver halide crystals), perhaps the question is moot. Because its basis and processes are computational, the very nature of digital information processing is to be without substance in the ordinary sense of the term.

(Of course, extraordinarily, anyone who has experienced a hard-disk crash is brought to a sudden comprehension of the computer's material and technological realities.) However, if the shift to digital capture and synthesis indicates a change of medium in "film" making, then we will want to know how to characterize their automatisms and their ontology with some philosophical precision. I will address this question more completely in the sections that follow.

The second difficulty involves what I call the paradox of "perceptual realism." (The third will relate this paradox to the question of theatrical projection.) Since the early 1980s, if not before, technological and creative innovations in digital image synthesis have been driven by a single, though somewhat paradoxical, goal: the achievement of "'photographic' realism," or what Lev Manovich has called "perfect photographic credibility."[5] Game design as well, though in a less singular way, has been driven by the desire to attain degrees of involvement and identification in game worlds commensurate with those of cinematic narrative, especially through manipulating subjective point of view as movement in space through time-delimited actions. Curiously, for an industry driven by innovation and market differentiation, the qualities of the "photographic" and the "cinematic" remain resolutely the touchstones for creative achievement in digital imaging entertainment. The "new" has not been sought in digital imaging as much as fresh means for producing familiar effects with a long cultural history, though often in very novel contexts. This is yet another way in which digital cinema positions itself in the long genealogy of photographic and cinematographic practice. Through a strategy that Phil Rosen has characterized as "digital mimicry," research in computer graphics has pursued an idea of realism wherein photography and cinema, as well as other images based on the geometry of linear perspective, function as perceptual and spatial defaults.[6] Through the desire to achieve perfect photographic credibility, perceptual realism in digital images reproduces and reinforces deeply recalcitrant cultural norms of depiction. Nevertheless, this desire is paradoxical, in that computational processes, and the automatisms derived from them, fuel powerful countercurrents that reconfig-

5. Quoted in Elsaesser, "The New New Hollywood" 192. On the question of perceptual realism in the development of computer graphics for theatrical cinema, see Stephen Prince's essay "True Lies: Perceptual Realism, Digital Images, and Film Theory," in *Film Quarterly: Forty Years—A Selection*, ed. Brian Henderson and Ann Martin (Berkeley: University of California Press, 1999) 392–411.

6. See *Change Mummified*, especially 304–314.

ure these norms, shifting the function of screens and challenging spectators to reconsider the very concept of the image.

That contemporary research in computer graphics is driven by the desire to produce "'photographic' realism" in synthetic images is itself curious, but no less so than attributing the ideal of a spatial "realism" to photography. The emphasis on perceptual criteria for judging the indiscernibility of synthetic and photographic images also exhibits some interesting assumptions concerning what defines our interest in photographs both before and after the digital era.

To consider a photograph or a digital image as perceptually real involves an assumption that such images are representational. Moreover, representation is defined as spatial correspondence. The terms of correspondence, what corresponds to what, are of special interest here. In an important essay on the development of computer graphics for narrative film, Stephen Prince notes that "a perceptually realistic image is one which structurally corresponds to the viewer's audiovisual experience of three-dimensional space. Perceptually realistic images correspond to this experience because film-makers build them to do so. Such images display a nested hierarchy of cues which organize the display of light, color, texture, movement, and sound in ways that correspond with the viewer's own understanding of these phenomena in daily life" ("True Lies" 400). In addition, Prince clearly implies that the viewer's audiovisual experience is not defined by phenomenological criteria as such; rather, both "understanding" and "experience" are defined by the mental or psychological work of cognitive schemata. Perceptual realism refers, first, to a set of criteria in reference to which computational algorithms attempt to replicate the spatial information that cinematography automatically creates through analogical transcription, especially as movement in and through space. Animating synthetic images involves complex calculations for applying correct algorithms for mass, inertia, torque, and speed, collision detection and response, perspective construction (edge and contour information, monocular distance codes, etc.)—in short, mathematically constructing a "screen geography with coherent coordinates through the projective geometry of successive camera positions" ("True Lies" 399).

In the history of cinema, the advent of digital synthesis renders this tendency even more curious as the desire to maintain an impression of reality as cued by objects and "worlds" that have no physical existence. Indeed, one of the defining features of digital cinema as experienced on screens today is the blending of capture and synthesis, combining images recorded from physical reality with images generated only on computers in the absence of any recording function or physical referent. Having a modular structure composed of discrete elements whose values are highly variable, the powers of the digital image derive from its mutability and susceptibility to transformation and recombination. Yet the criteria of perceptual realism reinforce, even exaggerate, *spatial* coherence. They strive to be more spatially similar and more replete with spatial information than photography itself. In a recent essay, "Realism and the Digital Image," W. J. T. Mitchell notes that the cultural function of digital capture today is optimizing rather than challenging or subverting the norms of depictive credibility. "If we are looking for a 'tendency' in the coming of digital photography," Mitchell writes, "it is toward 'deep' copies that contain much more information about the original than we will ever need, and super copies that can be improved, enhanced, and (yes) manipulated—but not in order to fake anything, but to produce the most well-focused, evenly lit image possible—in other words, to produce something like a professional quality photograph of the old style."[7]

Mitchell is undoubtedly correct about our conventional uses of digital capture devices. My deeper point, however, is that the technological criteria of perceptual realism assume, wrongly in my account, that the primary powers of photography are spatial semblance. The first paradox of perceptual realism, then, is the insistence on preserving, and even deepening and extending, an "impression of reality," thus prolonging Hollywood cinema's long-standing stylistic goal of producing spatial transparency or immediacy. This would not be an overcoming of the old realism-versus-formalism debates of classical film theory, as Prince suggests in his otherwise informative essay. Rather, the wish to construct completely imaginary spaces with the perceptual density of photographs grants full honors to the "realists," so long as the criteria applied are only spatial and perceptual. In this respect, the concept of realism in use by computer graphics professionals has a rather restrictive and circular definition. It does not correspond to an ordinary spatial sense of the world and actual events taking place within it, but rather to our perceptual and cognitive norms for apprehending a *represented* space, especially a space that can be represented or constructed according to mathematical notation.

This definition of "realism" mischaracterizes the powers of photography no

7. "Realism and the Digital Image," in *Critical Realism in Contemporary Art: Around Allan Sekula's Photography*, ed. Hilde Van Gelder and Jan Baetens (Leuven: Leuven University Press, forthcoming).

less than digital graphics. And here is a second paradox: the criteria of perceptual realism are defined by analogy with photographic images without themselves relying on analogical processes. If I am correct about the primacy of the temporal sense of photographic transcription, the insistence on the perception of spatial semblance here is surely consequential. It is as if the creation of digital imaging as a medium were willing the annihilation of past duration with respect to space in order to replace it with another conception of time, that is, the time of calculation or computer cycles. Moreover, although the processes of digital capture are fully consistent with our ordinary sense of recording actual events, the goal of both digital capture and synthesis is to constitute a space that is mathematically definable and manipulable. It is as if the algorithmic construction of space seeks, in its definition of realism, to correspond to a world defined only by Cartesian coordinates and their algebraic manipulation of geometrical shapes. Thus, the paradoxes of perceptual realism result from a circular logic wherein computer science projects an ideal of photography that finds in the photographic image only those qualities best expressed through computation in the form of spatial outputs. In the wish to render the digital image identical with "photography," it already imagines the photograph as if it were a digital image, or at least what the digital is capable of simulating as photography.

For this reason, the appearance of digital synthesis does not obviate the tension between formalism and realism in film theory, but it does shift the grounds for the discussion of realism in two ways. As even André Bazin knew well, every realism relies on formal effects, and no doubt, perceptually, these effects are cognitively conditioned. But cultural criteria are also needed to comprehend a shift in the nature of how effects of realism are produced, as Mitchell wisely points out. Automatic analogical causation grounds its sense in a special kind of indexical logic in which judgments of correspondence are anchored in physical reality and reference to the past. To say that these criteria were never relevant and to displace the problem entirely to a cognitive domain is to provide some interesting hints about the emerging ontology of the digital. The key point of reference now will be to mental events—not physical reality molded to the imaginary, but the free reign of the imaginary in the creation of images *ex nihilo* that can simulate effects of the physical world (gravity, friction, causation) while also overcoming them. If the criteria of perceptual realism have come to dominate judgments concerning the apparent realism of images, we need to know to what "reality" these criteria correspond. In its reliance on cognitive criteria for assessing effects of (spatial) realism produced by computer-generated imaging, perceptual realism bases its judgments on a correspondence between modeling algorithms and the cognitive schema on which they are based. Interestingly, this is correspondence to a mental or psychological reality, not a physical one, and refers only to the cognitive mechanisms through which represented spaces are perceived and comprehended. There is a circular reasoning here wherein research in computer graphics assumes that the cognitive processes for perceiving space and motion in represented images somehow correspond structurally and mathematically with the physics of space and motion as experienced in the natural world. This may or may not be the case. But by this argument the only problem that perceptual realism might actually account for is how synthetic spaces may be accepted as invisibly blended with captured spaces. As I will describe more fully later, this assumption indicates an interesting mutation in our ontological relations with digital images. In its presumed correspondence with the viewer's cognitive and perceptual structures, perceptual realism retreats from the physical world, placing its bets on imaginative worlds—in other words, a projection of mind into image that conflates mental images with perceptually real events. To introduce the problem of realism in this context involves question begging that assumes that analogical and digital processes construct space in the same way. (It also assumes that those spaces are perceptually equivalent, which may not be the case.) And it seems to imply that differences in representational processes are irrelevant so long as they correspond to or replicate cognitive mechanisms for recognizing space constructed through projective geography. Nevertheless, the automatisms of analogical and digital processes do differ in significant ways, as I will argue in the next section.

One last feature of perceptual realism as a strategy for producing computer-generated or computer-manipulated imagery should be addressed here. Current digital cinema invisibly combines graphical and animated elements, both synthesized and hand-rendered, with lens-captured elements. (Of course, this is possible only once all analog elements are scanned to a digital intermediate for postproduction processing.) Thus, a corollary to the reinforcement of the spatial and representational qualities of the image is, again paradoxically, a reassertion of its *graphism,* meaning the ability to erase and efface, to add and subtract, to alter perceptual values in a painterly or pictorial way. As Thomas Elsaesser has noted, "as a graphic mode, digital cinema joins painting also in another respect: it requires a new kind of individual input, indeed manual application of craft and skill, which is to say, it marks the return of the 'artist' as source and origin of the image. In this respect, the digital image should be regarded as an expressive, rather than reproductive medium, with both the software and the 'effects' it produces bearing the imprint and signature of the creator" ("Beyond Distance" 192–193). The image becomes not only more painterly but also more imaginative. Its powers of documentation are diminished or decentered in relation to the presentation of counterfactually conditional worlds. Recent Hollywood practice reveals a curious fault line in this respect. As innovations in digital synthesis or animation strive for ever-greater depictive credibility and visual transparency or immediacy, digital post-production practices in live-action films are producing ever more powerful effects of hypermediacy: very fast editing with "intensified" continuity, eccentric manipulation of rates of motion, enhancing the graphical values of the image through digital manipulation of color, and so on. Both science fiction and the action film are special-effects driven, and both are remaking themselves stylistically through the painterly and imaginative powers of digital creation and manipulation.

Because there are so many ways of producing or simulating the perceptual effects of "photographic credibility," the live-action movie—or rather, movies aesthetically interested in images captured from live performances—may become deemphasized as the norm of motion picture entertainment. Indeed, in special-effects-driven genres this is more and more the case. Ninety-five percent of the information in *The Phantom Menace* (1999), for example, was digitally synthesized—practically speaking, it is no more nor less an animated film than *Madagascar* (2005). As digital production makes other options possible or even more desirable, the idea of recording or capture as the creative manipulation of physical spaces and times may become optional rather than one of the constitutive features of cinematic language. Weakening or eliminating the indexical powers of photography shifts the balance, then, between causation and intention. In this respect, it is probably incorrect or misleading to attribute photographic indexicality or causality to digital synthesis. (I address below the difficulties of applying the concept of indexicality to digital capture.) The isomorphism of analogical processes is not fully coincident with digital ones; the continuity of transcription is not replaceable by digital synthesis. Analogical processes need only imprint these isomorphisms from a physical space, found or constructed, and combine them in imaginative contexts, which is why I have followed Stanley Cavell in insisting that photographic capture is not representation. And for this reason, the process of automatic analogical causation is indeed *necessarily* tied to physically existing spaces and times, even though captured elements may be recombined to produce imaginative worlds and counterfactual senses. Alternatively, digital synthesis is only optionally tied to the physical world through its capacity to construct spatial semblance.

(In this respect, I often feel that computer-generated and blended images can be very strange and hyperreal, but rarely *surreal.* The great discovery of Surrealist cinema was to present the uncanniness of ordinary objects displaced to unusual contexts, whether through *photogénie*—the act of being framed and photographed—or through recombination in staging or editing. Photography and film fascinated the Surrealists because of their powers to suggest underlying, uncanny, and unrecognized powers flowing through objects as ordinarily experienced. Photographic causation was an important tool for generating this effect as the projection of the ordinary into extraordinary contexts or combinations, just as the making of Surrealist objects often involved the transformation of everyday devices, as in Marcel Duchamp's readymades or Man Ray's irons equipped with spikes and Meret Oppenheim's teacups lined with fur.)

## 16. Real Is as Real Does

The criteria for judging the perceptual realism of digital images are less ethical or ontological than pragmatic. Confronted by the opening of his own film, one can imagine Forrest Gump opining, "Real is as real does" in perfect satisfaction with the digitally painted feather that floats before him. In this respect, the paradoxes of perceptual realism raise questions in a new domain. Does the replacement of the photographic by the digital matter if electronically projected digital images are effectively indistinguishable from 35mm print projection? Will the experience of theatrical moviegoing change in any significant ways?

From the standpoint of the industry, if audiences continue to buy tickets in the same numbers the answer is no. Alternatively, neither cognitive nor psychoanalytic theory has produced very clear indicators concerning whether or not the electronic arts—which have different technological conditions for reproducing space, light, and movement—set significantly different conditions for perception, involvement, and pleasure in the image. Nonetheless, these differences are phenomenologically significant for audiences in ways that are still difficult to anticipate.

In 2002 I was invited by Charles Swartz at the Entertainment Technology Center in Los Angeles to a test of what has now become the industry standard

Frame enlargement from *Forrest Gump* (Paramount, 1994).

for digital projection, Texas Instruments' DLP system. The test reel included fully synthetic images, various ratios of mixed photographically recorded and digitally captured or synthesized images, and, finally, 35mm original transferred to digital. My subjective impression of these images surprised me, and watching commercial digital projection today has not changed my opinion. To the extent that the images presented were created through digital synthesis, the better they looked in electronic projection. Indeed, these images seemed to surpass in brightness and resolution the quality of 35mm film, producing an impression often referred to as hyperreality. At the other end of the spectrum, fully 35mm original transferred to digital looked poor: the images were soft, lacking in resolution and clarity; contrast and apparent depth of field were reduced; and colors were blurred. High-definition digital capture was more difficult to judge. While often it seemed to rival 35mm resolution overall, by any number of criteria it also seemed "colder," less involving, and less pleasurable to watch.

Digital capture and synthesis and digital projection are changing the nature of the medium of motion pictures, but probably not in ways that will help theatrical exhibitors to attract new and larger audiences.[8] Unlike previous eras of technological transition (for example, the addition of sound, color, or widescreen), when stark perceptible differences were marketed as the hallmarks of new cinematic experiences, today the major studios appear to want

8. See the recent work of John Belton, especially "Digital Cinema: A False Revolution," *October* 100 (Spring 2002) 98–114.

the transition from film to digital to be as transparent as possible. Consequently, the gradual installation of digital projection systems in movie theaters seems to be happening rather quietly and surreptitiously.

For the entertainment industry, movies must remain movies and without significantly changing their aesthetic identity in crossing platforms. The marketing of the digital thus expresses some rather stark if badly understood ironies. I mentioned earlier my impression that digital cinema "wants" electronic projection. For a variety of reasons, my working hypothesis remains that when reproduced on an electronic or digital screen, 35mm original may never fully realize the phenomenological density of time, pastness, and causality of the projected film experience. More poignantly for film studies, this experience has been lost for at least a generation for the great majority of motion-picture audiences. Ironically, although the 35mm image remains the gold standard for visual quality among Hollywood professionals, the perceptual norm for the vast majority of spectators is videographic. It may be the case that contemporary spectators also "want" the videographic as the will to a new electronic, rather than photographic, ontology.

As the touchstone for the perceptual experiences of digital motion pictures, the goals of perfect photographic credibility and of perceptual realism thus present a double bind for the film industry. On one hand, it is unclear whether audiences will continue to pay premium prices to watch someone else's big-screen television, for indeed digital projection is nothing more than high-definition video, an experience increasingly available to home viewers. Theatrical exhibition will undoubtedly continue, though I suspect that the number of tickets sold will remain flat or shrink slightly for the foreseeable future. Will going to the movies soon become the economic and cultural equivalent of going to a Broadway show or to the opera, as a savvy auditor once suggested to me in Berlin? Perhaps. But the key point here is twofold. First, it remains to be seen whether and how the expansion of digital projection may push filmmakers to develop visual styles and aesthetic strategies that exploit the creative automatisms of the digital image in more imaginative and challenging ways. Consequently, it may turn out that the desire to reproduce the look and feel of the 35mm image in digital will turn out to be a failed strategy, and that more directors will follow the lead of Robert Rodriguez in signing their work as "digital files." Indeed, the full consequences of movies becoming "digital files" rather than "films" still needs to be worked out. Furthermore, as I have argued, home theater has already significantly overtaken commercial exhibition in popularity and economic importance. It remains, however, to understand whether a new aesthetic, and a new ontology, of motion pictures are emerging or have already emerged. And it may be the case that our new ontology in relation to digital imaging and digital processes are only with difficulty and incompletely realized in the context of theatrical projection.

## 17. Lost in Translation: Analogy and Index Revisited

No doubt there are many similarities between photography and digital imaging. Still, I am less certain than Tom Gunning and other recent commentators that digital photography is an extension of analogical processes, comparable to earlier innovations such as the replacement of wet collodion processes by dry plates or the appearance of fast exposure times.[9] Grasping the distinctiveness of the transition requires understanding how the digital relates to the analogical, as well as examining a more difficult assertion: that digital depictions are not "images," at least in the ordinary sense of the term.

The first step in tracing out the emerging ontology of digital imaging was to examine why it strives to be perceptually indistinguishable from a previous medium, namely, the photographic. All emergent media reproduce the form and effects of their predecessors to some degree, just as early film preserved the narrative sequencing and spatial conventions of lantern-slide lectures and the modularized tableaus of vaudeville presentations. Nonetheless, the persistence of the "photographic" in the digital is one of the most striking and widespread features of digital imaging, whether it is defined by capture (the recording of physical objects) or by computer synthesis. Obviously, there is something valued in the photographic, both culturally and aesthetically, that even the captains of the Hollywood film industry fear losing. Still, the conceptual criteria of perceptual realism, which are restricted to qualities of spatial semblance, are of limited use in helping to understand how photographic and filmic images are distinct, nor do they point the way to uncovering or creating new powers of digital imaging.

Another line of attack is suggested by characterizing the photograph as an analogical medium conceptually distinct from the digital, but here too the situation is cloudy.

There is a curious moment in *The Matrix* when Neo encounters Cypher,

9. See Tom Gunning, "What's the Point of an Index? or, Faking Photographs," *Nordicom Review* 25.1–2 (September 2004) 39–49.

Cypher2.tiff


```
MM*¸-2ÚIÍ2
v¯(1'20º∏DÜI1Ó¸ái
c`
¸Ä'
¸Ä'Adobe Photoshop Elements 3.0 Macintosh2006:02:23 11:16:45<?xpacket begin='Ôºø'
id='W5M0MpCehiHzreSzNTczkc9d'?>
<x:xmpmeta xmlns:x='adobe:ns:meta/' x:xmptk='XMP toolkit 3.0-28, framework 1.6'>
<rdf:RDF xmlns:rdf='http://www.w3.org/1999/02/22-rdf-syntax-ns#' xmlns:iX='http://ns.adobe.com/iX/
1.0/'>

 <rdf:Description rdf:about='uuid:22b8c447-a5f0-11da-b6d7-bcaba2d4e00f'
  xmlns:pdf='http://ns.adobe.com/pdf/1.3/'>
 </rdf:Description>

 <rdf:Description rdf:about='uuid:22b8c447-a5f0-11da-b6d7-bcaba2d4e00f'
  xmlns:photoshop='http://ns.adobe.com/photoshop/1.0/'>
  <photoshop:History></photoshop:History>
 </rdf:Description>

 <rdf:Description rdf:about='uuid:22b8c447-a5f0-11da-b6d7-bcaba2d4e00f'
  xmlns:tiff='http://ns.adobe.com/tiff/1.0/'>
  <tiff:XResolution>4718592/65536</tiff:XResolution>
  <tiff:YResolution>4718592/65536</tiff:YResolution>
  <tiff:ResolutionUnit>2</tiff:ResolutionUnit>
 </rdf:Description>

 <rdf:Description rdf:about='uuid:22b8c447-a5f0-11da-b6d7-bcaba2d4e00f'
  xmlns:xap='http://ns.adobe.com/xap/1.0/'>
  <xap:CreateDate>2006-02-23T11:05:17-05:00</xap:CreateDate>
  <xap:ModifyDate>2006-02-23T11:16:45-05:00</xap:ModifyDate>
  <xap:MetadataDate>2006-02-23T11:16:45-05:00</xap:MetadataDate>
  <xap:CreatorTool>Adobe Photoshop Elements 3.0 Macintosh</xap:CreatorTool>
 </rdf:Description>

 <rdf:Description rdf:about='uuid:22b8c447-a5f0-11da-b6d7-bcaba2d4e00f'
  xmlns:xapMM='http://ns.adobe.com/xap/1.0/mm/'>
  <xapMM:DocumentID>adobe:docid:photoshop:22b8c446-a5f0-11da-b6d7-bcaba2d4e00f</xapMM:DocumentID>
 </rdf:Description>

 <rdf:Description rdf:about='uuid:22b8c447-a5f0-11da-b6d7-bcaba2d4e00f'
  xmlns:dc='http://purl.org/dc/elements/1.1/'>
  <dc:format>image/tiff</dc:format>
 </rdf:Description>

</rdf:RDF>
</x:xmpmeta>
```


The two “worlds” of *The Matrix* (Warner Brothers, 1999).

played by Joe Pantoliano, on the flight deck of the *Nebuchadnezzar.* Watching the computer screens, Cypher does not observe the simulated world of the matrix. Having no need of an interface, he watches, rather, the symbolic code itself. "You get used to it," he says, gesturing to the constant flow of numbers across the screens. "I don't even see the code. All I see is blonde, brunette, redhead."

Unlike Cypher, however, humans have not yet developed the cognitive capacity to translate binary code into a perception. This is because digital encoding is not analogical: it does not produce an isomorphic impression of its subject. Where analogical transcriptions record traces of events as continuities in time, digital capture and synthesis produce tokens of numbers through a process of calculation, producing a mathematical equivalent—a symbolic expression—of what humans would call a "perception." However, machine-readable code is readable only by machines; there are no criteria by which the coding characteristic of "machine languages" can be even remotely characterized as a perception, nor would we ordinarily refer to such things as "images." (*The Matrix* craftily produces these notations—"the matrix"—as graphical *aesthetic* images displayed on a screen, mirroring in miniature the movie that takes its name from them.) Even programming languages must compile this code into something resembling a humanly manipulable alphanumeric or algebraic notation.

Two consequences may be drawn from this observation. One of these divides the analog and the digital into separate universes; the other bridges them.

The latter consequence is easier to comprehend. There are many points of exchange linking the analogical and the digital. Invented in 1833, telegraphy already used a digital code in an analogical carrier; today, digital photography presents an analogical message in digital form. All digital recording or synthesis requires digital-to-analog conversion to become humanly perceptible. In fact, there seems to be something distinctly human about analogical reproduction, which is one reason it remains the touchstone for judging the quality of image and sound reproduction. For this reason, the digital will never fully replace the analogical and will always have to find a working symbiosis with it. Indeed, essential to the aesthetic definition of digital processes is the capacity for outputting information in an analog form. (From the reverse perspective, rotoscoping and motion capture remain important tools for digital animation, since computers still have difficulty synthesizing "natural" movements—they require some kind of analog input.)

This is another way of saying that digital information requires an interface that can reproduce the qualities of analogical perception. But on a closer look, the interface also turns out to be as much a bridging concept as a mark of distinctiveness. One could argue that all two-stage arts, in Nelson Goodman's sense of the term, require an interface. However, it is an abuse of language to call a symphonic score the "interface" to an orchestral performance. A more precise definition would examine the necessity of interfaces for accessing information that is otherwise only with difficulty perceptible to human eyes and ears. Since recorded analog information is continuous with its source, analog interfaces would be required only in situations in which the record requires amplification and/or reconstitution. The grooves on a phonographic recording are isomorphic with the sound waves so preserved, but they are imperceptible to the ear (as well as the eye). They require amplification as well as modulation into electronic signals that will drive the speaker cones whose vibrations produce sounds. The film projector is a similar kind of interface—magnifying the image and reconstituting movement—as is the analog video monitor. The creation of interfaces does not follow the invention of digital computers.

However, the fact that digital information *requires* an analog interface already indicates the ontological distinctiveness of analogical and digital processes. For example, an analogical transcription of a sound can be sculptural (traced in vinyl), pictorial (a photographic record, the standard for motion picture sound recording until the 1950s), or a modulated signal (voltage values preserved as the redistribution of magnetic particles on tape). The distinguishing feature of what I have called automatic analogical causation is that the process of transcription is continuous in space and time, producing an isomorphic record that is indivisible and counterfactually dependent on its source. At the risk of superimposing a computational vocabulary on analogical processes (an all-too-frequent conceptual abuse), we can say that a necessary condition of analogical transcription is that inputs and outputs are continuous. The transcription may require amplification or modulation. Nonetheless, every analog copy preserves the isomorphism of its source, though with one caveat—it is subject to entropy. Indeed, an inescapable quality of all analogical media is that each subsequent copy and every instance of playback introduces noise to the recorded information.

Alternatively, the fact that digital information requires analog translation demonstrates its fundamental separation of inputs and outputs. In contrast to the continuities of analogical transcriptions, a "digital image" is always marked by a fundamental discontinuity as if riven by, yet encompassing, two separate dimensions. On the side of the image is what remains humanly perceptible and in cultural exchange with other images and signs. But on the side of the digital there is only machine language, characterized by Lev Manovich as "a computer file that consists of a machine-readable header, followed by numbers representing the color values of its pixels. On this level it enters into a dialog [only] with other computer files. The dimensions of this dialog are not the image's content, meanings, or formal qualities, but rather file size, file type, type of compression used, file format, and so on. In short, these dimensions belong to the computer's own cosmogony rather than to human culture" (*Language of New Media* 45–46). Analogical representations can take various forms, including pictorial, sculptural, and acoustical. But digital information is by definition symbolic and notational. Of course, an analog image can capture symbolic information as part of its spatial record of a given duration (as can a digital photograph), as witnessed by Walker Evans' wonderful photographs of billboards, posters, and storefronts. The profound difference between the two processes is that digital inputting itself produces symbolic notation and can be manipulated (or not) as such. Fully analogical devices reproduce or amplify a signal that is spatially isomorphic with their source in an act of transcription temporally continuous with that source. Analogical-to-digital conversion requires "rewriting" the source into a machine-readable notation that is neither spatially nor temporally continuous with its source. Timothy Binkley describes this situation with great clarity:

> A photograph retains pictorial information in its smooth layer of light-sensitive film which quickly responds to any illumination by undergoing chemical changes that record an image. This is an analog information format implanted in a physical substance. A computer stores meta-pictorial information in a fragmented array of discrete numbers, which cannot communicate directly with the depicted or the observing world: some kind of translation is required before this set of abstruse digits can record or represent anything visual. In this digital format, defined not by a physical medium but by a conceptual structure, pictorial space is approached analytically, fragmented into regular rows and columns of small dots called pixels (picture elements). The concrete physical grains of chemicals in a photograph are replaced by an intangible array of numbers . . .
>
> The end product is a photograph, but it visually "depicts" the numeri-

> cal contents of a frame buffer, and not necessarily the state of any real place at any particular time.[10]

The separation of inputs and outputs—analogical-to-digital translation and back again—is like communication across parallel universes. I will further characterize this discontinuity below.

We cannot completely distinguish digital images from chemical film by using the criteria of resemblance, such as those of perceptual realism or analogy. Can we do so through the criterion of indexicality?

Here again, a superficial look at digital capture finds little difference from photography. One reason is that the concept of indexicality is medium independent. In C. S. Peirce's logic the index is determined by causal relations, or in Peirce's terminology, "real connections." Yet more interesting are Peirce's frequent references to photographs as examples of indexical signs, while insisting that indexes have no necessary relationship of similarity or resemblance to their causes.[11] Deriving from the logical category of "secondness," the category of fact or singularity, indexes are signs of existence: the present or past action of a determinate force. The movement of a weathervane, the rise and fall of mercury in a thermometer, and footprints in the sand are indexical signs by virtue of the logical inferences they lead us to make from current or past causes, not from the substance or medium that carries them. It is also possible to characterize different types of indexicality by qualifying their causal relations. The movements of a weathervane or of mercury in a thermometer are examples of direct and continuous causation, what Peirce calls a "dynamical relation"; they give evidence of real-time changes in wind direction or temperature. Like footprints, the photograph is an example of inferred causation; that is, it is the present trace of a past action whose causal origins must be found through reasoned conjecture. In both cases, time qualifies causation.

At first glance, digital devices raise no special difficulties around the logic of indexicality. "Caused" by light reflected from its subject, a digital photograph would seem to be a no less powerful index of a past event than film. Nevertheless, the logic of digital capture, no less than digital synthesis, raises tricky

10. "Camera Fantasia," *Millennium Film Journal* 20/21 (Fall/Winter 1988–89) 10.

11. See, among other frequent references, "Dictionary of Philosophy & Psychology," in *Collected Papers,* ed. Charles Hartshorne and Paul Weiss (Cambridge, Mass.: Harvard University Press, 1931–1958) 2: 305; and *Semiotics and Significs: The Correspondence between Charles S. Peirce and Victoria Lady Welby* (Bloomington: Indiana University Press, 1977).

problems of reference and causation that are not so easy to resolve. Digital photographs certainly function as indexical signs, and in many ways reproduce the cultural functions and assumptions of chemical photography. But do they do so in the same way and with the same powers as "film"?

If analog media record traces of events and digital media produce tokens of numbers, the following may also be asserted: *digital acquisition quantifies the world as manipulable series of numbers.* This is the primary automatism and the source of the creative powers of digital computing. Alternatively, photographic automatisms yield spatial segments of duration in a uniform substance. Both kinds of photography produce convincing representations as a result of their quality of counterfactual dependence, wherein any change in the referent is reflected as a corresponding change in the image, and in both cases this quality relies on the logic of indexicality. But they may also be qualitatively distinguished according to the types of causation involved in the acquisition of images and by ascertaining whether the causal relations between inputs and outputs are continuous or discontinuous. Here (analogical) *transcription* should be distinguished from (digital) *conversion* or *calculation.*

If there is a difference to be found in "film," by my account it lies not simply in the criterion of analogy or the perception of space, but rather in the temporality of the process through which a substance continuously captures an isomorphic image or can be said to be caused by it. I have maintained that photographs transcribe rather than represent, and that the primary sense of this transcription is temporal; in short, photographs express duration and our present relationship to past events. Photographs and films capture blocks of duration in a uniform and continuous causality effecting physical transformations in the recording medium. Our intuition of this type of causality clarifies why photographs are often felt to be spatially convincing yet temporally perplexing or paradoxical. In Roland Barthes's compelling account, the photographic paradox is expressed as an oscillation between present and past perceptions, a (spatial) here-now overlaying a (temporal) there-then. And if the photograph is "never experienced as an illusion," this phenomenon owes less to its spatial qualities or to its perceptual realism than to "its reality . . . of the *having been there,* for in every photograph there is always the stupefying evidence of *this is how it was,* giving us, by a precious miracle, a reality from which we are sheltered."[12] Similarly, in *Camera Lucida* Barthes is struck not by

12. "The Photographic Message," in *Image-Music-Text,* ed. Stephen Heath (Glasgow: Fontana, 1977) 44.

the meaning of Time, but by its *sense,* not by the form of duration, but rather by its *intensity.* The present image expresses two absent currents of time, what has been in the past and what will be in the future, for example, the past historical existence of Lewis Payne who awaits his imminent execution. Deeply and phenomenologically attentive to the temporal and existential qualities of photography, like Cavell Barthes is profoundly sensitive to photography's strangeness—the recurrence of a present trace of a past event, a spatial presence indicating a temporal absence, both in the past and yet to come as a finitude that confronts us all. The sense of every (analogical) photograph is that of a historical document—the automatic transcription of a past state of affairs, not only recording the world, but expressing the world as past and passing, anticipating a future that will always become past. We are sustained in this perception by our implicit cultural understanding of the photograph as a certain kind of image: one whose past cause was continuous in time, producing in a measured instant an image expressive of a unique duration that perseveres in time.

This cultural understanding, however, has surely been changing for some time, as a result of both the widespread digital processing of images and the increasing popularity of consumer digital devices. Even though digital image capture is designed to produce outputs that are spatially indistinguishable from photographs, or even to exceed photographs in their ability to produce similarities, the criterion of time or duration may yet prove to be significant. This is why digital capture should be understood in contrast to analogical transcription as a process of calculation in which time is measured as the *conversion* of light into code. ("Quantizing" is the technical term.) In digital photography, the spatial link of physical causality is broken as well as the temporal continuity of the transformation. Hence my assertion of the fundamental separation of inputs and outputs in all cases in which a digital computer serves as a "medium." Here the logic through which indexicality is effected changes fundamentally. Digital capture involves a discontinuous process of transcoding: converting a nonquantifiable image into an abstract or mathematical notation. In digital capture, the indexical link to physical reality is weakened, because light must be converted into an abstract symbolic structure independent of and discontinuous with physical space and time. Moreover, transcoding introduces a temporal discontinuity in the recording process, experienced by most of us as shutter lag or other computational indicators of wait time: miniature clocks and spinning rainbow wheels. These signs are indexes of another sort; they designate the operation of computing cycles, applying algorithms while converting space and time into code. In this process, light does not become temporalized space; it becomes abstract symbolization. The singularity of an event present in space and in time is converted into an abstract universal; the uniform image becomes an assemblage of discrete and modular parts subject to numerical processing and manipulation. For this reason, source and notation, or input and record, remain conceptually distinct, separate, and irreversible. Obviously, changes in value made to digital notations are reversible; any series of changes made in the notation can be undone. But once analogical forms are converted into digital notation they can never be returned unambiguously to their original state. They have become information and retain the mercurial powers of information—an analog image is only one of a variety of outputs now available to them. Once space becomes information, it wants not to be preserved in an analogous record of duration, but to be transformed, manipulated, and exchanged. It cedes itself to other powers and new ontologies. The qualities of transcription, the sense of the photograph as a document or a transcription of a past state of affairs, are not broken here, but they are deeply attenuated. One feels or intuits in digital images that the qualitative expression of duration found in photography and film is missing or sharply reduced. Another consequence is that not only are the qualities of space unknown to digital information, but time itself is transformed as a purely quantitative function defined by calculation. Analog media transcribe time as duration; digital capture or synthesis consumes time as processing cycles.

Ordinary linguistic usage already recognizes the cultural shifts that have taken place in our relation to digital works. One speaks less of recording sounds or taking photographs than of capturing, acquiring, importing, or sampling them—terms that acknowledge acts that convert all inputs to information. These terms characterize analog-to-digital conversion as a one-way street in which the causal link to physical reality becomes weakened or attenuated. Consider the concept of "sampling." Cinematography samples movement in physical space as discrete units of one twenty-fourth of a second. But each unit in itself, as well as the succession of units in a single "take," involves temporally continuous isomorphic transcriptions. Inputs and outputs are continuous in such analogical transcriptions, and copies of these transcriptions remain isomorphically equivalent, though some information is always lost through successive generations of copies.

Whether in the form of image capture or image synthesis, digitization also involves sampling, but in addition the information sampled from the artifact must be quantified, or rather, quantized. Indeed, the quantification of information so produced also changes the nature of the sampling process. Scanning an image or capturing a digital "photograph" requires sampling light in a given frequency in the form of a grid with horizontal and vertical axes. The form of the grid is necessary to produce mathematically discrete units (pixels) whose variables can be assigned numerical values (luminance, color, etc.). It is significant that we want to call such captured elements information, for inputs to digital devices level every source (speech, music, text, image) to a common form: symbolic notation. Once scanned, an artifact can never be truly returned to a state of nondiscreteness. The process of quantification or numerization is irreversible, which is another way of saying that inputs and outputs are discontinuous in digital information. Moreover, these discontinuities produce perceptual or aesthetic effects. Given enough resolution, a digital photograph can simulate the look of a continuously produced analogical image, but the pixel grid remains in the logical structure of the image.

Two anecdotal but perceptually reasoned examples of the discontinuity between inputs and outputs in digital processes are surely welcome here. The search for a perceptually convincing "photorealism" is often presented as a quest to produce resolution equivalent to or exceeding that of 35mm film. But although the mathematical measures for resolution in analogical photography and digital capture or synthesis may be comparable (again, similarity), they cannot be said to be equivalent. The pixel is a mathematical unit appropriate to the mapping of Cartesian coordinates, but photographic resolution is an approximation of the resolving capacity of lenses, or their ability to produce analogical isomorphism at different scales. The chemical contents of a 35mm frame (the grain of the image) are not equivalent to 12 million pixels. Only in digital devices can picture elements be quantified in this manner. To insist that analogical images contain "information," and that these presentations can be quantified in mathematically discrete units, is already to succumb to the contradictions of perceptual realism by retroactively applying concepts of digital processing to a domain in which such measures are inappropriate. It is more precise to say that it would take 12 million pixels to make an electronic image perceptually *similar* to a 35mm photographic image.

A second example involves the printing of video on film. When video is printed to filmstock and projected at theatrical scales, why am I more disturbed when the video original was digital rather than analog? For all other differences, a structure of isomorphism is maintained in printing analog video to a photographic support. But the matrix or pixel structure underlying digital video is often magnified when printed to celluloid. A pixel array is like an image made of mosaic tiles: the position of the pixels is fixed, not random and shifting like projected film grain. The photographic display of digital materials (pretty much the standard in 2007) thus presents a situation that the cinematographer John Bailey already wondered about in 2001: "Imagine that the position and defining borders of the tiles remain static as the images on the tiles continually change. The question arises: is this pattern apparent, even subliminally? Does the static pixel array of digital video render images whose quality is fundamentally different from those created by the ever shifting, random movement of film grain? Is the dreamlike state of suspension that we associate with film inherent in its photochemical architecture?"[13] Indeed, the pattern is apparent, and there are good reasons for crediting Bailey's instincts here.

The abstract cosmogony of symbolic notation can output information as an image deployed in space and changing through time, but never in forms that would give unambiguous evidence of an existential link to a past state of affairs, for the recursive chain of analogy is broken.[14] In digital capture, transcoded information becomes abstract. Joining the numerical cosmogony of the computer, this information is communicable only through an interface, and can never regain direct contact with either the image or its source. A process of scanning or translation, this is a conversion of space and light into numerical values—a symbolic expression. In this manner, Peirce returns once again to take the measure of analogical photography and digital capture in a logical continuum that runs from indexicality to symbolization. Analogical processes have a privileged relation to indexicality; it is fundamental to their activity of transcription. But digital processes, requiring mathematic notation, have a privileged relation to symbolization. Because of the discontinuity of inputs and outputs, the force of indexicality in digital-capture devices stops when light falls on sampling devices, whether they be the charge-coupled receptors of digital cameras or the samplers of digital sound recordings. From this moment forward, light and sound become symbols, and therefore manipulable as such. A digital camera is therefore not a photographic apparatus;

13. "Film or Digital? Don't Fight. Coexist," *New York Times,* 18 February 2001.

14. For a fascinating discussion of the recursive or homomorphic nature of analogical processes versus the heteromorphic character of digital processes, see Timothy Binkley's "Refiguring Culture," in *Future Visions: New Technologies of the Screen,* ed. Philip Hayward and Tana Wollen (London: British Film Institute, 1993) 111–116.

logically, it is a computer with a lens as an input device. It is a device for converting inputs to symbolic notation.

The nature of automatic analogical causation is such that the "indexical trace," as Phil Rosen calls such transcriptions, always returns us to a past world, a world of matter and existence. Neither Erwin Panofsky nor Siegfried Kracauer was far wrong, then, in pursuing the intuition that the medium of photography or film is physical reality as such. André Bazin took this intuition in another direction: that photography and film express our desire to preserve an experience of time in duration against finitude. The will of the photograph is to conserve the past and to provoke memory. (The problem is that we have forgotten why the impossibility of return to the analogical *might* matter.) Alternatively, computational processes are indifferent to medium and to the referent in a way that conventional cameras cannot be, for film cameras are dedicated to the task of chemical contact with a profilmic event to which the camera is present. This observation qualifies my characterization of analog-to-digital-to-analog translation. The effects of perceptual realism produced in digital-to-analog conversion are not qualitatively equivalent to analog presentations, for they produce similarity rather than analogy. These are two different kinds of perceptual realism, which is why I have insisted not on spatial equivalencies but rather on the temporality of causation to distinguish two kinds of processes, transcription and conversion.

The practice of cell animation is often evoked to challenge arguments that the primary automatisms of film involve transcription and documentation. In the history of film theory, much conceptual confusion has been produced by staging these arguments as a distinction between realistic and fantastic uses of the filmed image. But this distinction is misleading. Regardless of the wonderfully imaginative uses to which they are put, and the spatial plasticity they record, cell animations obviously have a strong indexical quality. Simply speaking, each photographed frame records an event and its result: the succession of hand-drawn images and cells reproduced as artificial movement through the automatism of succession. Here, as in all other cases, the camera records and documents a past process that took place in the physical world. We are mistaken if we use the concept of animation to refer to the hand drawing of sequential images; it refers, rather, to photographing such images frame by frame and producing the illusion of motion by projecting them at a constant rate of movement. Every film is an animated film (automatism of succession) but, *pace* Lev Manovich, not for reasons of restoring pride of place to a so-called minor genre. Similarly, "digital 'animation'" is an oxymoron; it should be referred to more properly as computer synthesis or computer-generated movement.

Nevertheless, as in the case of *Mary Poppins* (1964), the graphical world is perceived to be distinct from the "photographical" because the filmed image asks us to equate images produced autographically (that is, hand drawn) with automatically recorded things and persons—drawn penguins dancing with a very living Dick Van Dyke. Both kinds of image function by a logic of analogy (discontinuous versus continuous variation), but the kinds of analogy are different and retain their distinctiveness when photographed. (A drawing is produced from a potentially infinite number of points expressed in a process of discontinuous variation; photography is an act of continuous variation produced in a unique duration.) The humor of such images lies in our knowing that they are existentially distinct though presented as belonging to the same filmed physical world.

In the strange new world opened after *Jurassic Park,* this perceptual distinctiveness is no longer present, and we are mistaken in assuming that a change has occurred in the nature of photography. It is rather the case that photographic transcription and succession have been replaced by *digital* "animation." Digital synthesis *produces* an image and animates it from an *abstraction*—numerical manipulation. Its only referent is the purely symbolic realm of numbers and algorithms as opposed to an event that occurs in a physical space occupying a certain duration. The telling example here is not *Who Framed Roger Rabbit?* (1988), but rather the most recent *Star Wars* films. If, in the fictional world they inhabit, Obi-Wan Kenobi and company are perceptually equivalent to characters such as Jar Jar Binks and Yoda, this is so because digital capture imports the actor's image to the world of digital synthesis, or the cosmogony of the computer. This is a reversal of the *Mary Poppins* effect, for the elements captured by digital cameras and those synthesized on computers belong to the same numerical universe; they are "ontologically" equivalent, as it were. These images are perceptually indistinct because, whether captured or synthesized, they are produced from the same kinds of data. Even if they were input from data tablets and painting programs, rather than captured from the human world, both now belong to the digital computer's world of symbol manipulation.

Analogical transcription and digital conversion or calculation mark the frontiers of two dimensions. But considering what happens to the photographed image as it passes from one dimension to the other, from analogical recording to digital information, probably pushes their distinctiveness too far where ordinary perception is concerned. This distinctiveness is real, however, and should create pause for deeper reflection. Yet we will have a better sense of what photography has become through processes of digital capture, editing, and diffusion by trying to map our culturally shifting sense of the image along a set of continua or sliding scales with which to measure or weigh the different kinds of emphases placed on these images in different kinds of uses. Thus, the distinction between transcription and transcoding should be qualified or tempered by applying other, related scales to our judgments of these images. I have already discussed how the enhanced graphism of digital images has rendered them more painterly; they are now more available to our creative intentions and less anchored to causal relations with the physical world. Similarly, our perceptual criteria for judging these images have become more spatial and less temporal, and less indexical and more iconic, although this iconism is an output for symbolic notation.

For these reasons, we are inclined to judge digital photographs by the criteria of perceptual realism, and as such to have faith that they are spatially similar to events we have witnessed and captured. In so doing, we often fail to recognize that our criteria for appreciating these images have shifted in ways both subtle and profound. Similarity has displaced analogy, and we have forgotten (or perhaps do not wish to remember) that these "outputs" may have no direct causal relationship to the events so witnessed or that the causal relation may be easily altered. The strength of spatial semblance tends to make us forget that the digital record is a symbolic form and thus, logically, is more similar to a written description than to a visual impression. The following parallel is strained, perhaps, but not completely unwarranted. Analog-to-digital conversion certainly entails a causal relationship, as does the outputting of the information so registered. But the reconstitution of an image from digital information is something like making a very detailed painting from the information given in a very precise description. In short, digital capture produces similarity, but not isomorphism or homomorphism in the ordinary senses of those terms; one cannot restore the historical force of analogism once the spatial and temporal continuity of indexical tracing are broken. Indeed, by these criteria digital capture and synthesis lose their distinctiveness, for there is no ontological difference between the information captured by charge-coupled devices and information constructed on a computer in ignorance of an originating state of affairs. Give me the instructions, and I will build you another image. It will impress you as being perceptually similar in all respects to the one you have captured, but, ontologically, it will be a homologon, and not an analogon, for the time of analogical transcription and the expression of duration is broken. But perhaps that is good enough for most.

The criteria of perceptual realism have led us to believe in digitally captured information as photographs, and perhaps they are in terms of our ordinary uses. But what these images do more precisely is to fulfill most of the spatial or iconic criteria by which images are judged in relation to similarity or semblance; the force of indexicality expressed by automatic analogical causation, however, is seriously challenged. And it is challenged all the more powerfully when we take advantage of the computer's powers to manipulate these records as information. For these reasons, photographs and digital images provoke in us two very different kinds of ontological curiosity. As Cavell or Barthes would have it, photographs inspire ontological questions about our relationship to the world and to the past, as well as to the limits of our existence and our powers of reasoning. For reasons I will soon explain, digital photographs have become for most of us much more utilitarian, more like simple records than historical documents of family events and histories. Moreover, digital outputs, when presented as photorealistic images, do make us uneasy or curious, but in a way that asks us to question the present identity—so mercurial, mutable, and transmissible—of information as the medium of our current epistemological and social relations. These are very large questions. And it may be that "photographs" no longer fuel our thought with the same energy as in a previous era. Indeed, what I have been trying to express here is, ontologically, the unbecoming of photography.

## 18. Simulation, or Automatism as Algorithm

> Before there was cinema. Now, and in the future, there is software.
>
> —Stephen Prince, *The New Pot of Gold*

Earlier I suggested that our current relation to digital screens was woven from three overlapping histories: those of photography and film, of electronic screens and transmission, and of computing itself. This observation echoes Lev Manovich's argument that digital visual culture remains cinematic, but only in one of its dimensions: "*the visual culture of the computer age is cinematographic in its appearance, digital on the level of its material, and computational (i.e., software driven) in its logic*" (*Language of New Media* 180).

The deepest paradox of perceptual realism in the emergence of digital cinema is its presentation of images that appear to be, and want to be, "photographic" only more so. Yet increasingly, there is no more photography or film, but only video displayed on electronic screens. By the same token, while DVD players and wide-screen televisions continue to dip in price and advance in home markets, the apparent differences between digital screens, capture devices, camcorders, and home computers begin to disappear. Fundamentally, all are variations on the same device: a computer connected to an electronic display. The contemporary image is thus inseparable from the computer. It retains the ideal of photographic or cinematographic appearance, yet its structure is symbolic and its forms and processes are computational, meaning ever more available to the creative intentions of information processing made possible by the separation of inputs and outputs. As Stephen Prince so aptly puts it, the new virtual life of cinema is driven by software.

Still, concepts of image, screen, time, space, and movement are as relevant to contemporary moving image theory as they were to classical film theory. This is so partially because digital imaging mimics photography and cinematography in producing the qualities of perceptual realism. We are inclined to treat concepts of representation, space, and development through time as if they were unchallenged by the ontology of the digital. Yet each one of these concepts has been transformed, both qualitatively and logically, by the long histories of electronic displays and computational processes. Clearly, the nature of "representation," or, better, the act of presenting, changes with digital processing. To comprehend what becomes of visual culture today, including the cinematic image, one must look past or beneath the present image, which is in fact no image at all, but information.

Roland Barthes once wrote of the photographic paradox as a message without a code. In becoming only message and code, the digital paradox is other than the photographic paradox, for a digital presentation is not an image, nor is it easily characterized by qualities of space or time in the ordinary sense. My suggestion here is that digital "images" have no qualitative relationship with either space or time; indeed, the fundamental sense of all digital information is to express value in a quantitative form. Fundamentally, time has no measure separate from computing cycles; space is relevant only to "memory" capacity, that is, the numerical amount of storage available on a hard disk or other kinds of digitally formatted supports. Thus, one profound consequence of the separation of inputs and outputs in computational processes is that digital information is in no way spatial, in the sense of extension given as a perceptible interval. Nor may information be characterized as an image or as a medium in the ordinary senses of those terms.

The persistence of cinematographic appearance, then, masks a deeper transformation at the levels of material and logic, which in turn challenge a conventional understanding of the nature of creative media. Timothy Binkley, for example, has referred to the computer as a nonspecific technology or an "incorporeal metamedium."[15] In the context of conventional arguments for medium specificity, computers certainly fail the criterion of substantial self-similarity, although, as I argued in Part I, in its virtual life film does as well. It is often argued that in simulating many functions, computers have no identity separate from mimicking other kinds of devices and media. In this they also fail the criterion of uniqueness, or the expression of a distinct artistic character derived from aesthetic a prioris. Yet, following Marshall McCluhan, one might insist that one test of the emergence of a new medium is that it always incorporates its predecessors as its initial content. This is key to Jay David Bolter and Richard Grusin's recent reformulation of the digital arts as a process of "remediation."[16] Here, the definition of a medium is that which remediates. The digital arts are then characterized by the different "how" of their remediation.

Nevertheless, computers are often disparaged as simulation devices. Gene Youngblood exemplified this perspective in commenting that "the computer . . . has no meaning, no intrinsic nature, identity, or use-value until we talk it into becoming something by programming it."[17] Alternatively, this statement may be the key to comprehending the automatisms of computing. As Alan Turing asserted in his early papers on the logic of computing, any process that can be reproduced in numerical form, and whose functions are amenable to calculation, can be simulated on a universal Turing machine.[18] A digital recording is not an isomorph but a metamorph. It does not so much record its source as convert it into a symbolic logic susceptible to algorithmic manipulation. Therefore, the primary automatism of universal Turing machines is

15. "The Quickening of Galatea: Virtual Creation without Tools or Media," *Art Journal* 49.3 (Fall 1990) 233–240.

16. *Remediation: Understanding New Media* (Cambridge, Mass.: MIT Press, 1999).

17. "The New Renaissance: Art, Science, and the Universal Machine," in *The Computer Revolution and the Arts,* ed. Richard L. Loveless (Tampa: University of South Florida Press, 1989) 11.

18. "On Computable Numbers, with an Application to the Entscheidungsproblem," in *The Essential Turing: Seminal Writings in Computing, Logic, Philosophy, Artificial Intelligence, and Artificial Life plus The Secrets of Enigma,* ed. B. Jack Copeland (New York: Oxford University Press, 2004) 58–90.

*simulation through calculation.* This process enables a new series of powers of synthesis and manipulation wherein, for example, computers can simulate analogical recording and editing devices in all their functions. But image or sound recording is just one more function that can be simulated by computers, and they will do this no more nor less well than any other kind of computational function that can be expressed as a logical algorithm. The very virtues of digital creations tend to erode or attenuate what for 150 years was assumed to be photography's cultural, historical, and evidentiary power as the singular expression of duration and the assertion of past existences in time. In another sense, they level this function, making it neither more nor less equal to the other kinds of functions that computers can simulate. Among their many other programmable uses, computers can record, but this is not their primary automatism. They are made to convert and transform before they function to transcribe and witness.

The difficulty of thinking of a computer as a medium, then, comes from an analogical presumption that creation through a medium involves physical causes and transformations, at least ones that are directly perceptible from a human perspective. This is another way of saying that in analogical media, inputs and outputs are continuous. But the power of computers—the enormous variety of the functions they serve and the transformations they effect—results from the fundamental separation of inputs from outputs. To become manageable by computers, the world must become *information,* that is, quantifiable or numerically manipulable, discrete, and modular. This is why I began Part III by asserting that there are no new "media"; nor does it make sense to examine the medium of computers in the presentation of "new media objects." One lesson to be learned from film's virtual life is that the very nature of a medium, whether analogical or digital, is to be variable, not identical with itself, and open to aesthetic and historical transformation. Computers push this virtuality in new directions. There are no new *media,* only processes or operations that may be performed on symbolic information. Computers do not produce objects or things, but processes—automatisms—transforming inputs and outputs. Understanding the automatisms of computing involves thinking beyond or beneath their outputs to consider more deeply their processes.

In this respect, not only is Cavell's definition of medium not incompatible with electronic or digital creation; it may be the best conceptual resource for understanding how processes of expression and self-expression are being transformed through our interactions with computational devices. One of the many desirable features of Cavell's rich conceptual characterization of automatisms is how they define a medium through the creative acts they make possible or inspire. Certainly, automatisms function as horizons or limits: subtract lenses or filmstock from photographic cameras, and you have begun to create a new medium by repurposing elements of a previous one. Other automatisms refashion a medium by imagining and putting into play creative potentials that were previously unrecognized or ignored, and, having discovered such strategies, search for variations on them. To recognize a computer as a medium is to begin to define conceptually the automatisms it makes possible, how they are alike or different from previous automatisms, or how they transform existing automatisms.

Computer algorithms thus provide a new conceptual basis for understanding the nature of automatisms. When considered as automated operations, the self-actualizing procedures of digital computers become even more independent of instruments than the mechanical operations of cameras. What Manovich calls "operations" are functionally equivalent to Cavell's notions of automatism, though of course without the philosophical content. Both distinguish operations or automatisms from our ordinary senses of a tool or medium. Operations refer to the basic creative functions enabled by information processing. Among the most familiar are copy (including ripping); capture or sample; select, cut, and paste; search; composite; transform; and filter. These functions differ from tools or instruments in two significant ways. "On the one hand," Manovich writes, "operations are usually in part automated in a way in which traditional tools are not. On the other hand, like computer algorithms, they can be inscribed in a series of steps; that is, they exist as concepts before being materialized in hardware and software . . . Encoded in algorithms and implemented as software commands, operations exist independently of the media data to which they can be applied" (*Language of New Media* 121). In this way, operations derive from the primary automatism of computing—simulation through calculation, a process founded conceptually in the separation of inputs and outputs. Expressed as an automatism, an operation performs a function on data, writing it to new outputs while leaving the original data intact. By the same token, the independence of operations from data also demonstrates that the power of automatisms is conceptual before they are expressed as functions or as creative acts. In this way, universal Turing machines provide a wonderful context for reconsidering definitional problems of media and medium specificity. Agnostic with respect to outputs, they challenge or throw into disarray previous characterizations of medium specificity. Yet in their conceptual basis, they seem to exemplify Cavell's more difficult notion of the variability of media as acts of creation through automatisms, acts that indeed may exceed their automatic nature, as concepts that precede the media that embody them.

The computer is a medium, then. (How could it not be?) And all its automatistic powers are derived from the separation of inputs and outputs required for the interactive control or manipulation of information through programmed algorithmic processes. Therefore, I will reserve the concept of *simulation* for processes of computational synthesis and modeling. This includes the modeling of causation in the mathematical rendering of physical processes, as well as accessing, controlling, and interacting with the physical world by means of a computational model. An algorithm is a kind of automatism, then, although, significantly, it may only manipulate information. In this the automatisms of computing are fundamentally distinct from those of film and photography, no matter how well computers simulate the functions of analogical recording at no matter how high a resolution. For the separation of inputs and outputs in digital computing also severs information from the physical world in its duration, or its continuity in time and space. Computers can and will produce ever more convincing homologons, or simulacra of physical world processes, but never analogons, or representations. Indeed, the difference between simulation and representation is key to understanding the persistence of the ordinary characterization of the image as cinematographic while the computer completely transforms its logic and functions. Moreover, to consider what happens to the image through the computational "medium" also means confronting some fundamental issues. The first involves characterizing the automatisms enabled by computing. Lev Manovich has made a good start in suggesting that the powers of computational creativity derive from five basic automatisms: numerical manipulation, modularity, automation (programming), variability, and interactivity. These may be considered in turn as producing three conceptual models for understanding the novelty of computational processes: the convergence of all media toward a numerically manipulable and distributable form, practically infinite manipulability, and, again, interactivity. Each of these powers fundamentally transforms the spatial and temporal experience of spectatorship. The transformation of the concept of screen is also important. No longer a passive surface for receiving projections, the screen now becomes a manipulable surface for executing algorithms. It be-

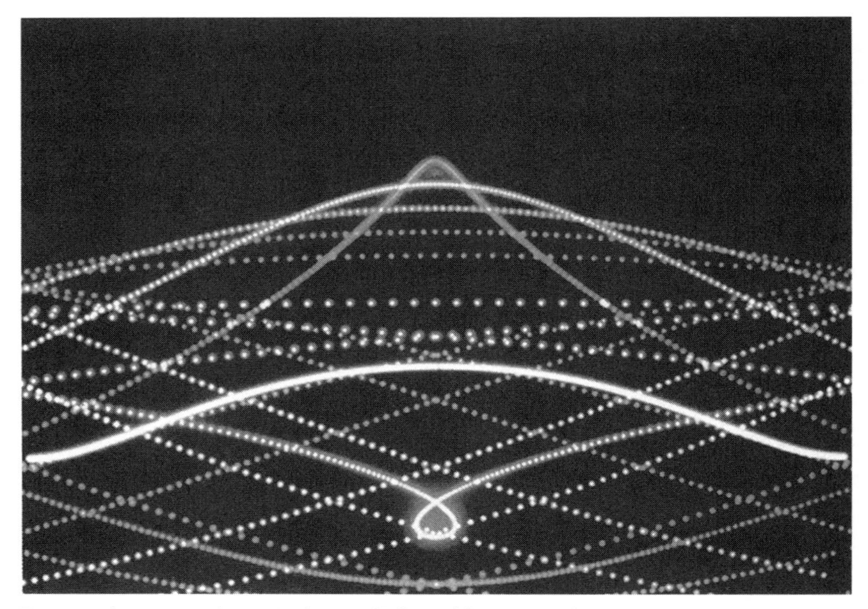

Frame enlargement from *Arabesque* (John Whitney, 1975)

comes a control interface, both graphic and textual, that executes commands and software operations while negotiating a new ontological relationship between human and machine.

The advantage of Manovich's distinctions are twofold. On one hand, they provide some points of navigation for understanding how digital automatisms are shifting our cultural conception of what it means to represent, both to make representations of the world and to represent ourselves to others. On the other, they demonstrate the continuity of certain concepts—image, screen, representation, frame—dear to film and art theory as baselines for comprehending these changes. But there is also a fundamental miscomprehension in Manovich that must be avoided, one that impedes our understanding of the radicality of his recognition of the separate cosmogonies of analogical transcription and digital notation. Manovich believes that the concept of representation is a stable one, whose function with respect to images is augmented with respect to computational processes. The ontology of information, however, is agnostic with respect to its outputs. It is a symbolic realm, meaning it is blind to all matters and patterns of thought that cannot be expressed in a logical notation. It is insensitive to the qualities of things and thoughts. While it is an expressive and logical realm, it does not "represent," at least in the sense in which we ordinarily take images to represent, that is, to stand for things that can be seen or imagined as being in the world (computers produce tokens of *numbers*). Of course, our concepts of perceptual or mental images are profoundly embedded in the assumption that images are produced through autographic and analogical procedures, and perhaps this assumption should be questioned. There is no space to digital information, and it does not represent; these facts help us to understand the standard assumption that images are continuous and extended in spaces real or imagined. And just as Benjamin remarked that the question inspired by photography and film is not "Is film art?" but rather "Has film changed our conception of art?," computers may indeed now ask us to question the nature of images.

## 19. An Image That Is Not "One"

> The video "image" does not exist as such, or at least, it does not exist in space . . . but only in time.
>
> —Philippe Dubois, *L'acte photographique*

The transformation of film into "digital cinema" exemplifies how the automatisms of information processing have transformed our contemporary notion of the image in its fluctuating existence as a signal traced on electronic screens. In the age of computers, the image is not *one*, meaning not identical with itself. Moreover, outputs to electronic screens confound our ordinary sense of what an image *is*.

The persistence of the cinematographic ideal is indeed strange, given that photography is rapidly disappearing from sight. Electronic screens are ever more ubiquitous, as already demonstrated by the displacement of theatrical exhibition; our ordinary experience of digital cinema is one of home viewing on various types of displays, from large-screen high-definition sets to video iPods. In hindsight, one understands better the rarity of experiencing film as projected in a movie theater. That the movies are now a mass medium as never before is also exemplary of the concept of the convergence of all media toward a numerically manipulable and distributable form. Thus, transcoding in Manovich's sense of the term refers not only to the conversion of all media types into digital information, but also to the programming or digital automation of all "cultural operations." Or rather, in my preferred philosophical vocabulary, this would be the algorithmic programming of the automatisms characterizing antecedent analog media: text processing; paint programs; image and sound capture, editing, and mixing; architectural modeling in two and three dimensions; and so on, all of which are amenable to presentation and manipulation via two-dimensional displays.

Ordinary language has created the neologism "'Photoshop'-ing" to describe the process of converting analogical automatisms into digital algorithms. Still, from one perspective it is surprising that photography and cinema should provide the predominant metaphors or analogies guiding the creation especially of computer gaming and other virtual worlds. It bears repeating that the model of perfect photographic credibility need not have determined the technological history of digital image simulation.

As exemplified in the pioneering work of John Whitney, analog and digital synthesis was first conceived as a process of abstraction. Often mischaracterized as "animation," these beautiful, hypnotic works were in no way dependent on the automatism of succession in the photographic sense, but rather were the products of algorithmic manipulations of a continuous electronic signal. The beginnings of electronic or computer art fully acknowledged that the basic automatism of electronic imaging was not taking a picture but modulating a signal. As a time-based medium, the electronic arts derive their powers from the ability to vary parameters that yield new outputs from given inputs.

History has not yet made clear why, already in the 1960s, photorealism was displacing abstraction as the driving goal of research in digital image simulation. Nevertheless it did, first by programming linear perspective into 3-D modeling software and later programming it directly into chips and graphics cards. Increasingly, the norms of perceptual realism derived from the conventions of standard Hollywood practice became the default perceptual mode for creating space and manipulating space in time, not only at the level of software design but also as engineered in the design of chips and graphics cards. In Manovich's accounts of this history, by 1996 researchers at Microsoft finally presented their goal as translating the heuristics of filmmaking into computer hardware and software—in short, converting "cinematographic expertise" into manipulable algorithmic functions. Transcoding the cinematic into the digital means that "element by element, cinema is being poured into the computer: first, one-point linear perspective; next, the mobile camera and rectangular window; next, cinematography and editing conventions; and of course, digital personas based on acting conventions borrowed from cinema, to be followed by make-up, set design, and the narrative structures themselves" (*Language of New Media* 86). Here the automatisms of film are reified into programmable functions. In this way, the conventions of cinema, especially contemporary Hollywood cinema, have become the platform for the creation of and interaction with virtual worlds. In addition, the perceptual availability of abstract hypermediacy in early computer animation has now been displaced "behind" the (transparent) immediacy of the contemporary digital image in its cinematographic appearance.

Today the creative language of digital creation is predominantly the language of movies. Thus, one way in which film's virtual life extends itself is through its rebirth as the predominant aesthetic template for computational interfaces and works. Cinema does not remain unchanged in the process, however. Through transcoding, filmic automatisms lose their concreteness as creative potentialities and become metaphors for digital functions. Splicers, glue, and editing tables disappear into the screen interfaces of Premiere or Final Cut Pro. But here the term "digital cinema" exemplifies a force that both reasserts and undermines the singularity of our understanding of what cinema was and has become. Our audiovisual culture remains "cinematic" in the sense that the most popular forms of digital media long to recreate and intensify cinematic effects of framing, editing, dynamic point of view, and mobile framing. Alternatively, as befits a medium whose inputs and outputs are discontinuous, transcoding is a one-way street; the perpetuation of cinematic algorithms in the deep structure of digital programming means the disappearance of film, and the rebirth of cinema in the form of programmable algorithms. The idea of cinema persists as a way of modeling time-based spatial forms with computers, but cinema is only one of myriad functions that computers can simulate or model. Understanding digital cinema, then, means defining and evaluating the automatisms that computers make possible. These may be automatisms that create filmlike effects, but they are no longer filmic automatisms. Our audiovisual culture is currently a digital culture, but with a cinematic look. And cinema, too, is increasingly just another element of digital culture.

Traveling from the Silver Age of film, through the Iron Age of video tape, we have now fully arrived in the Silicon Age of computers. The familiarity of cinema as a cultural form has eased this transition for us and remains in many ways our perceptual and aesthetic default for characterizing the image as such. But there are a number of reasons why the digital image is not *one*, that is, *an* "image," in the ordinary sense of the word. Some of these reasons should already be apparent. A graphical image is only one possible kind of output for digital information, and information processors are entirely agnostic as to the identity of their outputs, whether textual, pictorial, acoustical, or any hybrid combination of the three. Moreover, outputs lack closure. Numerical in their logic and modular in their structure, they are open to modification at any time and on any scale. Digital practices call for transformation, dissemination, recontextualization, and even transmutation into other kinds of perceptual outputs. Their identity is inherently multiple and open to viruslike mutations into ever-renewable series. In this way, digital practices respond not only to automatisms of convergence, but also to those of interactivity and practically infinite manipulability.

Finally, despite the predominance of dynamic graphical outputs, digital presentations are not spatial; at least, they do not occupy space according to our usual habits of perception or thought. Certainly, computers make images available as graphical or spatial outputs. But these "images" are never fully present to us and are always incomplete in space and in time. Otherwise, they would not be open to our creative intentions through programmable interactive manipulation. Digital presentations have no presence or identity that is not commensurate with the structure of electronic displays. Having disappeared into information, the image can be reborn or reconstituted only as an electronic signal.

Understanding fully the depth and extent of this transformation requires accounting for the present relation between image and screen. That the contemporary moving image is an electronic image, and not a photographic one, is an important and often-neglected point. The cultural presence of computers and digital imaging has profoundly changed the function of the screen. These changes were already prefigured in the rapid proliferation of video displays (televisions) in the U.S. domestic market between 1947 and 1955. The video or televisual display thus prepares and executes a conceptual transformation of the image as traditionally understood. We are still coming to terms with the enormity of this sea-change in our everyday sense of the image. Film and photography occupy a long history of pictorial conventions that electronic imaging has displaced and transformed. Common sense still considers an image as a perceptual presentation that occupies space as a stable volume in two or three dimensions. In other words, paintings or sculptures occupy our visual field as an apparently unchanging whole—their mode of existence is to be fully present to us, and with us, in time and space. Photography already shifted the terms of the image's mode of existence in confronting us with past time in present space, and film altered these terms yet again in producing movement as the dual pursuit of an image absent in space yet moving in time. From photography to film, the canonical sense of a frame as delimiting a stable image deployed in two dimensions is displaced by a dynamic frame expressing movement and mobile perspectives.

Electronic images are inseparable from displays, however, and as such produce a new kind of dynamic "space." This is a simple observation, but it has important consequences. Cinema requires a screen to receive a projected image, yet it remains perceptible as an independent object—photograms on a 16mm or 35mm strip are viewable with the unaided eye. For many years, film editing was accomplished by sight alone or by the simple illumination and magnification of movieolas. The electronic image, however, is more intimately tied to a display, itself an electronic device. In this respect, the electronic image is not "one," or identical with itself, since it has no visible presence for us or to us without the aid of a display. Its becoming visible is inseparable from the presence of an output device, and in this way analog video anticipates the computer's separation of inputs and outputs. The appearance of television already marked the disappearance of the image in its photographic appearance. The medium of cinematography is light; the medium of videography is electricity. "Digitality," if such a neologism is to come into existence, is the algorithmic manipulation of symbolic functions. These are three stages in the virtual life of images, as it were, in which the spatial form of registered light gives way first to a modulated signal (a continuous variation of input to output) and then becomes transcoded as digital information. Where analog video registers light values and records them as analogous changes in voltage values, digital video samples light values and encodes them as symbolic notations of color, intensity, and position, with individual pixels corresponding to memory locations dynamically updated on computer screens. Not only does image become information here, but also the separation of inputs and outputs in graphical computing means that the life of images corresponds not to transcriptions of the world, but to the writing of information outputs to screens. In this way, digital "images," or rather, graphical outputs, differ from both painting and photography in their mode of existence. The appearance of the image is anchored neither to its "medium" (paint or filmstock—two kinds of physical and chemical existence) nor to a direct causal connection to past or present states of affairs. Therefore, the information in a digital file is not comparable to a film strip stored in cans. It has no physical existence and does not suffer change in the same way. Digital records may be printed, of course. But their "natural" ontological state is to be manifested on electronic displays.

Here, time and causality are once again transformed, shifting the mode of existence of digital outputs as well as our interactive relations with them. The cinema screen is a passive surface that receives projections. It is a surface for reflecting the projection of the past as a passing present. The sense of pastness, and of time's passing, is key for understanding film's particular expression of the skeptical attitude as a consciousness divided from the world by the window of perception, a division experienced as confronting the gulf of past time. With electronic imaging, however, the screen does not simply receive an image; it actively produces it and causes it to become dynamically in the present. Filmic projection presents one way of overcoming skepticism in that the powers of automatic analogical causation support belief in past existences in time. The electronic image screens us no less powerfully from this world, yet the terms of its response to skepticism are quite different. Whether radar screen, video monitor, computer monitor, or instrument display, the novelty of the electronic screen is the ability to express change in real time. Unlike photographs and films, which as indexical traces are the present expressions of past events, a radar screen or video surveillance image is counterfactually dependent on changes in the present that are nonetheless divided from us in space by distance or scale. Unlike the passive surface of the cinema screen, video displays constantly react to electrical excitation and so qualify causality differently. Film is an isomorphic projection and passive record of past causation. An analog video recording also preserves an indexical trace, but in playback we are perceptually present to a continually changing causation, the excitation of phosphors traced on an electronic display. If we are perceptually attentive to causation, the indexical trace of the film screen returns us to the past, while on electronic displays tracing sustains us in the present: images are presented in the form of a constant and repetitive process of scanning. Following the canonic frame of pictures deployed in a static two-dimensional space and the dynamic frame of film, which introduces time to the image in the form of duration and mobile viewpoints as a moving image of the past, the primary automatism of the electronic display is the ability to display change in real time; in other words, the video screen holds our perceptions as the expression of causal changes in the immediate present.

Related to film through the automatism of succession, the electronic image nonetheless differs from film in the temporality of this automatism—the expression of change in the present as opposed to the present witnessing of past durations. Moreover, the presentation of the image on detached displays differs in yet another way from standard and dynamic framing. The passing present of the unrolling film strip is a historical expression, the presentation of past duration or duration past. Before a real-time display the viewer occupies the same duration as the changes witnessed, even if she is divided from them in space. Now a video display may function like film to present a record of the past, as when we watch a prerecorded tape or DVD; but the nature of time with respect to the image, and with respect to the impression of movement presented by changes in the image, differs in substantial ways. In cinematography, as in photography, all parts of the image are exposed simultaneously. We cognitively construct the impression of movement from the passing images. We add movement to the image, as it were, with the aid of the projector, but the individual images themselves persist as wholes with their own unique durations. An electronic image, whether analogical or digital, never displays a spatial or a temporal whole. Unlike the film screen, which passively receives images, the electronic display actively constructs images in time; or, more correctly, it displays signals that produce an image through sequential scanning. Rather than producing a whole spatial field, in NTSC interlaced scanning, for example, an electron beam traces first the odd lines of a 525-line display, exciting light-sensitive phosphors along the way, and then the even lines. The different parts of the display correspond to different phases in time such that there is never a moment when the entire image is spatially or temporally present to us. We perceive an "image" because the sequential phosphors (600 pixels per line) continue to glow in overlapping durations and because the scanning process is so rapid (one-fifteenth of a second for a field; one-thirtieth of a second for a frame).

Digital "images" present an even more powerful paradox. Though output to electronic displays, their fundamental form is symbolic notation, tokens of numbers that neither occupy space nor change through time.[19] The film projector produces movement by animating still images. But as presented on electronic displays, the image *is* movement or subject to continual change because the screened image is being constantly reconstituted, scanned, or refreshed. Being in a constant state of reconstruction through a process of scanning, the electronic image is never wholly present in either space or time. Moreover, it is

19. John Belton has also pointed out to me that the quantification and compression of digital images significantly abridge the presentation of time and space on electronic screens: "In looking at a movie that has been digitized, temporal and spatial data have been omitted via the sampling that is part of both quantification and compression. Part of the image that remains constant over several frames is therefore given to us in frame one, then replaced in successive frames by a numerical code that refers us back to frame one. For that particular part of the image, we are seeing one brief moment of time and space again and again"; correspondence with the author. See also Mangolte, "Afterward: A Matter of Time" 264.

fundamentally discontinuous; that is, it is never identical with itself in a given moment of time. This means that the "video image" does not exist as such, or rather, that it does not persist in space as an undivided unit of time. A discontinuous, fluctuating, and pointillist image, both spatial and temporal unity are unknown to it.

Therefore, the electronic image is a time-based image not only because it is capable of succession, but also because it is never fully present in space or in time; it occupies a state of continuous present becoming. Thus, even a "photograph" displayed on an electronic screen is not a still image. It may appear so, but its ontological structure is of a constantly shifting or self-refreshing display. Electronic images are in constant movement or states of dynamic change, even when they appear to be static. In this manner, the electronic image challenges not only commonsense notions of what an image is, but also what an object or aesthetic object might be as a static presence in space and in time. In a sense there are no new media "objects" or images. A better term might be "elements," which may vary in terms of their outputs and underlying algorithmic logics. Thus, it bears repeating that electronic art involves not the making of a thing, but variations in a process or transformations of a signal.

When the video display becomes a digital interface, another mutation takes place in the nature of electronic screens: the variability of the video image, its receptiveness to real-time change, becomes nonlinear and interactive. The screen is not only a surface for expressing images; it also functions as a control for executing instructions. Perceptually we are placed before a surface amenable to two quite different cultural functions—one extending our relationship with analogical images, and one presenting us with new opportunities for the interactive manipulation of information. The digital display offers simultaneously the potential for passive immersion (as in watching a movie) and the possibility of active, general-purpose control. Indeed, users alternate at will between these two functions. As Lev Manovich deftly describes this situation, the latter enables us "to perform complex and detailed actions on computer data," while the former "positions the user inside an imaginary universe whose structure is fixed by the author." In this way,

> The concept of a screen combines two distinct pictorial conventions—the older Western tradition of pictorial illusionism in which a screen functions as a window into a virtual space, something for the viewer to look into but not act upon; and the more recent convention of graphical human-computer interfaces that divides the computer screen into a set

> of controls with clearly delineated functions, thereby essentially treating it as a virtual instrument panel. As a result, the computer screen becomes a battlefield for a number of incompatible definitions—depth and surface, opaqueness and transparency, image as illusionary space and image as instrument for action. (*Language of New Media* 90)

The variability of the electronic image thus corresponds to the multifunctionality of digital displays, which call, alternately, for passive and active responses on the part of the viewer. One consequence of the multivalence of digital screens is a capacity to react to them simultaneously as image and as information. The digital screen is no longer a passive surface receiving representations or presenting them. Rather, as appropriate to the separation of inputs and outputs in information processing, as well as the symbiosis of the digital and the analogical, the surface of the screen now vacillates between two different but related purposes: providing a perceptually convincing image—that is, a representation—and providing efficient access to information. The function of control is added to that of presentation as the screen becomes both an interface and an instrument panel open and available to a multiplicity of functions. Among the most powerful automatisms enabled by digital screens is thus real-time interactions with either virtual functions or actual processes and persons separated from us in space. What the digital screen empowers in its alternation between image and information, representation and interface, is action at a distance in the present, that is, in simultaneity or real time regardless of geographical separation. Yet it is important to recognize that, whether our interlocutors are virtual or actual, in this situation we are interacting with a digital homologon. Simulation is the logical term for describing this homologon in contrast to processes of analogical transcription, and in this can be understood another attribute of the computer as a medium. Computers are agnostic as to whether the interactions they enable, or functions they simulate, execute actions in the physical world or only result in internal changes of logical states. In this respect, the lesson of the Turing test is not whether computer communication will become indistinguishable from human expression; rather, it is already the case that computers consider every action to be symbolic and will not distinguish between human or physical processes and virtual ones. Computational algorithms may model processes and aspects of the physical world according to the criteria of perceptual realism. However, these models have no causal relations or references to physically existent objects or states of affairs. And when they do, we must understand the qualitative differences effected by causation in a situation in which informational inputs and outputs are discontinuous. We should not fear that computers will become conscious. But we should continually evaluate the quality of our communications and interactions where "real connections" are mediated predominantly by interaction with symbolic worlds and control interfaces.

Returning to Carroll's useful terminology, we can now better understand the distinctiveness of electronic outputs from photographic or cinematographic images as differences in their presentation of two-dimensional images and apparent movement, as well as in the nature of detached displays. These differences may be evaluated as different relations to time and causality, and all indicate a shift in medium according to the creative automatisms these elements enable or empower conceptually. Indeed, the appearance of digital screens has completed the transition to a new mode of existence for images.

I have discussed at length Cavell's definition of film as a succession of "automatic world projections," which produces a phenomenology that Cavell characterizes as "viewing." Equally interesting in comparison to my remarks on the nature of electronic screens is Cavell's definition of television as *"a current of simultaneous event reception."*[20] Through the constant flow or continuity of time, which encompasses the discontinuous modalities of live presentation, replay, and retransmission, television presents events standing out from the world, especially through the condition of liveness: "in live television, what is present to us while it is happening is not the world, but an event standing out from the world. Its point is not to reveal, but to cover (as with a gun), to keep something on view" (*The World Viewed* 26). And these events are not viewed, but rather *monitored*—a requirement of our attention in time. Digital events may require another definition. One variant of this definition might be *a process of simulation through algorithmic information interactions.* And through this process of interactivity, we seek less to view or monitor than to control or command.

As we trace the genealogy from classic and dynamic screens to real-time displays, can we also not infer a shifting ontology of time? The advent of digital images as a perceptual norm has once again made photography strange to us, although this curiosity is becoming more and more archaeological. Our ontological relation to digital screens moves us to ask once again why we found photographs and films to be compelling as past experience and as an

20. "The Fact of Television," in *Cavell on Film,* ed. William Rothman (Albany: State University of New York Press, 2005) 72.

experience of the past. At the same time, our ontological fascination with video displays needs also to be evaluated ethically. What draws us to computer screens and televisual displays? As two possible responses to skepticism's division of consciousness from the world by the window of perception, the film screen and the digital screen present two different relations to duration and causality. Electronic screens give the perception of a continually changing present that can never be whole, or wholly present to us, in any of its instants. In addition, through digital screens our relation is not to an image, but to function or force—that of control and the management of information. We do not ask of digital screens that they provoke contemplation of the past and passing time as we do of film; we want them to sort, organize, give access to, and act on information in the present. We desire them to manage time or to make time more manageable as there is less and less of it. Thus the paradox of cheap recording: we can store more and more information without having the means to access and edit it in ways that are meaningful to us. This is the essential double bind of computers, in which more and more calculating power chases greater and greater storage capacity. This paradox leaves open the ethical questions: to paraphrase Nietzsche, "What do electronic images want?" and "What do we will in wanting them?" In the sections that follow, I will examine these questions through the concept of the transvaluation of photography, the return of film to contemporary art practice, and the digital event.

## 20. Two Futures for Electronic Images, or What Comes after Photography?

From the moment that *National Geographic* committed the original sin of digitally shifting the apparent distance among the pyramids of Giza on the cover of its February 1982 issue, much ink has been spilled over the crisis in photographic "authenticity." However, as William Mitchell has explained in *The Reconfigured Eye: Visual Truth in the Post-Photographic Era*, one should really wonder why and when viewers ever attributed visual authenticity to photography. Mitchell's own title, however, promulgates a number of false problems. One cannot judge visual presentations to be deceitful if they have never been capable of *telling*, much less telling the truth. And fifteen years after Mitchell's path-breaking book, it seems strange to characterize contemporary visual culture as "post-photographic" when more and more images are being captured daily.

We live not in a "post-photographic" era, then, but in an age in which pho-

Abu Ghraib documentation (2003).

Sam Taylor-Wood, *Pietà* (2001), 35mm/DVD, 1 minute 57 seconds. Copyright © the artist. Courtesy Jay Jopling / White Cube Gallery, London.

tography and cinema have rapidly become both more than themselves and something else entirely. Here are two diverging directions for the virtual life of film: as information and as art.

In my view, photographs have earned the right philosophically to lay claim to a documentary function, even when producing barely recognizable spatial images. But this is not the same claim as an expression of visual truth or authenticity. (What has changed, perhaps, is the nature of "documents.") Although the functional differences and similarities between pictures and propositions have worried contemporary analytic philosophy for some time, simply speaking, pictures are not statements. Depictions, even photographic ones, cannot be judged to be truthful, though under certain conditions they may be considered deceitful or at least misleading. A photograph can neither lie nor tell the truth; it only denotes (automatically registers space) and designates (is causally related to a past state of affairs). One may want to assess or evaluate the accuracy, resolution, or amount and kinds of information relayed by an analogical transcription, but this will not amount to a statement that could be judged truthful or not.

Nor does it make sense to characterize these combined functions as authentic or inauthentic. Given the existence of standardized procedures of automatic analogical causation, faith has and may still be placed in the photograph's ability to produce similarity. These automatisms, all of which are reproduced in processes of digital capture, deepen and extend long-standing technological norms based on commitments to unaltered spatial consistency, temporal unity, and the precise recording of spatial relationships obtaining in a past state of affairs. Ordinarily, and in full knowledge of the vast amount of visual information that may be omitted or uncaptured, straight photographs usually convince us that the image viewed is analogous in all relevant features to the scene witnessed by the photographer through the viewfinder. While in ordinary language straight photographs are habitually characterized as "truthful," "authentic," or "faithful" renderings, in actuality these are often expressions of a yearning to account for our ontological perplexity before the spatial presence of past time; and these expressions are often mischaracterizations, as I have put it, of a wish to give a spatial or representational account of a temporal perception. In this manner, our ontological yearnings frequently confuse epistemological questions with ethical conundrums concerning how to place ourselves in the world and in relation to the past through these images. Past time grips us in photographs, but not in ways that are usefully characterized as truthful or authentic.

If we are provoked to new ontological questioning by the computer's mediation of representation and communication, the problems confronted there have nothing to do with either "truth" or "realism." These are philosophical canards to which photography was never capable of responding. But this is not photography's fault, for the questions are badly posed to begin with. To insist that photographs transcribe or document the past is not to claim that they are truthful accounts of the past. Questions of truth or falsity may not be resolved by depictions. Moreover, the documentary force of photographs (often retroactively disappointing), what they can tell or relate about a past state of affairs, is always conditioned by institutional contexts and criteria of evaluation that are bracketed by phenomenological examination. Although we can evaluate the *sense* of photographs, like all depictions they cannot express *meaning*. "Realism" presents another set of problems as a concept that confuses spatial correspondence with temporal indication. The strange idea that photographs could be truthful or not is a misconstrual of correspondence theories of truth, a misunderstanding arising from the spatial emphases of perceptual realism. Painting may aspire to spatial descriptions that are as exacting as those of photography. We may be temporarily fooled by Chuck Close's painterly recapitulation of Polaroids and other styles of photorealistic painting. But the force of our conviction in the past has a temporal sense before a spatial one. Moreover, this is a force and sense produceable only through automatic analogical causation. (Photography is not painting, and, moreover, the beauty of Close's painterly magnification of the Polaroid image, of the painterly translation of scale, is to return us perceptually to the surface and texture of painting itself.)

This confusion is compounded when images automatically produced are taken up in syntactic or semantic combinations; for example, when commitments to spatial unity are revoked in combination prints and photomontages, in subtraction of information from the negative, or when images are combined in series with captions and other written or spoken documentary reports. In these cases, the range of extensions to automatically captured images changes: no longer this world's historical past, but a marshaling of these spatial features to project other possible worlds, which may be fictional and counterfactual or, more unkindly, deceitful or tendentious. Cameras have no intentions, nor can they be mistaken or correct. These instruments do not lie or dissemble, although photographers and editors do. When images are marshaled as statements in evidence of historical events, we are concerned with being assured not only that standard procedures have been followed in their mode of picturing, but also that their new propositional functions follow constitutive rules of evidence: commitment to defend the claim, preparedness to document the claim, and sincerity of defense. Like all other forms of documentary evidence, whether linguistic or depictive, photographs demand corroboration. In important situations in which they must give evidence—whether scientific, historical, or political—we do not let them stand alone, but ask questions about provenance, intention, and context. In these situations, the linguistic contexts of photographs are usually found to be more misleading than the images themselves.[21]

If I am correct that the indexical force of digitally captured images has become diminished in comparison with photography, this does not mean that faith in such images as historical "documents" has been lost or that we necessarily approach them with increased skepticism, although, frankly, we probably should. Digital photographs are still taken to be perceptually real and indeed may capture more information at higher resolutions than is possible in chemical photography. To my knowledge, no one seriously challenged the Abu Ghraib images as faked or even unrepresentative of the deplorable situations they documented. And even the low-resolution pictures captured by cell phones in the London Underground during the attacks in the summer of 2005 remain compelling historical images of those events.

In the twenty-first century, automatic recordings are still taken to be documents, and more so than ever. The waning of indexicality means only that digital images are increasingly and more powerfully susceptible to the computer's powers of symbolic manipulation and transmission. It is a tribute to the power of the cultural association of photographs with a documentary function that digital capture is still considered to be "photography." However, to begin to comprehend the automatisms of digital imaging, one must understand not only the power of these images to convince as being spatially "real," but also how the temporality of computers in relation to electronic imaging has asserted new powers through these images. Through the waning of indexicality, new ethical stances in relation to time and to history emerge in our encounters with digital imaging.

The idea that photography has become more deeply itself and something more besides is demonstrated by the cultural history of the Abu Ghraib docu-

21. For an overview of the ethical and legal ramifications of treating photographs as "evidence," see Mitchell, *The Reconfigured Eye* (Cambridge, Mass.: MIT Press, 1992), especially chaps. 3 and 9. The analytical debate about examining pictures as propositions was opened in a special issue of *The Monist* 58.2 (1974) devoted to Nelson Goodman's *Languages of Art,* especially John G. Bennett's essay "Depiction and Convention" 255–268.

ments. On one hand, the immediate cultural impact of these images has shown that our belief in the documentary powers of digital capture is undiminished. On the other, they exhibit powers possible only in the age of computers. Like all other forms of digital information, these images express a new, accelerated relationship with time—of copying and transmission—where the present gains in density and scope. Indeed, the images from Abu Ghraib are provocative examples of how the powers of digital capture and diffusion have transformed not our sense of the past, but our relationship to the history of the present and what it means to occupy *present* time. In the ontology of photography, the past is felt as an ontologically distinct and often unbridgeable temporal dimension. As Barthes's examples showed, even the future implied in such images is a future of the past, though as a power of recurrence always present with us or to us. In a contemporary context, digitally captured images, rather, shape a past felt to be historically present with us and to which we feel connected or embedded; in other words, they express an immediate, cumulative past that remains part of our historical present.

Although one or two images have become emblematic of the images from Abu Ghraib, it is significant that there are thought to exist as many as 1,800 digital images and four videos recorded from October through December 2003. Most remain unpublished. Not only were the abuses, as well as prison life in general, easily and substantially recorded by several sources and stored on computers; they also were quickly copied, recontextualized as screen savers and calendar images, and, of course, shared and transmitted within the prison via CD-ROM and, subsequently, across the globe via the Internet. Because of time and date stamps, an often-ignored feature of digital capture, precise time frames and chronologies of recorded events could also be established.

Undoubtedly, those who captured images at Abu Ghraib naively never intended their pictures to become public, or at least not to be seen by a public larger than their immediate community of friends and colleagues. But embedded in the programming of digital capture devices and their connectivity to computers are other, more powerful intentions—algorithms or automatisms—that have transformed the ontology of "photography" both quantitatively and qualitatively. On one hand, the programming of digital cameras has preserved, deepened, and extended cultural norms of perceptual realism and personal documentation, making it yet more commonplace to capture more and better images at greater rates of speed. We may continue to believe that we possess these images as personal property and can control their circulation in the form of copies. And, in this respect, we still live in a generation that takes the digital camera for a photographic apparatus. But, as I have explained above, digital capture devices convert images into *information*, and in so doing they accelerate and amplify their powers as *communication*, a process limited only by the availability of computing cycles, storage capacity, and bandwidth.

For all the ink spilled in the 1990s over the possibility of producing false and misleading images that appear to be spatially consistent and perceptually real, the dominant cultural uses of digital capture are better understood through examining how computational processes have transformed and augmented the temporality of digital capture, copying, and transmission. Captured to electronic screens and transmitted over computers, digital images, like those taken at Abu Ghraib, are the nephews of television rather than of print journalism. The temporal powers they express are closer to video than to photography. These include the quantitative accumulation of images captured cheaply and at prodigious rates, the capacity for real-time monitoring and instant random access, and the possibility of instant editing and (re)transmission. In every case there is a compression of time in relation to the image, with the duration of photographic acts and automatisms becoming shorter and shorter as well as cheaper and cheaper. Thus, one consequence of the proliferation of the means of digital capture as well as the ease and rapidity of the capture process is to expand and deepen our relationship to the present as multiple sources scattered in space document and transmit it. Quantitatively, the number of digital images captured, literally from all points on the globe, has increased exponentially. In this respect, they function as an incessantly proliferating mapping of our present whose dimensions and scales are powerfully expansive. It is as if every individual on the globe capable of purchasing a capture device were participating collectively in a project of visually documenting our immediate present. We are immersed in this present as part of a global, serialized community in which the individual "photographer" is now one among many inputs contributing to a larger collective process of the spatial and temporal mapping of everyday life.

One way to characterize digital documentation, then, is to examine how the image is treated more and more as information to be accumulated, stored, sorted, and analyzed. Computational processes have driven a vast augmentation in the velocity of capture and diffusion of images. An immense archive of our immediate present is accumulating on memory cards and hard drives, documenting situations that are more often banal than eventful. However, the proliferation of devices means that if an event occurs, there will surely be a "camera" there to capture it—indeed, more than one, and most in the hands of "amateurs." I place amateurs in scare quotes because we have all become, to a greater or lesser extent, professional users of consumer digital devices. The tremendous speed and global scale of capture and diffusion have made daily life luminous; our entire present is a potential image for someone. (Often I have wondered in how many photographs and videos I inadvertently figure as, during my daily walks to class or to Widener Library, yet another tourist bus pulls away from Harvard Yard.) Moreover, the distributed nature of cellular and computer networks has greatly enhanced the possibilities of producing multiple copies and distributing them on a potentially global scale. Retrospectively, Walter Benjamin's cinematic utopia, in which every person could lay claim to the right of being filmed, had to wait for the computer to really come into existence. We are all extras now in the images and movies of others.

Just as Henri Bergson imagined the passing present as being doubled at each moment with a piling up of virtual images of our immediate past, our immediate present is passing into a vast archive of digital images. And what the computer has wrought, it must also store and access. As memory capacity increases, images accumulate on hard drives with ever-increasing density. If computers are responsible for the velocity and scale of the acquisition of images, they are also indispensable for accessing, selecting, sorting, and retrieving this information when required and if possible. In this respect, the powers of this continuous global mapping of daily life are more virtual than actual. Ease of capture and the numerical proliferation of images have made problems of storage and editing ever more challenging. Users tend not to edit and preserve photographs as family records, but rather to take, distribute, and dispose of them for purposes of immediate personal communication. And indeed, I believe that most users of digital devices have not thought through the future or potential uses of their images; that is, what it means to produce a personal image archive as a database that can be easily accessible by others. These databases may be volatile and often disposable, yet we have the capacity to preserve them if we wish. Indeed, they often preserve themselves through copying, transmission, relay, and recontextualization in ways that cannot be anticipated.

In worrying about the capacity of computers to transform images, we nearly forget their more powerful and prosaic will to copy and transmit. Digital-capture documents and digital documentation express new powers—not only deep and superior copies, but also an increasing ease and velocity of dissemination. In even the most private digital document, then, lies the capacity to proliferate throughout the public sphere, distributed on networks in innumerable copies and archived on uncountable servers. These documents carry within them highly specific metadata concerning authorship and times and dates of creation and modification, as well as other information. In this manner, the belief in the disposability or even triviality of images captured at Abu Ghraib provoked the downfall of the individuals and institutions that wished to suppress this information. For in the age of computers and computer networks, the ability to suppress and monitor information plays a game of leapfrog with the global velocity and decentralized movements enabled by packet-switched networks. In this respect, the distributed nature of capture and diffusion produces the possibility of continual surveillance wherein citizen documentation must counterbalance governmental abuse. In the curious case of the Abu Ghraib photographs, self-documentation by individuals resulted in the unveiling of systemic abuse in U.S. Army detention centers. The digital proliferation of capture, copy, and distribution means, one can hope, that such documents will continue to overflow the will to contain them and will remain available for ethical and political evaluation. One key difference, though, is that digital images may no longer be capable of producing the existential or ontological perplexity of which both Barthes and Cavell were so keenly and philosophically aware. Digital photographs have become more social than personal, and more attuned to the present itself than to the present's relation to the past and future. Symbolic and notational at their core, they provoke discussion of images as *information*. In this they solicit often-healthy debates (would that all images did so) about provenance, reliability, accuracy, and context. Less *puncta* and more *studia* perhaps, where their personal and existential force fades their capacity to provoke moral outrage and debate may grow. Or they may reduce us to silence and inaction. The hermeneutic circle of interpretation becomes here an ethical circle of responsiveness or unresponsiveness. As images become information, computers tend increasingly to make personal photography public communication. And this public information often returns to us as private moments before screens, where the electronic image calls for ethical deliberation and response, whether successful or not.[22]

The powers of digital imaging are the powers of computing. For the mo-

22. On the ethical dilemmas posed by electronic images, see Tom Keenan's essay "Publicity and Indifference (Sarajevo on Television)," *Publications of the Modern Language Association* 117.1 (January 2002) 104–116.

ment, users are less concerned with creatively transforming the symbolic information that constitutes these images than with "correcting" or enhancing them, thus reinforcing the spatial and perceptual norms of realistic or representative images. As or more importantly, the digital image is submitted to a temporal domain expressive of computers and computer networks that has augmented and speeded up the automatisms of select, copy, paste, sort, modify, and transmit. Everyone has become a photographer who not only captures images but also edits and distributes them, and the logarithmic increase in the capture and dissemination of images means, in crucial situations, that the demands for corroboration and ethical evaluation must be higher.

The example of Abu Ghraib expresses in microcosm the current situation and place of digital capture in our global present. Ease of digital capture, storage, and distribution has produced a powerful and curious dialectic wherein the image serves not as documentation of the past, but as an incessant mapping of the present. Our immediate historical present is reproduced and transmitted with ever-increasing density. What form or what use these records will have for future historians is anybody's guess. One may hope there will be fewer Abu Ghraibs in our future. But if there are, the chances are greater such abuses may be exposed.

The ethics of consumer photography have been changed by digital devices in ways that are difficult to identify and evaluate. And if the near-universality of consumer digital capture devices has made everyone photographers, then what becomes of the professional art photographer? How has her creative mode of existence been transformed by the automatisms of digital capture, editing, and transmission?

This is a deep and complex question worthy of a book of its own. Certainly, the increasing powers of digital mimicry, of the computer's ability to reproduce and simulate the automatisms of photography, mean that straight photography continues to exist, only more so and more rapidly. The straight photographer continues her creative work in much the same way, even if darkrooms give way to Photoshop and digital printers.

The more difficult ethical problem is to examine what the photographer becomes when photography becomes something else. (The same question may be asked of the cinematographer.) This question is illuminated by the increasing tendency of galleries and critics to refer to "lens-based practice." In the century spanning the careers of Eugène Atget, Berenice Abbot, Germaine

Krull, Walker Evans, Robert Frank, Gary Winogrand, and Lee Friedlander, photography was defined not only as the practice of a singular art, but also as a mode of existence or style of life. To seek out images was to become a traveler—whether urban *flâneur,* cross-country road-tripper, or foreign correspondent—in search of contingent encounters with the flux of history and everyday life. The city stroll or road trip was emblematic of the photographer's dual obsession with capturing events in the fleeting course of time and registering the surface materiality of physical existence. Akin to the Surrealist concern with the "marvelous," in the genre of straight photography singular images were often valued as the capture of unique and unrepeatable moments of (past) existence, contingent encounters preserved spatially against the ineluctable flow of passing time all but unnoticed or forgotten if not for the photographer's decisive and fortuitous act of recording. The desire to capture time's unrepeatability as well as the singular and evanescent nature of events and encounters inspired the ethics and aesthetics of straight photography. No doubt, the fact of the camera's having built-in automatisms ready at a moment's touch to transcribe time and register space encouraged this attitude or style of life. Despite its poetic imprecision, one can still sympathize here with Siegfried Kracauer's characterization, in his *Theory of Film,* of the mode of existence of the straight photographer as an empathic witness, observer, or explorer and of photography's inherent affinities with the unstaged, the fortuitous, endlessness, indeterminacy, and duration or the temporal continuum of physical existence.

In the past thirty years at least, the ethic of straight photography has become decentered or displaced. That there is no longer photography but rather lens-based practice exemplifies a new promiscuity in the creation of images. The increasing availability of electronic images and the ability of the computer to simulate many different kinds of devices and interfaces has unhooked the lens from specific apparatuses, such as the film camera, and transformed it into just another input device. The photographer has become an artist in ways that free her from commitment to a single device and involve her in new senses of the image. In this situation, the singular makes way for the multiple: the artist does not make *an* image, but rather works the intervals passing "between images." In any number of strategies, so precisely noted and remarked upon by Raymond Bellour, contemporary art has become increasingly attentive to the complexity of the spatiotemporal variables both defining and crossing between still and moving images in ways that completely transform their usual structures of creation and reception.[23] Increasingly, the individual print becomes one element to be ordered and combined in hybrid situations. In this way, art since the 1970s has both implicitly anticipated the computer's automatisms and responded to them in remarkable ways. In contemporary artists as different in style and sensibility as Victor Burgin, Isaac Julien, and Sam Taylor-Wood, one finds the tendency to work in more than one medium—for example, image capture (both chemical and digital), video (both single and multiple channel)—as well as in different film formats (super-8, 16mm, and 35mm), while often mixing media and multiplying channels and screens in complex, hybrid arrangements. The spatial unity of the photograph is respected less and less, giving way to new creative acts inspired by the retrospective awareness that photography has always been a time-based medium. The image may register duration, imply or occupy time as one element in a sequence, or be situated in complex arrangements with moving-image media whose own relationships to time and duration are yet more varied and complex.

The career of the London-based artist Sam Taylor-Wood is exemplary of this trajectory. A sensitivity to photography's registration of time, reminiscent of Futurism's fascination with the abstraction of movement through long exposure times, is already evident in her 1992 print *A Gesture toward Action Painting*. By 2000, however, the singular fully gives way to the multiple in Taylor-Wood's approach. *Contact* is a wall-sized collage (660 × 260 cm) consisting of hundreds of contact prints, color and black-and-white images of various sizes, and Post-it notes complete with artist's notations and editing marks culled from a decade's work. The focus on the fine-grained print is replaced with multiple and recombinable images crafted as an artfully arranged database wherein time is laid out in spatially complex sequences that are impossible to take in at a glance. The scale and density of the work impose a time of reading. *Contact* displays an aesthetic memory as a great jumble of carefully arranged fragments, whose system of connections and combinations is practically infinite, and where each reading is deeply personal for the responsive eye seeking out its proper duration.

The *Soliloquy* series (nine works, 1998–2001) anticipates these complex arrangements. Directly referencing Renaissance altarpieces, with their principal images and predellas, each work in this series combines a large C-type print

23. See *L'Entre-Images: Photo, cinéma, video* (Paris: La Différence, 1990); and *L'Entre-Images, 2: Mots, images* (Paris: POL, 1999).

"captioned" below with a smaller, 360-degree panoramic sequence. *Soliloquy I* (1998) is exemplary of the series. The main image shows a young man asleep on a divan in a modest apartment or bedsit; the predella presents a sequence of images in a richly tiled room with men and women posed in ways both erotic and surreal. Each work first divides time between the spatial unity of the main image and its juxtaposition with the predella as if doubling a present exterior time with an internal time of dream or fantasy. The panoramic predellas then distend time in other, uncanny ways. The panoramic image itself requires a certain duration and, laid out as strip, spatializes time as a linear sequence, thus implying a narrative. But this narrative is oblique, progressing not as a sequence of frames or shots, but as a continuously unfolding duration in the perceptually "real" but impossibly plastic space of fantasy. Some images in the series are digitally retouched: figures are repeated; limbs have been elongated unnaturally. The effects are subtle, however, and the influence of digital tools is only indirect.

In the early twentieth century, photography changed painting, but not in a manner so direct that painters copied photographs. Now the increasing presence of digital tools and electronic communication is changing creative approaches to photography and film, but nothing of interest comes from looking for direct causes and effects. Oblique relationships are always more interesting. Here digital and electronic media have amplified awareness of concepts and effects of seriality, multiplicity, and recombination with respect to earlier concepts of spatial unity and presence of past time. We are still seeking ways in which art photography seeks out new relationships of time unthought in the analog era.

In this respect, it is as if one of Taylor-Wood's concerns throughout this ten-year period was how to return duration and the image of change to photography or film in a period when, in a consumer or amateur context, digital capture was beginning to transform our quotidian encounters with the image. This will to restore duration to acts of viewing is played out in several strategies. Taylor-Wood's approaches to the question are both varied and interesting, as each one calls for the creation of different automatisms that generate works in series of increasing temporal complexity.

Through her work of this period, photography, video, and film are combined in complex relations of exchange or reversal. The series *Five Revolutionary Seconds I–XV* (1995–2000; color photographs on vinyl with sound) resembles the *Soliloquies,* but with a key difference. The 360-degree panoramic "takes"—each one a five-second revolution of the camera—make up the main images. Instead of predellas, the images are now combined with soundtracks. These are documentary recordings of the photo shoot, lasting anywhere from ten to forty-five minutes. As in the *Soliloquy* series predellas, the panorama implies a dramatic sequence unfolding like a scroll with implied spatial frames. Again, these are carefully arranged mise-en-scènes, conveying a strong yet ambiguous narrative sense that cannot be taken in in a single glance (the works vary from around 757 to 792 cm in length). The five-second pan registers a precise duration for the sequence; the sequence is then laid out as if it were a film strip but without the presence of distinct frames. The body in movement of the viewer from left to right (or the reverse if she pleases, as the registered space is circular) makes a sequence of the image, which itself rests immobile. Here it is not film that moves through the projector, but rather the viewer's body in movement that must animate the sequence.

There is also an affective discrepancy between the prosaic sounds from the set and the series of panoramic images, each of which suggests dramas, fictions, and emotions of varying intensities. Part of the uncanniness of the implied fictional world is the recognition that such clearly diverse characters and situations are occupying the same physical space. As Taylor-Wood relates, "I [also] think about those photographs as showing different states of being simultaneously—you have one person who's bored, a person sleeping, someone taking drugs, two people having sex—you have the embodiment of all these different states of being within one room. It's like encapsulating one person in one room but within eight different bodies, each one not communicating with the others."[24]

The idea of multiplying states of being is reproduced in the layering of sound with image. The reading time of the image and the hearing time of the sound express temporal divisions, both narrative and phenomenological. The acoustical time of the soundtrack is an indexical trace documenting an event with its own unique history, and this history is counterpoised with our desire to read a fiction into the sequence. Like an unfolding film strip, the soundtrack enfolds the spectator in a linear and irreversible duration. The sequence and staging of the image, however, express an ambiguous fictional time, a time of personal and imaginative reading spatialized or frozen in the present. Between image and sound, the present duration of reading is in tension with the past time of making; an indexical trace through sound and in time continually

24. Claire Carolin, "Interview with Sam Taylor-Wood," in *Sam Taylor-Wood* (Göttingen: Steidl, 2002).

rubs against the affective fictions suggested by the images. Between seeing and hearing, we occupy two temporalities and distinct narrative registers—that of fiction and that of the document. The image has frozen duration and is entirely present to us in space, yet requires us to restore time to it with a series of moving glances. The soundtrack unfolds as a temporal event with its own irreversible movement through time, and its presence in the space surrounding us cannot be avoided. While the acoustical (past time) envelops us as a continual presence and as ineluctable movement, we must restore time to the present image through physical movements and imaginative responses. History and fiction, film and photography, enter into a complex series of exchanges here—two states of becoming juxtaposing incompossible yet causally related worlds. The soundtrack acknowledges that the photograph documents a specific historical event occupying a unique duration, and each repetition of the soundtrack returns us to that historical moment. Yet the work as a whole propels us into movement, both physical and imaginative, that extracts differences from each repetition. In this Taylor-Wood is emblematic of a contemporary approach that makes of photography a new kind of movie. Here the image is an immobile sequence detached from the ineluctable temporality and spatial presence of sound. And from the same event, sound extracts history as the continual return to a unique moment in the past, and the image expresses fiction or emotion as an always new and unrepeatable experience in the present.

The display of the photographic image as a scroll that cannot be taken in at a glance is a way of restoring time and motion to the body in acts of viewing. The immobile viewer no longer receives a film, but rather animates a sequence of images as if to make the body itself a projector. Taylor-Wood's film and video work takes up these complex approaches to the body and duration while pushing them in new directions. One multiplies perspectives on the same event by disjoining the linear sequence of time in film or video into distinct spatial frames. The other seeks to register the moment of qualitative change in a given duration. In both cases, there is an emphasis on the event and unique duration, sometimes in a single frame or multiplied across several screens. The photographer's obsession with time has not changed, but her qualitative sensitivity to time has been transformed in two ways: either to occupy duration as a moment in the present (to register the unlocatable moment where a change takes place), or to split the present into multiple perspectives in or on time.

*Third Party* (1999, 16mm transferred to DVD, sound, 10 minutes) exemplifies the latter strategy. This installation is the logical outcome of Taylor-Wood's other multiple screen works such as *Killing Time* (1994, video, sound, 60 minutes), *Travesty of a Mockery* (1995, video, sound, 10 minutes), *Sustaining the Crisis* (1997, 16mm, sound, 8 minutes 55 seconds), or *Pent-up* (1996, 16mm, sound, 10 minutes 30 seconds). The last is exemplary of an ontology of monadism implicit in her work wherein the distinctiveness of separate framings and autonomous locations find themselves rejoined in a common duration. This installation involves five contiguous screens lined up on one wall. Each frame contains a single character in quite different and obviously geographically segregated environments: a woman walking down a London street in a reverse traveling shot; an elderly man sitting alone; a young man in a white interior; a young woman, alone, talking to herself at a bar; and a disturbed young man on the patio of a city flat. Each character speaks, but in a self-involved, agitated, and disturbed or slightly mad way, until the viewer begins to realize that they are engaged in a strange dialogue (or perhaps voicing seriatim the same monologue), responding to one another within and across their isolate framings.

*Third Party* follows a similar strategy though within a single diegetic location. The overall event involves a party staged on set using professional performers, among them Ray Winstone and Marianne Faithfull. The staged action lasts for ten minutes, the time of a single camera magazine. Like Jean Eustache in *Numéro zéro,* Taylor-Wood is concerned with recording continuous duration. But here the same event is filmed simultaneously and in sync from seven different perspectives, each with its own framing and scale. The installation is set in a rectangular room with a single entrance, and images are projected on all four walls. The seven perspectives are displayed in the following manner:

1. Entering the room, the viewer is confronted with a huge close-up of Marianne Faithfull that fills the wall opposite. On the right-hand side there are two projections.
2. On one end of a couch, we see a woman's torso minus the head, gesticulating in an animated manner.
3. Seated on the other end of the couch in a separate framing, the actor Ray Winstone looks on suspiciously . . .
4. . . . at the actress Saskia Reeves, projected opposite him on the left-hand wall. She is facing left and chatting flirtatiously with a young man in the image situated at a right angle to her.

5. This is the actor Adrian Dunbar, who addresses his eyeline to her left.
6. To the immediate left of Marianne Faithfull's image, a girl (Pauline Daly) dances to the party music.
7. Finally, between Reeves and Daily on the left-hand wall there is a table framed in close-up and projected at a smaller scale than the other images. The image frames an ashtray surrounded by beer cans and wine glasses. In the course of ten minutes, it fills to overflowing as glasses are raised and lowered.

All the camera positions are stationary except for position two, taken with a handheld camera that leaves and refinds Dunbar, sweeping the space and the other actors. Nor are the actors necessarily fixed in their frames; Winstone leaves his frame in position three to watch the dancing girl in position six.

The installation is not dissimilar in approach from Mike Figgis' *Time Code* (2000), except there is no linear narrative to follow and the parallel actions occur in the same diegetic space. Moreover, the relation of the viewer to space is different, requiring again a mobile and fragmented perspective sustained by a body moving in space. *Third Party* refers to cinema in its use of professional and recognizable actors, its studied mise-en-scène, and its implication of a narrative situation, but in a way that pulls the spectatorial situation of cinema inside out. *Time Code* requires the stilled spectator of the movie theater to perform the synthetic act of understanding four simultaneously occurring actions in a single frame. In *Third Party,* rather, it is as if the simultaneous actions are projected on a crystal with seven facets. Placed inside the crystal and free to move within it, viewers may combine frames in any order they please. On one hand, the images are displayed as a database from which multiple perspectives and sequences may be constructed and recombined; on the other, the sound that envelops us returns us through hearing to a linear if looped duration—the sequence repeats every ten minutes. This is another variation on an ontological monadism, in which each character is framed spatially as a separate world, even though each world communicates across a unique duration. And the viewer, occupying his or her own *durée* and unique point in space, must discover ways to recombine these fragmentary perspectives and construct a sense for them.

Taylor-Wood's single-channel works and her turn to 35mm film are emblematic of another interesting exchange between the photographic, the cinematic, and the electronic in contemporary art. Here Godard's choice to film in fine-grain black-and-white in 2003's *Eloge de l'amour* runs parallel to the renewed interest in celluloid in contemporary art practice. Just as DJ and mix culture created new conditions of existence and creation for vinyl in the 1980s and 1990s, in an era dominated by electronic and digital imaging, photography and 35mm film are finding new forms of life in the art gallery and museum. There is a lesson here for the virtual life of film. As celluloid disappears from contemporary theatrical cinema, it reemerges in new forms in the return to 35mm filming in certain kinds of art practices, and in the persistence of experimental filmmaking devoted to both 16mm and super-8 formats. Silver is becoming perceptually scarce, and 35mm film may be becoming an artisanal medium. Fabricated from a precious metal and installed in galleries and museums, where they are meant to be viewed in unique situations as autonomous artworks, films are regaining a sense of aura, and, finally, film is becoming Art. Yet art's potentially critical functions may still come into play as well. The turn to 35mm as art object, and art practice's complex investigations of the phenomenology of the viewing experience in moving-image media, could also express a countervailing desire—that is, the yearning for duration and uninterrupted time, for perceptual depth, and for a sensuous connection to physical reality in a universe dominated by simulation and information saturation.

Sharon Lockhart, the Dutch artists Jeroen de Rijk and Willem de Rooij, and Sam Taylor-Wood present three variations on this idea. Self-defined as a photographer and filmmaker, and showing experimental work in alternative theatrical settings, Lockhart occupies a genealogy running from structural film and Andy Warhol through James Benning, Yvonne Rainer, and Chantal Akerman. From *Goshogaoka* (1997), with its six ten-minute segments of highly choreographed actions by Japanese school-age basketball players, to her more recent *No* (2003), a static framing in three contiguous takes of two Japanese farmers who gradually pile and spread hay, moving from the background to the foreground of the image and back again, Lockhart demonstrates a fascination with the choreography of quotidian acts deployed in a continuous duration. In most respects, her practice eschews the digital in favor of orchestrating duration with respect to actual landscapes, architectures, and the actions of physical bodies deployed in time. As in my earlier account of Eustache's *Numéro zéro*, these films owe an obvious debt to Warhol's experiments with continuous duration and a commitment to celluloid's automatisms of analogical transcription.

Unlike Lockhart but like Taylor-Wood, de Rijke and de Rooij identify themselves as gallery-based artists rather than as experimental filmmakers. They share with Lockhart, however, a commitment to 16mm and 35mm film and a fascination with landscape and continuous duration whose minimalist formal rigor still owes much to structural film. To this date, they have also produced only single-screen works. Exemplary of this work are their films *Bantar Gebang* (2000, 35mm color with sound, 10 minutes) and *I'm Coming Home in Forty Days* (1997, 16mm color, 15 minutes). The latter consists of three shots as a ship circumnavigates an enormous iceberg floating in Greenland's Disko Bay. Lasting just over a minute, the first shot marks the transition from anchor to movement as the boat gets underway; the second shot is a long take lasting ten minutes. In one way, the work's main concern is to multiply signs of indexicality. For the whole of the film the image remains in precise focus throughout the presented depth of field. The frame line of the image bobs gently, giving evidence of the boat's own rocking motion, and the image promotes a deep perceptual immersion attentive to subtle changes in the quality of light, the movements of water, and the mobility of the frame itself, revealing small and unpredictable events emerging from and disappearing to offscreen space. The form, color, and light quality of iceberg, water, and sky shift constantly with the changing perspectives of movement. The seascape produces its own photographic drama of light playing against water, icebergs, and sky, whose contours in the image are gradually lost and refound. The film registers as well changes of state too slow for the eye to perceive—processes of freeze and thaw in which water becomes mass and ice returns to water. In the final shot, lasting about two minutes, this romantic and contemplative landscape suddenly gives way to an abstract image: a translucent green color field. In a first viewing, the spectator is unsure where the camera has gone or what it "represents" after the flow of starkly beautiful natural images. But this, too, is an indexical image rendered in clear focus: the camera has plunged under water.

In some respects *Bantar Gebang* is a simpler, more minimalist film, yet its effects are complex. Here the image registers—through qualitative changes in the brightness and quality of light and in a long shot of people and animals awakening and moving—a transition in time: the shift from dawn to daybreak expressed as a single ten-minute take with a fixed frame. Again, the film immerses us deeply in all the rich sonic and visual details expressive of a transition in time given as a unique duration; but here the scene is very different. For Bantar Gebang is the name of an impoverished shantytown constructed on a trash dump outside Jakarta. It is among the few living sites available for poor inhabitants displaced by inner-city development. The frame captures a perception caught in a temporal paradox: giving us an image of change of great sensual beauty, it also registers an environment where little historical change takes place beyond the repetitive daily struggle for survival.

In contrast to Lockhart's work, these films are closer to a documentary approach. Although they present carefully chosen images framed in dramatically compelling ways, they are observational in tone and little alter the recorded sites. One might think of them in the best sense as moving photography—they produce aesthetic effects from the registration of a unique event occurring in time. Indeed, the central concern of these films is to focalize, enhance, and deepen our sense of a perception occupying a unique duration. This goal is emphasized through de Rijke's and de Rooij's insistence on strictly controlling the viewing spaces of their moving-image works. These works are meant to be installed in museums or galleries rather than shown in theaters; the exhibition spaces are designed and constructed as minimalist sculptures and are meant to be experienced as artworks in their own right. Often they are simple white rooms with benches, the projection booth is soundproofed, and the walls are dimly lit so that the size and dimensions of the space remain visible. The rooms are spare and functional. They are meant to contain and separate the viewing experience from all external distractions and to focus perception on the event of the screening itself. The films are not looped. Projections have clear beginnings and endings scheduled at regular intervals, indicated at the entrance to the rooms. These are less exhibition spaces than sculptural time boxes—they are containers for constraining and focusing the perception of time as a spatial experience. In this way, the design of the rooms performs a sort of phenomenological bracketing wherein spectators are meant to immerse themselves in the experience of duration given in the films.

Each of these artists is concerned in a different way with restoring an expanded sense of duration to contemporary aesthetic experience. In shaping and controlling the entire experience of projection and viewing, de Rijke and de Rooij seek an intensive experience of duration—that each viewer shall encounter the same duration in the same space. Alternatively, Taylor-Wood's installations explore the mobility of a body that must make its own sense of the fragments or facets offered to it. Asking that each viewer makes of duration a unique experience, this is a differential expression of duration. However, this experience is not uniquely attached to the idea of film as a medium. In Taylor-Wood's work, the decision to work in 16mm or 35mm seems a reasoned choice but not a commitment. Very often, her works shot on celluloid are displayed on laserdisc or DVD; sometimes, as with her dance film, *16 mm* (1993), the presence and sound of the projector in the gallery are an essential feature of the work. Clearly, the choice of film as a creative medium is not a commitment to celluloid projection as a viewing medium. Indeed, as I have explained above, Taylor-Wood works *entre-images,* creating media from automatisms inspired by the translation or transposition of one spatial and temporal material into or onto another, setting up systems of exchange between photography, film, video, and electronic display. Indeed, only electronic displays—DVD and video projection—provide the necessary control and synchronization of serialized and fragmented segments of duration that are so much a part of her multiple-channel work.

Alternatively, whereas Lockhart or de Rijke and de Rooij explore duration as an external perception in the physical space of landscapes and bodies, Taylor-Wood's single-channel works echo her photographic images in their obsession with the surface perception of qualitative changes of state that are either indiscernible or interior and invisible. The 35mm film *Pietà* (2001, 1 minute 57 seconds) exemplifies one simple strategy. Seated on a row of steps, Taylor-Wood struggles to cradle the actor Robert Downey Jr. in the well-known religious pose of spiritual support. But here we are concerned with the real physical weight of the actor's body and with the incapacity of Taylor-Wood to sustain that body for more than a short time. The mark of the film's time and the extent of its duration are the measure of Taylor-Wood's ability to hold Downey up while recording the moment of change when she collapses under his weight. An earlier work, *Noli Me Tangere* (1998, 16mm, sound, 3 minutes 50 seconds), also expresses duration as framed by the body's capacity, and incapacity, to resist gravity. Installed in a gallery, the images present a man filmed front and back simultaneously who seems to struggle to hold his arms upright. Only at the end of the work, when the man collapses upward, do we realize that the image displays an acrobat in a handstand turned 180 degrees.

Still more compelling are the works in which an external perception of duration is meant to express otherwise invisible and internal changes of state—explicitly, qualitative emotional changes—as they are displayed across the body. *Hysteria* (1997, 16mm, silent, 8 minutes) documents changes or shifts in extreme emotional states in a single eight-minute take. Structurally similar to her more recent and misunderstood *Crying Men* series of photographs, in this work a professional actress and friend was asked to work from the memory of a recent bereavement. The work is about qualitative changes in emotional states, of the indiscernibility between laughing and crying, of movement from one to another in a pendulum whose shifts in direction are unpredictable though registerable on the screen in their states of becoming. One does not feel this work to be exploitative, nor is it concerned with the trained body's capacity to emulate emotion. The lack of sound is important, providing a certain distance and restraint. What we experience here, in a duration analogous to the "performance," is the return of memory and emotion as a physical experience, the body becoming itself a photograph or index registering in time the manifestation of past experience.

*Breach* (2001, 35mm, silent, 10 minutes 30 seconds) follows a similar strategy. Again the film is silent, with a static framing in one long take. In rehearsal, the actress was asked to endure a series of insults hurled at her from a person offscreen. In the finished film, we witness in silence the actress' distressed reaction to these insults as a memory of the immediate past, a memory that returns to the body as a cycle of change from a complete breakdown to reassertion of self, a transformative series of becomings from weakness and defenselessness to strength and self-repossession. That both films are without sound is important. In this way attention is refocused on often subtle physical changes in series. Memory and the past return to the body as physical waves of emotion that rise up from an interiority that can be perceived in the other only from an exterior state of silence. What links most of Taylor-Wood's screen works, whether still or moving, is a concept close to Stanley Cavell's characterization of the filmic or photographic image as "somatograms" that register thought and emotion as surface manifestations of interior movements erupting across the body in ways as subtle as they are violent. These somatogrammatic images register the powers of intensive or expressive duration "as the camera's knowledge of the metaphysical restlessness of the live body at rest."[25] This is what photography calls thinking.

It is curious that Taylor-Wood more often than not presents this work on video or DVD, yet insists that it be made in 16mm or 35mm film. And despite variations in approach and practice, one finds in all four artists the will to restore duration and becoming to our phenomenological experience of works of art. For these and other contemporary artists, film—with its automatisms of analogical causation, succession, and projection—seems to have the unique capacity to register and examine change with real phenomenological depth, and to sustain this image of change for us in new and innovative ways. All four artists depart from and reconstitute these automatisms in significant, creative ways. Yet all derive their powers of creation from what Gilles Deleuze has called the concept of the "dividual." The turn to film and the persistence of celluloid are valued here not only for their spatial conveyance of an experience

25. "What Photography Calls Thinking," in *Cavell on Film* 126.

of duration, but also for their ability to register changes in physical and emotional states in sequences of infinitesimally small and indivisible differences emerging from an arc of continuous change or qualitative becoming. As digital capture, with its own particular capacities for creation and communication, makes photography more and more like information, and as our experience of filmic duration disappears from theatrical movie houses, film reappears in the art gallery and museum, seeking out a new virtual life.

## 21. The Digital Event

> If the replacement of the analog by the digital isn't a matter of time anymore, time is still at the heart of the difference between the two.
>
> —Babette Mangolte, "Afterward: A Matter of Time"

No doubt, the prevalence of DVDs on home cinemas and computer screens has changed our understanding of the cinematic image and what it will become in this century. We still enjoy the immersive experience of movie watching, yet the ability to control the image interactively and to access contextual information in DVD databases is also valued. The DVD is a new historical form for cinema in more than one sense. Even so, as long as celluloid projection is still common in movie theaters (and it will already have become less so by the time this book reaches print), some final conjectures on what the cinematic image has and will become may be useful here.

In an engaging and provocative essay written in honor of Annette Michelson, "Afterward: A Matter of Time," the cinematographer and experimental film/videomaker Babette Mangolte asks one of the most compelling questions I have read in the last ten years: "Why is it difficult for the digital image to communicate duration?" "Why," she elaborates, "is the brightness of the LCD screen, the relentless glare of the digital image with no shutter reprieve, no back and forth between one forty-eighth of a second of dark followed by one forty-eighth of projected image, with no repetitive pattern as regular as your own heartbeat, unable to establish and construct an experiential sense of time passing? And why could the projected film image do it so effortlessly in the past and still can?"[26] In many senses, this is the question around which all the arguments of this book turn. Perhaps it is more appropriate for work that

26. In *Camera Obscura, Camera Lucida: Essays in Honor of Annette Michelson*, ed. Richard Allen and Malcolm Turvey (Amsterdam: University of Amsterdam Press, 2002) 263.

originates on digital video, or even for our experience of home viewing on digital screens today. Yet, as film disappears into an aesthetic universe constructed from digital intermediates and images combining computer synthesis and capture, and while I continue to feel engaged by many contemporary movies, I still have a deep sense, which is very hard to describe or qualify, of time lost. Ironically, since in 2007 most commercial films are still released to theaters on projected celluloid, reprinting to an analogical support seems not to be able to return to digital movies the experience of watching film.

On the very evening in 2003 when I saw Jean Eustache's *Numéro zéro* for the first time, I had the always-pleasurable experience of dining with my friend the artist and theorist Victor Burgin. In trying to come to grips with my undoubtedly overheated enthusiasm for this film, Burgin interrupted me with the quip: "Why didn't he just shoot on video?" As Sony PortaPak technology was becoming available at the time of the film's making, this teasing question was no doubt a valid one. I have tried, more or less to my satisfaction, to respond to Burgin's question in the conclusion to Part II. In the meantime, another aesthetic challenge was raised to my intuitions concerning time, duration, and the film image—Alexandr Sokurov's 2002 work, *Russian Ark.* Like *Numéro zéro, Russian Ark* is a work inspired by reflection on the problems of history and time's passing, as well as the utopia of recording continuous duration. This work finds deep inspiration in the aesthetic qualities of film; it is meant to be a sort of time capsule for Russian history, culture, and art analogous to the senses of history embedded in the Hermitage collections and the architecture of the Winter Palace. Shooting in continuous duration is meant to highlight this examination of Russia's past as a nonchronological exploration of historical memory conveyed by the wanderings of the cultured French intellectual, based on the life of the Marquis de Custine, and the invisible witness of Sokurov's "speaking" camera. In these senses, Sokurov's movie is an astonishing accomplishment and a work I find deeply interesting. However, whether viewed projected in a theater or watched at home on a high-definition screen, it does not involve me in time. This experience became less perplexing to me when I realized that Babette Mangolte had asked the question, a question posed to me by my viewings of *Russian Ark* but which I was not able to articulate precisely: "Why is it difficult for the digital image to communicate duration?"

In this particular respect, *Russian Ark* is for me a failed film, though in many other respects it may be an eminently successful work of digital cinema. Wishing to record continuous duration, and unable to overcome the physical limitations of the conventional 35mm film magazine's inability to hold more than twenty-two minutes of raw footage, or even of portable high-definition video cameras to record for more than forty-six minutes, Sokurov and his talented cinematographer, Tilman Büttner, adopted the novel solution of recording an uncompressed high-definition signal directly to hard disk. Lasting eighty-six minutes, the raw material thus obtained is a tour de force of mise-en-scène and Steadicam framing. Nevertheless, the difficulty of this work for me, and for many instances of digital cinema, is that Sokurov and Büttner accept at face value Burgin's ironic suggestion while ignoring that the assumptions of perceptual realism are indeed paradoxical. *Russian Ark* is a movie that places its bets on the spatial equivalency of photography and high-definition digital video. In so doing, it places in perspective their difference in time.

There is, then, a contradiction in *Russian Ark*'s conception. The movie is mistakenly characterized as an uninterrupted sequence of eighty-six minutes' duration, nor is it a "film" in any conventional sense of the term. I express no aesthetic prejudice in saying this. Rather, to explain why the movie cannot be considered one long take or a single shot goes a long way toward explaining how digital cinema transforms both of these concepts. The key to resolving the discrepancy between *Russian Ark*'s self-presentation and its ontological expression as digital cinema is to understand that it is a *montage* work, no less complex in this respect than Sergei Eisenstein's 1927 film *October*.

Recorded on 23 December 2001 after three false starts, *Russian Ark* is a work captured in one go, as it were. And in watching the "making-of" featurette included with the DVD, titled *Film in One Breath*, it is fascinating to observe the epic orchestrations of mise-en-scène required to record this movie. However, what strikes me most is the comment of the movie's producer, Jens Meurer, that the finished work includes more than 30,000 "digital events." Indeed, comprehending the nature of the digital event is central to understanding what is or will become digital cinema.

In what does the digital event consist? Digital capture, synthesis, and compositing are the three principal creative operations of digital cinema. Digital capture may be considered as analogous to video recording in a number of ways. Yet, even here the image is not "one," for light recorded on charge-coupled devices is already fragmented into a discrete mosaic of picture elements, which are then read off as distinct mathematical values. The process of conversion or transcoding separates the image into mathematically discrete and modular elements whose individual values are open to any number of programmable transformations. The separation of outputs from inputs, and the process of calculation converting light into code, unravel the unity of the profilmic spatial event unfolding in a unique duration. As befits the mathematical basis of information processing, the digital event corresponds less to the duration and movements of the world than to the control and variation of discrete numerical elements internal to the computer's memory and logical processes.

Several aesthetic conclusions may be drawn from this abstract, technological description. First, as constituted through digital capture or synthesis, the image is always "montage," in the sense of a singular combination of discrete elements. Even an unaltered digital still is already a work of montage in this respect. Second, as I have already related, digital conversion is a one-way street: the output from digital capture can write movement back into the image, but it cannot restore duration to a projected film, for the continuity of automatic analogical causation is broken. Here an answer already begins to appear for Mangolte's provocative and astute question. Because the spatial unity of the image in time can no longer be assured or attested to by the digital image, and because the powers of indexicality are weakened and decentered by the process of digital conversion, the expression of duration is transformed—it becomes other to the powers of film and calls for a new medium. These are not lesser powers, but they do differ significantly from film's conveyance of past time. We no longer seek to overcome our temporal alienation from the past in digital cinema, first because the causal chain of analogy is broken, and second because the electronic screen expresses another ontology, which I have characterized as an increased attention to the present and to the control of information. This is one fundamental way in which *Numéro zéro* is of a different species than *Russian Ark*. *Numéro zéro* is composed of a continuous alternation of ten-minute takes in about eleven shots (not counting its prologue). Alternatively, there may be "takes" in digital cinema, but there are no shots. Or rather, what was previously considered a shot has now become a highly variable element open to interactive manipulation at the most discrete levels. In this respect, cinema has become more like language than image, with discrete and definable minimal units (pixels) open to transformations of value and syntactic recombination.[27]

27. Manovich proposes a provocative formula, which puts the case in an interesting way: "Digital film = $f(x, y, t)$ . . . Since a computer breaks down every frame into pixels, a complete film can be defined as a function that, given the horizontal, vertical, and time location of each pixel, returns its color. This is exactly how a computer represents a film . . . For a computer, a film is an abstract arrangement of colors changing in time, rather than something structured by 'shots,' 'narrative,' 'actors,' and so on"; *Language of New Media* 302.

In its numerical basis, digitally acquired information has no ontological distinctiveness from digitally synthesized outputs that construct virtual worlds mathematically through the manipulation of a Cartesian coordinate space. In turn, this is why compositing—the combination of captured and synthesized elements—is such a powerful creative option for fabricating imaginary worlds. In terms of digital operations or automatisms, compositing refers to a process wherein a number of different digitized elements, whether captured, synthesized, or applied as algorithmic filters, are assembled from a variety of sources and combined ideally into a perceptually seamless artifact. Selection of elements and their compositing is often an interactive process, which is in principle open-ended (practically infinite manipulability). A digital event, then, is any discrete alteration of image or sound data at whatever scale internal to the image. Elements may be added, subtracted, or refashioned interactively because the data components retain their separate, modular identities throughout the "editing" process.

Compositing, and the automatisms that can be created from it, then, best characterize the digital event in its difference from the shot. A telling example is presented in the section of the *Russian Ark* that takes place in 1943 during the 900-day siege of Stalingrad. Against the advice of the invisible witness, the Marquis enters a mysterious room, passing from the First World War to the Second, where he will find, according to the character present, only coffins and corpses. (The character is meant to represent the director of the Hermitage during the Second World War.) Empty picture frames are piled willy-nilly against both walls as the worker fashions his own casket. The formerly bright colors of the Winter Palace have gone dark here, taking on the bluish cast of night. It is winter; a window is broken, and snow falls gently through the air and onto the floor.

The featurette helpfully presents this scene both in the form of the raw, captured image and in its completed state after it was worked over in post-production. One sees clearly in comparison the addition and subtraction of a number of discrete elements: a color filter has been applied; implied lighting elements have been changed; both the hole in the window and the falling snow have been laid in digitally; even a perspective algorithm has been invoked to change the relatively normal view to wide angle, thus distorting space expressionistically. In a sense, this is what Eisenstein would have considered as dividing the shot into a "montage cell," though without Eisenstein's insistence on the presence of contrasting or opposed compositional elements to bring forward differences in perceptual and semantic value. Indeed, the style of most digital compositing is to suppress this difference in the apparent spatial

Raw data from *Russian Ark* (Egoli Tossell Film and Hermitage Bridge Studio, 2002).

Frame enlargement from *Russian Ark*.s

unity of the constructed image. Still, the "Casualties of War" section of *Russian Ark* illustrates well how the separability of image components into discrete layers brings something fundamentally new to digital images: the possibility of what Manovich calls "spatial" montage. This is neither vertical nor horizontal montage in Eisenstein's senses of the term, but rather something like a palimpsestic combination of data layers. The concept is hard to comprehend because in fact these combinations are not spatial at all in the ordinary sense of the term. Rather, they are applications or transformations of discrete mathematical values through different kinds of operations. One tends to think of compositing by analogy with cell animation: one overlays a blue cell to transform color, or a cell transparent but for the effect of falling snow to add this element. Fundamentally, however, what makes compositing possible is that the separate layers are not spatial wholes but numerically defined values. *All* compositional elements are discrete in a composite and, given the proper algorithm, can be changed or reversed at will: colors, angles, perspectives, positions of objects, and so on. With respect to a visual image, space has changed meaning here. Space no longer has continuity and duration; rather, any definable quality of the defined space is discrete and variable. What is combined in "montage" is no longer just contiguous spatial wholes as blocks of duration, for any definable parameter of the image can be altered with respect to value and position. Nor must the combined elements be recorded from preexisting artifacts (matte paintings, for example). Captured and synthesized elements are as easily composited as any others.

Compositing is certainly anticipated in matte shots and other forms of combination printing in film, as well as in chromakey video processes, but it is also important to note significant differences. Combination prints are assembled from analogical components, meaning each component is a discrete spatial whole whose individual elements are inseparable from that whole. This is really a case of combining two separate shots, but in space rather than in time. What differentiates digital compositing is the discreteness of the information manipulated, the separability of elements into discrete layers, and the modular organization of the artifact on different scales. Digital synthesis produces an image of what never occurred in reality; it is a fully imaginative and intentional artifact. Optical printing and chromakeying combine elements recorded from physical spaces and join them through an effect of spatial montage—an imaginative and intentional effect created from causal elements, as it were. Compositing combines the two, but in a way that produces something ontologically strange or curious. What appears to be photographic, and therefore causal, is simulated and therefore intentional. We are perceptually convinced of the apparent spatial unity and coherence of discrete digital events so combined because the causal and analogical world of profilmic space has been pulled into the universe of numbers. Composited outputs appear "seamless" or perceptually real because all the elements now belong to the same ontological order—that of symbolization and its openness to intentional acts. What looks photographically "real" has actually shed its indexical or causal qualities. Our previous perceptual criteria for realism have now ceded fully to imagination, fantasy, and the counterfactual powers of possible worlds. When photography becomes simulation, it yields to a new imaginary that is unconstrained by causal processes; creation from physical reality gives way to the composition of "elastic" reality.

Despite the intrinsic separability of image components and the potential for controlling an infinite number of layers with respect to any of their variables or values, under the pressure of perceptual realism the predominant aesthetic of compositing stresses smoothness, continuity, and seamless boundaries between combined elements. In ordinary practice, the automatism of compositing has thus produced three distinct aesthetic criteria: *invisibility of layers* (and thus the apparent uniformity of space, or space defined as the seeming unity of all its contents or elements); *continuity of movements* (or the sense of movement as smoothly obeying the physical laws of natural space); and the *devaluation of filmic editing*. Elaborating the last criterion sheds light on all the others. Analog "shots" define discrete spatial wholes, and thus film editing entails combination of those wholes. Time in film is expressed not only by the duration of the shot, but also in associations of shots that may imply continuity, ellipsis, simultaneous and parallel actions, or displacement toward the past or the future. As a spatial record of duration, the history of film has demonstrated a constant fascination for the *durée* as lived time, both physical and psychological, and has developed a rich variety of automatisms for expressing that experience. We are used to conceiving images as uniform extensions in space. Where film editing may be characterized as the addition of spatially discrete wholes (shots; automatism of succession), the modularity and discreteness of the numerical image allow it to be separated into or combined with a potentially infinite number of digital events that can be manipulated in a great variety of ways. Having not yet forgotten that "photorealistic" digital images may have had no past relation to a physical space and thus are no longer bound by physical causal processes, we continue to be surprised and disturbed by perceptually convincing viewpoints unanchored by gravity and by spaces that appear to morph, disassemble, and recreate themselves according to an astounding variety of parameters. Alternatively, and as exemplified in first-person gaming, movement in the digital image is best characterized by a single continuous trajectory through an apparently three-dimensional space. Film editing is a logical consequence of the automatisms of analogical transcription, which lend themselves to producing discrete spatial wholes. But once converted to numerical form, the digital image, whether captured or synthesized, may vary in any of its parameters. Logically, it does not suggest or require the necessity of "cuts" as discrete sections of space and duration. And so, from the perspective of a filmic culture, one of the most unnerving and often thrilling aspects of digital space is the sense of controlled, continuous, and open-ended movement. Cuts or breaks in duration are not anticipated because they are not necessary; the management of duration comes from interactive relations with remote controls and screens, not from "editing."

And here is another strange effect of the curious ontology of digital worlds, at least from the perspective of a filmic perception: movement through virtual space is badly characterized as a mobile frame, for it is not a record of movement through physical space, but a synthesis of motion perspective according to the criteria of perceptual realism. Indeed nothing *moves,* nothing endures in a digitally composed world. The impression of movement is really just an impression—the numerical rotation and transformation of geometrical elements. Here the sense of time as *la durée* gives way to simple duration or to the "real time" of a continuous present. The real-time interactivity of first-person games is also linear and teleological; it is ends-directed, pragmatic, and marked by the continuity of elapsed time in the quantitative measures of points accumulated, prizes won, and levels superseded. (Games like *Myst* present the possibility of a different kind of immersion in digital time, one characterized more by memory and thoughtfulness as well as by movements whose objectives are more oblique and less time delimited.) Moreover, the first-person perspective of gaming, and the way it holds the user in present time, differ qualitatively from similar effects in film. For example, typically a subjective traveling shot in film is one kind of long take, but not characteristic of the mobile frame itself. It lends itself to the multiplication of points of view and, through the camera, enjoins the spectator to partake of a multiplicity of perspectives through mobile viewpoint. Alternatively, perceptual immersion in virtual worlds amplifies a certain form of skepticism. Indeed, it produces a form of monadism in which there is no present other than mine, the one I occupy now; there is no presence other than myself.

It is striking that the logic of continuity (of space, in space, and through space) should so dominate the aesthetics of compositing and the combination of digital events. As I have already suggested, while maintaining the first-person emphasis of most computer gaming, the virtual world created by the makers of *Myst* and its follow-ups stresses more the separateness and hybridity of combined elements. No doubt, this is still a strategy of immersion motivated by the implied narrative's concern with dimensions, frontiers, and parallel worlds. Indeed, a striking difference between *Myst* and action games is that it *has* a narrative that is both spatially elaborate and temporally complex. Solving its puzzles interactively is the user's route through that narrative. In contrast to *Russian Ark,* one might consider a work like Eric Rohmer's *L'Anglaise et le duc* (2001). Here strategies of compositing are directed toward an aesthetic of the "separability of elements," not necessarily in the Brechtian sense, but rather as a meditation on history in general, as well as the specific history of digital cinema and the virtual image in their long and complex genealogies with earlier versions of reproducible images and perspectival techniques. In this movie, we are drawn into a fascination for interpreting history as a retroactive reading of documents that maintain their pictorial and literary integrity and opaqueness, as the viewer is made aware of the origins of the work in Grace Elliot's memoir of the French Revolution, and of the compositing of actors with paintings and other visual artifacts fashioned in the style of eighteenth-century France.

But to return to my main point; in so closely following the criteria of perceptual realism, the automatisms created from the technology of compositing have created their own continuity aesthetics parallel to or inspired by the continuity strategies of Hollywood filmmaking—with the exception, of course, that this is no longer predominantly a strategy of editing and of combining discrete spatial elements recorded only from physical spaces. Undoubtedly, the most paradoxical conclusion to be drawn from the example of compositing is twofold. On one hand, the filmic conception of the shot as a "block of duration," or as a spatially whole and irreducible element of filmic expression, has been significantly challenged. In digital cinema, the image is always "code," that is, a combination of logically discrete elements completely open and available to changes in value, both perceptual and semantic. On the other, in digital cinema there is no longer continuity in space and movement, but only montage or combination.[28] For these reasons, in digital cinema postproduction becomes more important than production, that is, shooting on a physical set. As Manovich correctly explains, the distinction between creation and modification is no longer relevant as it was for photography and film. Production becomes just the first step in postproduction: "reordering sequences in time, compositing them together in space, modifying parts of an individual image, and changing individual pixels become the same operation, conceptually and practically" (*Language of New Media* 301).

*Russian Ark* is a movie that embodies these paradoxes on many levels, though not in ways that the work is often willing to acknowledge. The time and space given in the image are less an expression of the long take and continuity in movement than a complex example of creative acts of compositing and "spatial" montage whose aesthetic relies on the modularity and variability of the digital image. The movie cannot be considered a single long take because it is a highly composited artifact and therefore not spatially uniform. What it gives us in eighty-six minutes is not a "shot" as ordinarily conceived, though Sokurov and his camera operator may think so. (In this respect, I am continually struck by students' responses to the work, which apprehend its spectatorial experience as something more akin to that of firstperson gaming, or of a CD-ROM museum visit, as the experience of moving room to room along a continuous visual trajectory.) What the digital event signifies here is that, ironically, *Russian Ark* is a "montage" film as are all expressions of digital cinema. But here montage is no longer an expression of time and duration; it is rather a manipulation of the layers of the modularized image subject to a variety of algorithmic transformations. This is what I call the digital event. While marketed as a heroic feat of recording in a physical location, the movie is better characterized, like most digital cinema, as an aesthetic of postproduction, highly subject to computational processes and the imagina-

28. This is, of course, a complete reversal of Manovich's own conclusion, where he states: "In computer culture, montage is no longer the dominant aesthetic, as it was throughout the twentieth century, from the avant-garde of the 1920s up until the postmodernism of the 1980s. Digital compositing, in which different spaces are combined into a single seamless virtual space, is a good example of the alternative aesthetics of continuity; moreover, compositing in general can be understood as a counterpart to montage aesthetics. Montage aims to create visual, stylistic, semantic, and emotional dissonance between different elements. In contrast, compositing aims to blend them into a single whole, a single gestalt" (*Language of New Media* 144). Manovich is using montage in the limited sense of the editing style of Soviet cinema's golden age. I invoke the term in the more general sense of editing or combination of elements.

tive intentions of its authors. Indeed the recording strategy of the movie and its accomplishment are almost unthinkable without the corrections and additions of setting, lighting, perspective, and other compositional elements made possible through techniques of digital postproduction.

## 22. Transcoded Ontologies, or "A Guess at the Riddle"

> Everyone can see the future, but no one remembers the past.
>
> —Alexandr Sokurov, *Russian Ark*

While I do find it difficult to overcome my nostalgia for the analogical world (and it is in the nature of analogical worlds to provoke a yearning for the past), I mean to make no judgments against the cosmogony of computers, nor do I wish to imply that analogical images and sounds are better or worse than digitally produced or altered works. Rather, it is important to understand that digital information expresses another will to power in relation to the world. This will is neither better nor inferior, but it is different both in its values and in its modalities of expression. No doubt, it attenuates or even blocks an earlier photographic relation to past worlds, for the digital will wants to change the world, to make it yield to other forms, or to create different worlds. Before the digital screen, we do not feel a powerlessness, but rather express a will to control information and to shape ourselves and the world through the medium of information. This is also a will to measure the world and communication, or to take measure of it, and so to manage it according to mathematical means.

The most difficult question, then, relates to the ethics of computational interactions; that is, evaluating our contemporary mode of existence and addressing how our ontology has changed in our interactions with computer screens. What epistemological and ethical relations to the world and to collective life do simulation automatisms presuppose?

To respond fully to these questions is the task of another book than this one, which I, as a *cinéfils*, may not be capable of writing. Yet, perhaps a guess at the riddle is possible. This may involve a retreat from the sensuous exploration of the physical world and the material structure of everyday life to probe imaginative life and a new kind of sociality. In this way, the retreat from physical reality is balanced against the potential for, as Pierre Lévy describes it, a global "collective intelligence."[29] Emerging from a filmic ontology, new relations with space and with time are developing that involve expectations of interactivity and control. (Children at the movies these days want to pause, rewind, or alter the volume of sound—it is unthinkable that they should relinquish their desire to control time before the screen.) As a screen technology, this is not an overcoming of skepticism, but a different expression of it. In the world of computers and the Internet, we have little doubt about the presence of other minds and, perhaps, other worlds. And we believe, justifiably or not, in confidence or anxiety, in our ability to control, manage, or communicate with other minds and worlds, but at a price: matter and minds have become "information." In this sense, the cultural dominance of the digital may indicate a philosophical retreat from the problem of skepticism to an acceptance of skepticism. For in the highly mutable communities forged by computer-mediated communications, the desire to know the world has lost its provocation and its uncertainty. Rather, one seeks new ways of acknowledging other minds, without knowing whether other selves are behind them.

The digital "image," to the extent that it is one, also partakes of this ontology. Forged in the logic of information, the ethics of perceptual realism is based on a vision of a world that is entirely mathematical in nature; or rather, it is a nature that is mathematical before it is or could be imagined as physical. And if we feel duration less in the numerical image, this may be because through symbolic expressions we want to control time—not to preserve an image against the flow of time, as in photography, but rather to overcome time and to have dominance over it. We do not seek an experience of duration in such expressions, especially one in which world and being are recalled to a common duration. Rather, we seek to manage time in relation to information and as information.

This is why a new philosophical perspective is required for these kinds of images, if they can still be called such. In a book devoted to the image and to the future of cinema, it bears repeating that information displaces image as the *potentia* of this ontology while forming the basis of its new automatisms, spiritual or otherwise. In a world defined by the heady accumulation of information, the will to access and control this world from behind interactive screens defines the desire of the new ontology. Manovich characterizes this will as a "database complex"—the irrational desire to preserve and store ev-

29. *Collective Intelligence: Mankind's Emerging World in Cyberspace*, trans. Robert Bononno (New York: Perseus Books Group, 1997).

erything on computers—but this definition jars with experience. "[The] subject of the information society," he writes, "finds peace in the knowledge that she can slide over endless fields of data, locating any morsel of information with the click of a button, zooming through file systems and networks. She is comforted not by an equilibrium of space and colors, but by the variety of data manipulation operations at her control" (*Language of New Media* 274–275). I find it odd that Manovich would characterize this process as one of finding peace or comfort. For me, it expresses a profound intensification of time and of time's immediate passing. This is, rather, a deep immersion in the present where one struggles to control both the amount of information one receives and knowledge of how to sort, store, and retrieve it properly; and one is always in a hurry.

Alternatively, comfort might be taken from the apparent inability of digitally synthesized images to become fully indistinguishable from photographic or cinematographic ones. But this attitude also blinds us to the temporality of digital screens and the ontological questioning they do provoke. In this respect, synthetic imagery is neither an inferior representation of physical reality nor a failed replacement for the photographic, but rather a fully coherent expression of a different reality, in fact, a new ontology, which Manovich describes as "a world reduced to geometry, where efficient representation via a geometric model becomes the basis of reality" (*Language of New Media* 202–203). The temporal character of this "efficiency" is important. Whereas the photograph catches us up in the recurrent presence of a past event and a future that will already have happened, and the electronic screen sustains us in an expansive present, synthetic or digital expressions always have an air of science fiction about them. They anticipate a future world that has already emerged in the present, and which we confront with exhilaration or anxiety. We recognize the perceptual power of photography and film retroactively as a disappearing or vanished world; we are drawn to digital and interactive screens as a will to grasp a future that is always running ahead of us and pulling us forward in its slipstream. Our disappointment in failing ever to know the world or others now becomes the perpetual disappointment of failing to attain the more nearly perfect (future) knowledge of computers and computer communications, whose technological evolution always seems to run ahead of the perceptual and cognitive capacity to manipulate them for our own ends. It is the failure to arrive at what always comes ahead.

It may well be that the photographic persists in the digital as a way of managing the force of this future shock. The image of photography persists in digital capture, and the idea of cinema persists in the term "digital cinema," as a way of easing the transition to a different world, now both here and yet to come, whose mode of existence is difficult to evaluate, much less envision. In a telling anecdote recounted in *The Language of New Media,* Manovich relates that the problem of designing computer-generated imagery for *Jurassic Park* lay not in achieving the resolution of 35mm film, but rather in strategically degrading the image to give it an "analog" appearance—in other words, in making the future image conform to our expectations of a more historically familiar practice. Spielberg's dinosaurs were the paradoxical expression of a future that had already arrived and overtaken us; we saw ourselves there as *revenants* from the past. As computer-generated images, these dinosaurs were models for a new mathematical perfection in imagery, as well as the product of a more-than-perfect computer vision. Free of the limitations of both human and camera vision, computers are capable of producing images with potentially unlimited resolution, detail, and depth of field that are free of grain or noise of any kind, and rendered with intense color saturation, sharp edges, and perfect geometric forms. The lesson of *Jurassic Park* is that we still find such images uncanny, "unnatural" or "inhuman." To appear to be "perceptually realistic," that is, to conform to the standards of realism established by photographic images, synthetic images must, ironically, be degraded to appear more noisy and analog. In other words, "reality" is still recognized only in its photographic appearance, and we are barely prepared for the new ontological situation emerging within composited images. Thus, a final paradox of perceptual realism, of creating digital images in the form of photography or cinematography, is expressed as a will to retard the future or to slow the velocity of its becoming.

The cosmogony of the computer draws us into its world through the shifting status of image and screen. The modularity, incompleteness, and mutability of the digital electronic image, as well as its inseparability from an interactive screen, are equally expressive of this temporal state that draws us toward the future rather than engaging us with the past. Here the spectator is no longer a passive viewer yielding to the ineluctable flow of time, but rather alternates between looking and reading as well as immersive viewing and active controlling. In daily practice, these are undoubtedly overlapping states of being—the viewer becoming user and user becoming viewer, with the transition between the two being indiscernible. The "super-vision" of synthetic images is complemented by the "control vision" of interactive screens. Computer gaming thus accelerates and amplifies a potential that already lies within the more simple screens and interfaces of video and DVD watching. Vision becomes an activity that is always anticipating menus of possible actions that must be responded to in split-second decisions. This is another way in which the immediate present becomes oriented to an already emerging future. Our relationship to the screen is to anticipate future events to which we must respond, and our corresponding action produces effects that generate the possibility of new future events, all within a highly condensed time frame. (What enemy lies around the next corner? Do I have email or am I hailed for a chat? And so on.)

In this respect, our mental attitude toward computers recapitulates the separation of inputs and outputs characteristic of information processing itself. As game designer Will Wright puts it, "playing a game is a continuous loop between the user (viewing the outcomes and inputting decisions) and the computer (calculating outcomes and displaying them back to the user). The user is trying to build a mental model of the computer model."[30] The variability of information outputs is thus correlated with our highly variegated relations with digital screens, which alternate rapidly between information and immersion, transparency and opaqueness, viewing an image and running a program, representation and control. And with respect to these screens, identity is rendered as a variable, aggregate, and modular form that constantly remakes itself as selections from a menu of options. To the extent that computers pervade nearly every activity of everyday life, these qualities have become structural features of everyday life. Interactive gaming thus anticipates the immediate future that we all inhabit, ready or not, where expressions become data structures and actions are formulated as algorithms.

As a corollary to Babette Mangolte's pondering—"Why is it difficult for the digital image to communicate duration?"—I want to conclude with the as yet unasked and perhaps still unanswerable question that continues to hover beneath my inquiries into the virtual life of film. Why have digital presentations not yet provoked the same kind of ontological perplexity and inquisitiveness that so strongly characterized classical film theory, and which return to haunt us today? Perhaps the new media still run ahead of philosophy, as I argued in *Reading the Figural.* One would think that people of my generation, who have witnessed as adults the displacement of the photographic by the videographic and the digital as default perceptual norms, would be more alert to this question. But perhaps we are not yet ready to raise these questions; hence my guess

30. Quoted in Chris McGowan, *Entertainment in the Cyber Zone* (New York: Random House, 1995) 71.

at the riddle. Just as the photographic persists in the digital as a way of warding off future shock, digital cinema extends the ontological questioning provoked by film but only in a diminished form, a form that may indeed express resistance to the future. The experience of duration has lost its preciousness; causal links to physical reality have become weakened. But more important, the unidirectional temporality of cinematic narrative—what is most strongly perpetuated in classical narrative form—comes into conflict with the most original and powerful automatisms of digitality—namely, interactivity, control, modularity, and programmability.

The will of digital practices is other to representation in our ordinary sense of the term. Through computers, we are less inclined to make a thing that stands as a token for another thing, but rather, to continually gather up elements, to copy and transform them, to recontextualize and recycle them, and to copy and share them, to transmit our results, and then to start all over again. The will to share, copy, and transmit relies less on a notion of the individual or of relations of identity than in the always virtual presence in time of a collective monad or a collectivity of monads—highly volatile and ever-evolving communities linked by common interests. The most powerful effect of networked communications is to make possible these many-to-many interactions, which occur simultaneously on local and global scales, by eliminating space in the framework of a common time. Real-time interactions are the ideal state, here, or alternatively, the attempt to reduce as much as possible the delay between message and response, thus holding the community in a perpetually reassertive present. New forms of skepticism and acknowledgment are forged in these virtual communities. Virtual collectives still require the power and anonymity provided by a screen that shields them from the world and its others. But in contrast to the film screen, which holds us in a present relation to the past and sustains our belief in a past world through the qualities of automatic analogical causation, digital screens require us to acknowledge others through efficient communication and exchange: I think because I exist in a present time of exchange with others, who are not present to me in space. Film's overcoming of skepticism relied on a perception of the shared duration of people and things as expressed in the condition of analogy, a condition wherein space functions as the conveyer of duration rather than representation. But movement through synthetic worlds actually degrades representational space to preserve time as fewer computing cycles; time as duration yields to time as calculation. In most virtual worlds images are rendered more simply, with less detail and complexity, when movements are invoked; when the mobile frame is stilled, absent information is returned to fill in the image. Here the passing of time in duration or the spatialized time of analogy is replaced by the quantitative subtraction and addition of information. In another sense, in reconfiguring the image as variable control interfaces, online communities also eliminate "representational" space (as well as geographical space), not in order to rejoin the world but to create a different world, which is still quite suggestively characterized by Pierre Teilhard de Chardin's concept of the noosphere. This noosphere is less the description of metaphysical unity or identity, however, than the assertion of a power expressed as coexistence in time, or as multiplying coexistence in an ever-changing state of simultaneity. Thus are characterized our new strategies for overcoming isolation with computers, with others, and with others through the medium of computers.

As befits their accelerated temporality, so far digital media have developed primarily in the form of communication not art, though this situation is sure to change. In our multiple quotidian uses, they amplify, multiply, and accelerate the transmission of information, rather than inspiring self-examination of the will expressed in these qualities or actions. Digital expressions are finding it difficult to become philosophical, to become something other than information. But, for future minds, they might. In this transitional moment, in seeking "photographic realism" digital imaging simulates an experience that it in fact displaces. Theatrical cinema will continue along these lines in a digital form for many years to come, first because of the temporal attractions of filmic narrative form, and also because the powers of digitality will inspire new cinematic forms and stylistic possibilities that will renew cinema itself. Film has already disappeared as a phenomenological experience—of this there is no doubt. But for the foreseeable future, cinema will persist, evolve, and undergo new transformations. As such, it remains the baseline for evaluating our aesthetic experience of moving images and of time-based figural expression. Before it becomes a genuinely antiquarian enterprise, film study or cinema studies may enjoy a robust existence for some time to come. Digital cinema, for the most part, can and will only prolong the lines of questioning originating in classical film theory, pushing them in certain directions without fundamentally transforming them. Alternatively, we must look for the more powerful expression of digital automatisms in other creative acts: in videogames and the varieties of online interactions, but also, and more importantly, in the digital arts. We are drawn to electronic screens no less powerfully or significantly than we are, or were, to the reflective screen of the movie theater. So perhaps something new is felt in relation to digital screens. And if a relationship to digital screens is now constitutive of our modernity in the sense of what disturbs or provokes us in the self-understanding of present life, perhaps this is because our ontological situation *is* being transformed. Newness relates again here to ontological perplexity—how to place or situate ourselves, in space and in time, in relation to an image that does not seem to be "one." Ontological provocations in digital creation may appear more clearly once these acts free themselves from the cinematic metaphor or significantly transform it. And, ironically, those of us whose subjectivity was forged in a cinematic culture—Béla Balázs' "visible humanity"—may not be capable either perceptually, psychologically, or philosophically of evaluating this experience. It is not *our* ontology. We seek a new generation of philosophers.

## 23. Old and New, or the (Virtual) Renascence of Cinema Studies

> [What] movies did at first they can do at last: spare our attention wholly for that thing now, in the frame of nature, the world moving in the branch . . . It is not novelty that has worn off, but our interest in our experience.
>
> —Stanley Cavell, *The World Viewed*

As I asserted in the beginning of this book, in periods of intense economic and cultural competition from other media, cinema incorporates an image of its rival the better to remake the narrative and social image of its aesthetic identity and to differentiate itself economically. At the same time, the marketing of the new is also the reassertion of something already well established: the preservation and enhancement of the psychological structures that have informed the pleasures of cinema viewing throughout its history. Film history helps us cut through the dissemblances of "digital paranoia" to understand how theatrical cinema has entered a phase of technological innovation and accommodation in which, rather than fading away, it is in fact renewing and renovating itself. Yet some things persist.

Surprisingly, David Bordwell is among my many friends who made the informal argument that films like *The Matrix* represent something fundamentally new in the history of cinema—the emergence of a postclassical style influenced by electronic and digital media. But on re-viewing the film, I am very much struck by another idea. Certainly *The Matrix* was highly innovative, and is now much copied, in its use of digital technology to manipulate space and movement in ways that were simply not possible with earlier photographic processes. And, as Bordwell pointed out to me, the absence of establishing shots and the rapid, elliptical nature of the editing seem to require a spectator who knows how to orient her- or himself in this post-music video space. However, this disorientation occurs strongly only during the first act of the film, that is, before Neo "wakes up" to find he has been dreaming in a digital simulation. On a second and third viewing, one becomes more struck by the resolutely classical nature of the narrative architecture on which all this baroque stylistic innovation is overlaid. By most criteria, *The Matrix* is a classical Hollywood film as Bordwell himself has so well defined it, at least in terms of *syuzhet,* or plot patterning, if not precisely in style. (In fact, it is clearly more classically constructed than *Citizen Kane,* one of Bordwell and Thompson's textbook examples in *Film Art.*) Among other criteria, its narrative causality is character centered; it is clearly divided into three acts organized according to the canonic story formula of undisturbed stage, disturbance, conflict, resolution of conflict; it has a double plot structure intertwining the action and romance storylines, and a plot pattern organized by segments, themselves causally related in distinct phases; and the end is marked by a strong sense of closure. *The Matrix,* in sum, has the rigorous structuring of a Proppian fairy tale. Its basic narrative architecture is instantly recognizable despite its bravura stylistic features and the density of its intertextual references. Moreover, its ideological project is so transparent as to be clichéd. In this case, either the definition of classic Hollywood cinema is so overbroad that it loses explanatory power, or we must assume that, narratively, there is little new in films like *The Matrix* and *Revenge of the Sith* (2005). The "classical" era has yet to release its grip on popular narrative cinema, digital or not.[31]

In like manner, earlier periods of technological change involving sound, color, and widescreen can be seen not as revolutions, but rather as additions or enhancements to the basic psychological and cultural experience of cinema. Despite structural adjustments at the levels of technology, the organization of the workforce, the structure of exhibition, and economic strategies of finance and distribution, the social and technological architecture of theatrical film viewing and the basic structure of classical Hollywood narrative have remained remarkably constant since 1917. While television and video certainly present different social and technological architectures of film viewing that

31. Indeed, this is the thesis of Bordwell's recent *The Way Hollywood Tells It* (Berkeley: University of California Press, 2006).

compete directly with those of theatrical exhibition, economically they have functioned more as new and lucrative channels of distribution. Perceptually, cognitively, and psychologically, television, video, and now the Internet present very different ways of viewing the same kind of narrative material in three different technological contexts. Financially, however, they serve to feed the same system: the multinational entertainment industries. In Hollywood cinema, and in cinema studies, both the excitement and the anxiety fueled by the emergence of digital media are inspired by the possibility that they will *replace* and eventually *supersede* the cinematic experience. But again this paranoia is an old one. Hollywood has learned to coexist peacefully with, and to profit enormously from, radio, television, and video. It is undoubtedly learning to do the same with the leisure hours consumed by the Internet, computer gaming, and home theater.

One response to film's virtual life is to cry, "Film is dead. Long live cinema!" Whether analog or digital, what we have responded to visually and narratively as "the movies" persists on cinema screens today and will for some time to come. Movies are as perceptually real to us as films, and, for the most part, they immerse us with equal power in compelling fictional worlds. In this respect, perhaps there are not many who will mourn the passing of film as an analogical art, or who will even recognize that the prince is long buried. Still, in Part II I also asserted that like the other arts of analogy, film did matter to us for reasons both phenomenological and philosophical as the expression of a past regained, although this sense of the past is becoming increasingly distant from us.

In the same breath I now want to emphasize that there is something "new" emerging in the new media that challenges us to rethink the fundamental concepts of film theory. (Indeed, one of the most important lessons of the virtual life of "film" is recognizing that all three responses to the current and past life of moving images are equally compelling and forceful.) This is evident, for example, in the nonlinear (though not necessarily nonteleological) narrative structure of multiuser and simulation gaming, whose interactive and collective nature mobilizes the spectator's vision and pleasure in novel ways. Not only does online gaming require new ways of conceptualizing the placement of the spectator; multiuser domains, where users participate collectively in the creation and modification of the game/narrative space, also ask us to rethink notions of authorship. Interactive media promote a form of participatory spectatorship relatively unknown in other time-based spatial media. Webcams are promoting new forms of self-presentation and new modalities of pleasurable and also perverse looking. A certain concept of representation is also changing profoundly, though, as I have argued, in digital imaging the criterion of "perceptual realism" remains a curious constant even as the indexical image is replaced by a computational simulation that enables new forms and modalities of creative activity. Finally, the various media that derive their power from distributed computing represent fundamentally new technological organizations of the time and space of spectatorship, in both its singular and collective forms. The collective audience organized in the unified space and linear time of the film projection has been dispersed into the serialized space and unified time of broadcast media. And in turn, the one-to-many model of broadcasting is yielding to the many-to-many model of distributed computing characterized by an atomized space and asynchronous time whose global reach is vaster yet more ephemeral.

It would be foolish to believe that we are encountering any of these "new" media in their mature form. Part of the excitement of the critical study of digital culture is the possibility of recognizing that we are witnessing the birth of a medium or media whose future is as difficult to imagine as another future was to my sociologist at the nickelodeon. Despite or perhaps because of their rapid economic, cultural, and aesthetic emergence, the digital arts lack concepts for critical and social assessment. The velocity of the changes taking place since the Internet became a cultural phenomenon toward the end of the 1980s, and the even faster spread of the World Wide Web since 1994, have rapidly overtaken the capacity of academic disciplines to comprehend them. Nearly twenty-five years had to elapse after the emergence of cinema as a mass, popular medium and a major American industry before the first large-scale sociological inquiry—the Payne Fund Studies—took place. The academic and educational response to radio and television as new communication technologies was somewhat quicker but nonetheless can still be measured in decades. However, unlike my young sociologist at the nickelodeon, we are not bereft of critical resources for comprehending the broad outlines of these new media; to the extent that they share lines of descent with the history of film, there are nearly 100 years of international film theory and historical enquiry to serve as a critical resource for their evaluation.

Here the old (cinematic) and the new (electronic and digital) media find themselves in a curious genealogical mélange whose chronology is by no means simple or self-evident. As "film" disappears in the successive substitutions of the digital for the analog, what persists is *cinema* as a narrative form and a psychological experience—a certain modality of articulating visuality, signification, and desire through space, movement, and time. Indeed, while computer-generated imagery longs to be "photographic," many forms of interactive media long to be "cinematic." Nonetheless, watching a movie on broadcast television or video, much less the Internet, is arguably not a cinematic experience. At the same time, although there have been mutations in the forms of spectatorship, the fundamental narrative architecture of film persists, and, despite competition from video and the Internet, theatrical film viewing shows no signs of disappearing soon. The unity or homogeneity of the cinematic spectatorial experience peaked long ago, in 1946, and since that time has fragmented and branched off into other distribution streams. Yet it remains the baseline for understanding and evaluating other spatial time-based media. For this reason, neither television nor digital *studies* has emerged with a coherence separate from a fundamental grounding in *cinema* studies; therefore, critically understanding the evolution of film narrative and new variations in cinematic spectatorial experience still relies on the core concepts of film *theory.* To address critically what television, video, and interactive digital media are becoming means both defining their significant technological and aesthetic differences *and* understanding that they emerge from similar genealogical roots with photography and film. Here the virtual life of film is defined in part by the twofold virtuality that breaches the Maginot line dividing the arts of time or discourse from the arts of space or image.

In this respect, we can see how the history of film and film theory reaches out to the larger concerns of visual studies. There is an obvious alliance here between cinema studies and media studies on the one hand, and the emerging field of visual studies on the other. But implicit in the idea of visual studies is either to return film studies to the history of art or to resituate it as an extension or part of a larger (multi)media studies. However, I would like to suggest a more radical idea.

While cultural conservatives consider film and interactive digital media to be debased creative endeavors, from another point of view they may be understood as raising fascinating philosophical problems that are less evident, and less interesting, with respect to other, more established arts. Moreover, despite their ostensible differences, film and digital media do so in similar ways. As I argued in *Reading the Figural, or Philosophy after the New Media,* cinema shares with new media a line of descent characterized by their powers of the "figural." This is why I include film among the new media, and claim that the key concepts of film theory define the best horizon for assessing both what is new and at the same time very old in the new media. In figural media, older distinctions of spatiality and temporality, visuality and expression, autographicality and notationality are collapsed or reconfigured in ways that require both the deconstruction of previous philosophical thought and the creation of new concepts. Thus, I am quite serious in including photography and film in a history of new media that follows the same genealogical declension, no matter how complex, as should be evident from my discussion of virtuality throughout this book. For these reasons, it seems clear that twentieth-century culture is fundamentally an audiovisual culture the history of whose forms and concepts are concomitant with the history of cinema and film theory. This idea enhances rather than detracts from my interest in the electronic arts as well as the new digital media and communications. For example, in his book on Michel Foucault, Gilles Deleuze argues that the historical transition from sovereign to disciplinary societies, and now to what Deleuze called our "control societies," can be analyzed by qualitative changes in how the nature of power is articulated through audiovisual regimes. Deleuze wants to restore and emphasize the status of visuality in Foucault's philosophy by arguing that discourse is not the only object of Foucault's analyses, and indeed that discourse always passes through the visible. Foucault's analysis of the Panopticon, whose organization of power in relation to vision comes to represent the disciplinary societies of the nineteenth century, is exemplary in this respect. Therefore, changing articulations of the visible with respect to the expressible—shifts in modes of envisioning and representing, positions of seeing and ways of saying—organize relations of knowledge, power, and subjectivity in different ways in different historical societies. Power is exercised through vision as well as through discourse, and the modalities through which this power has been both expressed and challenged in the twentieth century are largely concomitant, I would argue, with the history of the emergence of cinema. Indeed one fascinating dimension of Deleuze's cinema books, both historically and conceptually, is their suggestion that the semiotic history of cinema itself has already witnessed large-scale changes—from the movement-image to the time-image, and now the emergence of what Deleuze calls the "silicon-image."

The history of film theory therefore remains a keystone for understanding the problems raised by electronic and digital media for aesthetic and social theory. As I stated earlier, there are no "new media," but only a multiplicity of hybrid forms linked by their basis in computational operations or automatisms. Grouped together by the automatisms that make them possible, perhaps they may be referred to as computational arts, in the same way that varieties of now-overlapping moving-image experience could be called "cinematographic." Nonetheless, although this perspective may reflect the prejudice of a *cinéfils* and proud cousin of Serge Daney, in my opinion the multiple forms of new media do not yet have the semiotic and cultural coherence of cinema as an audiovisual medium. Undoubtedly, this will come, and perhaps cinema may one day dissolve or fray into a variety of new computational arts. But for the moment, it remains the baseline for comprehending the varieties of new media.

Thus, the history of cinema, and the concepts of film theory, become the most productive context for defining the audiovisuality of our past and current centuries. And in this manner, cinema studies suddenly asserts its central role in any humanities curriculum, once we relinquish an outmoded aesthetic argument and start to value figural media for the new thought they produce. At the same time, the new media also challenge cinema studies and film theory to reinvent themselves through reassessing and constructing anew their concepts. To reassert and renew the province of cinema studies also means defining and redefining what "film" signifies. Hence the apparent paradox of asserting the continuation and renewal of cinema studies in the face of the disappearance of what most self-evidently defines it—celluloid as a means of registering and projecting analogical images. I agree with Anne Friedberg that cinema studies now finds itself in a transitional moment wherein *screens* become display and delivery formats whose form and dimensions are variable (theatrical film, television, computer), *film* is relegated to a storage device variable as to its medium (celluloid, 1/2 inch magnetic tape, DVD, video servers, etc.), and *spectators* become "users" manipulating interfaces, either as simple as a remote control or as complex as data-gloves and head-mounted displays. The convergence of media that occurs in digital technologies also encourages us to widen considerably cinema's genealogy to include the telephone, radio, television, and the computer as parts of a broader audiovisual regime.[32] Equally interesting in Friedberg's observations is not only the concise expression of the variety and complexity of changes taking place, but also the resolute continuity of certain concepts—*screen, film, spectator*—which already

32. Anne Friedberg, "The End of Cinema: Multimedia and Technological Change," in *Reinventing Film Studies,* ed. Christine Gledhill and Linda Williams (London: Hodder Arnold, 2000) 440. Equally interesting is her suggestion that as film loses more and more its identity as a discrete object, the more the field has turned to film history as a way of reasserting its identity and continuity. However, the way in which this turn to history has taken place might miss the more radical consequences of filmic temporality.

have a long and complex history. In the best critical work on digital culture, then, one finds the recirculation, and indeed renovation, of certain key concepts and problems of film theory: how new forms of image emerge in relation to factors of movement and temporality; the shifting status of "'photographic' realism" as a cultural construct; how questions of signification are transformed by the narrative organization of time-based spatial media; and the question of technology in relation to art, not only in the production and dissemination of images, but also in the technological delimitation and organization of the spatiality and temporality of spectatorial experience and pleasure.

Screen, film, spectator; image, movement, and time; representation and the problem of "realism," or the relation of image to referent; signification and narrative; technology and art: the form and vocabulary in which these questions are posed has changed continuously in the history of film theory as a series of conflictual debates. Yet the basic set of concepts has remained remarkably constant. Moreover, the real and remarkable accomplishment of cinema studies, I believe, is to have forged more than any other related discipline the methodological and philosophical bases for addressing the most urgent and interesting questions, both aesthetic and cultural, of modernity and visual culture. Only the history of film theory gives us the basis to understand and to judge the extent and nature of the changes taking place in photographic, cinematographic, electronic, and interactive digital media. Suddenly, the questions and debates of not just 100 years of cinema, but of nearly 100 years of film theory, become the baseline for comprehending both what is entirely new in the emergence of interactive digital media and computer-mediated communications *and* what endures as the core experience of narrative-representational cinema. Film has not died yet, though it may become thoroughly "remediated." Nonetheless, the main questions and concepts of film theory persist, and we should pay careful attention to how they define a certain history of thought, how they can be used to reexamine that history, and how they form the basis for a critical understanding of new media and old. And at the same time, the core concepts of film theory are being recontextualized in ways that extend and render more complex their critical powers.

I am thinking again of my young sociologist passing by the nickelodeon. Both the academic status and the cultural status of university cinema studies still suffer from the time lag between the emergence of film and cinema, and their serious academic study. A whole new industry and art emerged in the early twentieth century without a philosophical or sociological context to imagine its social impact and consequences. Despite its richness and complexity, the history of film theory in the first half of the twentieth century was largely a matter of playing catch-up. Fortunately, the new digital culture is not emerging in a similar theoretical vacuum. For that same history positions us to comprehend better the complex genealogy defining both the technological and aesthetic possibilities of computer-generated imagery and its commercial and popular exploitation. The history of film and of film theory thus becomes the most productive conceptual horizon against which we can assess what is both new and yet very old in the new media. Film theory, then, is our best hope for understanding critically how digital technologies are serving, like television and video before them, to perpetuate the cinematic as the mature audiovisual culture of the twentieth century, and, at the same time, how they are preparing the emergence of a new audiovisual culture whose broad and indiscernible outlines we are only just beginning to distinguish.

# ACKNOWLEDGMENTS

This book began as a question posed to me in 1999 by Barry Ife, then vice-principal of King's College London: Will film studies change if its object becomes digital and electronic rather than photographic? This issue was of key concern to us at King's as we were creating a new film studies program in a new millennium. Like many deceptively simple questions, it became more complex, persistent, and perplexing the more I thought about it. Eventually I took up this problem as the subject of my inaugural lecture at King's in February 2002, "Dr. Strange Media, or How I Learned to Stop Worrying and to Love Film Theory." Thereafter my thoughts kept unfolding and developing until I realized that a book needed to be written. In 2002 *The Virtual Life of Film* was proposed successfully to the Film Scholars Fellowship Program of the Academy of Motion Picture Arts and Sciences. I am especially grateful to the Academy for its invaluable financial and intellectual support in the planning and writing of this book, and for the forbearance of my old friend, Greg Beal, the Program Coordinator, for the length of time it took to complete it.

The book itself took form in a number of conversations both formal and informal. I am particularly indebted to Laura Mulvey, who shared her thoughts freely with me, especially as we prepared our one-day conference "Cinema: Dead or Alive?" for the Screen Studies research group at the School for Advanced Studies at the University of London in February 2003. Various arguments for the book took shape, were revised, and were rethought in discussion with audiences in a variety of venues, including the conferences "Film Denken" (sponsored by the Synema-Society for Film and Media, Institut für Wissenschaft und Kunst, and by the Philosophisches Institut, University of Vienna); the Archimedia "Film Archives in the Digital Era," sponsored by the Amsterdam Filmmuseum; "Ontologies of the Literary Work and the Moving

Image," at the University of Oulu; "Media Aesthetics: The Concept of Medium in Aesthetic Practices/Aesthetic Effects in Media Practices," at the University of Oslo; "Lookalikeness: The Moving Image and its World," at Duke University; and "Interval (2)," at the Slade Research Centre, Slade School of Art, London; as well as invited lectures and seminar discussions at the following institutions: Department of Visual and Environmental Studies, Harvard University; Comparative Media Studies, Massachusetts Institute of Technology; Film Studies Program, Yale University; Film Studies Program, Mt. Holyoke College; Ustav filmu a audiovizualni kultury, Masarykovy University (Brno, Czech Republic); the Seminar on Ecology, Technology, and Cybernetics at the Humanities Center, Harvard University; Film Studies Program, University of Pittsburgh; Cinema Studies Program, University of Pennsylvania; Film and Media Studies, Swarthmore College; The Photographer's Gallery, London; University College London; and Vanderbilt University. I am also grateful for comments and conversations with students in my seminars on cinema and digital culture at Harvard University and at King's College London.

Several cherished friends took time to read carefully parts of the manuscript and to comment critically on my arguments, including Dudley Andrew, Mark Betz, the late and dearly missed Reni Celeste, W. J. T. Mitchell, Toril Moi, and Michael Westlake. Dan Reynolds worked long and hard at verifying citations and correcting editorial mishaps. Additional thanks are due to Bobby Allen, Emily Apter, Martha Banta, Victor Burgin, Verena Conley, Tim Corrigan, Jim Costanzo, Melissa Davenport, Jane Dye, Steven Eastwood, Thomas Elsaesser, Jane Gaines, Sam Girgus, Lee Grieveson, Liv Hausken, Judy Irola, Anton Kaes, Pekka Kuusisto, Brigitte Mayr, Ludwig Nagl, Linda Norden, Francette Pacteau, Vladimir Padunov, Dana Polan, Eric Rentschler, Eivind Rossaak, William Rothman, Michael Sanchez, Charles Swartz, Petr Szczepanik, William Uricchio, Eva Waniek, Charles Warren, Tom Wartenberg, Patty White, Ken Wissoker, and Catherine Yass. Lindsay Waters, Executive Editor for the Humanities at Harvard University Press, has been an invaluable friend and editor throughout the process of putting this book into print. I am also deeply grateful for the attentive and perceptive criticisms and suggestions provided by John Belton, Sean Cubitt, and Stanley Cavell.

Sophie Greig and the White Cube Gallery, London, and Callen Blair and the Matthew Marks Gallery, New York, were instrumental in providing images and other documents pertaining to Sam Taylor-Wood's works. Sam Taylor-Wood kindly granted permission to reprint an image from *Pietà*. I would also like to thank the Artists Rights Society and the Man Ray Trust for their kind permission to reprint two of Man Ray's works.

Different versions of Part I have previously appeared in print in the *Publication of the Modern Language Association* 116.5 (October 2001), *Cinérgon* 15 (2003), and in two collections: *Inventing Film Studies,* edited by Lee Grieveson and Haidee Wasson (Durham: Duke University Press); and *Film/Denken—Film & Philosophy,* edited by Ludwig Nagle, Brigitte Mayr, and Eva Waniek (Vienna: Synema, 2004). I am grateful to the editors of these publications for their indulgence in permitting republication here.

Finally, to Dominique Bluher and Sarah Rodowick, thanks once again for your affection and patience.